5

Romantic Understanding

Romantic Understanding

The Development of Rationality and Imagination, Ages 8-15

KIERAN EGAN

ROUTLEDGE
New York and London

First published in 1990 by
Routledge
An imprint of Routledge, Chapman and Hall, Inc.
29 West 35 Street
New York, NY 10001

Published in Great Britain by

Routledge
11 New Fetter Lane
London EC4P 4EE

Library of Congress cataloging in publication data

Egan, Kieran.
    Romantic understanding: the development of rationality and
    imagination, ages 8–15.
    /Kieran Egan.
        p.   cm.
    Includes bibliographical references.
    ISBN 0-415-90050-6; ISBN 0-415-90348-3 (pbk.)
    1. Middle schools—Curricula.   2. Romanticism—Study and teaching.
    3. Creative thinking—Study and teaching.   I. Title.
LB1623.E34 1990
373.2'36—dc20   90-34389

British Library cataloguing in publication data also available.

To
Catherine Paula Egan
with love

Contents

Acknowledgments

I am most grateful for the kindness and for the intelligent criticisms given to drafts of this book by Richard Angelo (University of Kentucky), Michael Apple (University of Wisconsin), Robin Barrow (Simon Fraser University), Suzanne de Castell (Simon Fraser University), Carmen Luke (James Cook University), Geoffrey Milburn (University of Western Ontario), David Nyberg (State University of New York at Buffalo), June Sturrock (Simon Fraser University), and John Willinsky (University of Calgary). The book is significantly better as a result of their help. In addition I am greatly indebted to a number of teachers who have experimented with these ideas. In particular I am most grateful for the time, energy, and professional expertise of Pierre Blouin, Sandy Chamberlain, and Scott Sayer (British Columbia), Tim Watson (Worcester, England), and Di Fleming (Melbourne, Australia). Eileen Mallory has "processed" the manuscript and revisions with her usual supernatural speed, accuracy and good cheer, for which I am most grateful. Susanna Egan has read and edited and commented on two drafts, apart from having contributed ideas from her own work cited in the text, for which gratitude seems a small return, but, unlike any of the above, she gets to share the royalties.

Introduction

My aim for this book can be divided into three overlapping parts: first, to characterize a somewhat distinct kind of understanding, which I call romantic (and also to clarify what I mean by a kind of understanding); second, to establish that this kind of understanding can and should be evoked, stimulated, and developed during the middle-school years (approximately ages eight to fifteen); and, third, to show that, in attaining romantic understanding, students today recapitulate its prior attainment in cultural history, particularly as it appeared in Romanticism during the late eighteenth and early nineteenth centuries. Throughout, I hope to make clear that focusing on the recapitulation of a "kind of understanding" can provide a new way of addressing some persistent educational problems, a way that takes us past some of the difficulties that currently hinder our ability to make educational practice more generally effective.

By romance I do not mean simply those attitudes and forms of expression one sees in "romantic novels" or "love stories" but rather those intellectual, emotional, aesthetic, and other characteristics that come to the fore during the period of Romanticism. It is relatively easy to list some of these characteristics; they include delight in the exotic, emphasis on individualism, revolt against the conventional, stress on the importance of imagination, intoxication with the sublime in nature, intense inquiry about the self, resistance to order and reason, glorification of transcendent human qualities, and so on. It is less easy, however, to build a coherent picture of Romanticism and romance. The difficulty is in part due to another of their prominent characteristics being a protean intellectual and emotional ferment, seen more in its shifting, troubled energy than in any distinct and stable properties; in part it is due to the limited grasp we have on complex cultural movements and on complex forms of understanding, and to the limited vocabulary that has been developed to articulate that limited grasp.

The nature of romance, and the defining characteristics of Romanticism, are matters of dispute in literary criticism and literary history. This is an area of scholarly inquiry marked by an unusual range of disagreement, extending even to what phenomena constitute its subject matter. There is an inherited canon of romantic writers and artists, central to which—to take only English literature—are Blake, Wordsworth, and Coleridge, and, in the following literary generation, Shelley, Keats, and Byron. But one cannot precisely mark what they have in common which clearly excludes, say, Jane Austen (for this dispute see McGann, 1983) or Robert Southey (see Butler, 1987, for an argument for enrolling Southey centrally in the canon). If we turn to the critical literature for a description of precisely what was new in their work we find a similar range of disagreement and difficulty in characterizing it. That Romanticism represented something powerful and new, though that something is very hard to pin down precisely, was evident long ago. Matthew Arnold, reflecting in 1850 on Byron's impact on a yet later literary generation, observed:

> He taught us little; but our soul
> Had *felt* him like the thunder's roll. (cited in Allott and
> Super, 1986, p. 138)

In Chapters 1 and 2, nevertheless, I will begin to characterize what I mean by romantic understanding by plunging first into the literature on, and constitutive of, Romanticism. My aim is not to give an abbreviated account of the disputes about Romanticism, nor to give an abbreviated account of Romanticism itself—though it might prove useful to start with one. Rather I want to consider Romanticism in terms of the new intellectual capacities that were generated within it, and I will try to characterize these as far as possible in terms of the technical resources that were generated to aid thinking. This rather opaque phrase, whose meaning will, I trust, become clearer as we go along, is intended to alert the reader to expect a focus on Romanticism that does not dwell on the more familiar literary and artistic categories. Second, as my aim is the elucidation of what I mean by romantic understanding, my focus will be on how native mental powers—which seem to be much the same for all people everywhere—are shaped into very distinct forms and uses in particular cultures due to the technical resources generated in the culture's history to aid thinking. It is, then, some particular technical resources whose development supported the movement we know as Romanticism that provides my starting point. In "technical resources that aid thinking" I include both the technological and material conditions of a society which affect how people make sense of the world and of their experience, and also the related developments in literary, artistic, philosophical, scientific techniques and in means for their communication and for the dissemination of ideas.

From this plunge into Romanticism I will try to emerge with some ideas that will help towards a better grasp on romantic understanding. Before leaving Chapter 1, I will indicate why any of this might have relevance to the practical problems of modern education.

In Chapter 2, I will take further this pursuit of the technical resources of thought that give Romanticism and romantic understanding their particular character. I will focus on the technologies of writing and the printing press, and consider how the resources they provided to thinking affected the development of Romanticism and romance. In particular I will explore the sense in which romance might be seen as a kind of aftershock of widespread literacy. These might seem somewhat exotic inquiries for a book devoted to practical problems of middle-school education, but I hope the results will show rather that dealing with such cultural stuff provides a direct route to central educational problems.

Additionally, and relatedly, I will try to show in Chapter 2 that while in common usage "romance" tends to be contrasted with "rationality" (another complex and troubled term) the notion of romantic understanding that I will elaborate involves not only a sense of imaginative wonder but also the rational capacities to explore systematically whatever is the object of imaginative engagement. Indeed, I will try to show that the sense of imaginative wonder which is a significant constituent of romantic understanding is in large part a product of the evocation, stimulation, and development of the basic tools of rationality.

The second part of my aim is to establish that the middle-school years are the appropriate period for the development of romantic understanding. In the process of education students cannot, of course, learn everything at once. We have to break down what we think it is important for them to learn into some sequence. The sequencing of the curriculum typically embodies in varying proportions two principles which we might simply call logical and psychological.

The logical principle operates by disclosing prerequisite sequences in areas of knowledge and accommodating the curriculum to these. The structuring of the curriculum according to this principle is largely an epistemological problem. The task facing someone hoping to have a practical impact on the curriculum by drawing on this principle has been described as follows: "What is needed is a much more careful examination of what the logically necessary features of areas of knowledge are and, in particular, the extent to which learning a subject involves adherence to what can loosely be called rules of logical order" (Hirst,

1974, p. 120). In the more exclusively logical schemes, such as Plato's, the ages at which particular knowledge or experience are engaged is determined by estimates of the time it will take to master each segment of the curriculum.

One difficulty in using the logical principle for sequencing the curriculum is that, even in the case of a logically tight field such as mathematics, it seems possible to begin at almost any point to build the network of skills and knowledge that accumulate to mathematical understanding. In other words, as Philip Phenix has made clear, even establishing logical priority in a discipline does not entail temporal priority in instruction (Phenix, 1964, p. 285). Any complex field of knowledge is, furthermore, amenable to an indeterminate variety of structural characterizations—in some of which prerequisite logical orders will be quite different from those of others. The kind of prerequisite logical orders that might be useful for determining the sequences of the curriculum might seem discernible in some restricted areas of mathematics and the physical sciences but remain so elusive in fields such as history or the visual arts that we cannot hope to derive clear guidance from them for the sequencing of the curriculum.

Applying the psychological principle involves trying to sequence the curriculum in a manner that conforms with the intellectual development of the student. From a study of what tasks students are typically able and unable to perform at different ages, inferences are made about sequences of intellectual development. From these, in turn, inferences are made about the kind of knowledge that students will be able or "ready" to learn at various stages of the developmental process being elucidated.

One difficulty with the psychological principle, evident with even the most sophisticated developmental theories such as Piaget's and Vygotsky's, and their current convergence, lies in the imprecision with which characterizations of intellectual development impact on subject matter. However fully we might want to accommodate the sequence of the curriculum to the cognitive dispositions apparent at various ages, the difference between how we describe cognitive processes and intellectual development and how we characterize knowledge makes the task of conforming the latter to the former problematic. The educator who wants to draw on such theories for sequencing curriculum is further bedevilled by the disputes persisting among psychologists about how secure their generalizations may be about what students can and cannot learn at particular ages. Especially pertinent are the claims that the psychological theories are in some significant degree not describing some natural developmental process to which educators must conform, but rather are describing a process which is in part at least a product of social and cultural contingencies, prominent among which are what educators have been doing. To try to conform to apparent implications of such theories, consequently, would be to try to conform to the results of past socializing and educational practices—which, for the most part, any curriculum revision is deliberately trying to improve on.

But clearly some logical and some psychological principles are indispensable if we are to sequence the curriculum sensibly. Educationalists have constantly tried to bring both kinds of principle to bear, though this has not proved at all as straightforward a task as it seems it should be. It seems that we ought to be able to bring together—to take just a couple of modern examples—the epistemological principles articulated by Paul Hirst and the psychological principles elaborated by Jean Piaget, and let each play its appropriate role. But the difficulties that attend each separately still obtain, and furthermore they seem quite resistent to coming together. At a profound level they seem to embody assumptions or presuppositions that act like magnetic poles that repel each other. The most influential attempts to find a way of articulating a principle that embodies both a logical and psychological dimension are derived from John Locke. From perceptual experience, he argued, come simple ideas which the mind has the power to compare, unite, elaborate in an almost infinite variety of ways, and so use to construct new complex ideas (Locke, 1690/1961). From his development of this notion we have inherited a very general principle that has profoundly influenced curriculum design. It finds its starkest twentieth century form in the notion that we should begin with the simple and move towards the complex. This notion involves a logical principle for organizing knowledge into sequential structures and a psychological principle based on a conception of how the mind works and, in particular, learns.

It continues to have a profound influence on educational practice even though the ideas it was derived from—especially Locke's conception of the mind as a *tabula rasa* amenable to almost infinite environmental determining—are no longer taken seriously. The flaw at its basis opens it up to serious question at the level of present day implementation.

Even so, I want to try to clamber onto Locke's shoulders and articulate principles for sequencing the curriculum that involve both logical and psychological components and that transcend the problems that attend each component when pursued separately. Focusing on the recapitulation of kinds of understanding, I think, makes this possible. Indeed I have used "understanding" in my title because it entails an epistemological and psychological dimension. One must have some knowledge in order to understand something, but in order to understand that knowledge we need to integrate it into some meaning structure; its significance must be grasped, it must take a place in the life of the knower. A metaphorical way of putting it is to say that, once understood, knowledge becomes a part of what we think with, before incorporation into a network of understanding it is what we think about (Gowin, 1981). And, indeed, understanding "is the highest goal of learning" (Scriven, 1976, p. 217).

Romantic understanding, then, will be elaborated in such a way that it will provide principles for sequencing the curriculum that are unlike those presently current. In particular I will try to show that coalescing logical and psychological principles can provide us with a new way of sequencing and structuring the middle-school curriculum. In Chapters 3 to 7 I will describe characteristics of students' understanding in the middle-school years, and try to show why it makes sense also to see, during those years, a predisposition towards what I am calling romantic understanding.

The use of "romantic understanding" as the overall label for students' thinking, feeling, perception, etc., between approximately ages eight and fifteen suggests that sufficient common features across the age range justify the single term. This is not to deny, however, that there are also significant changes within romantic understanding. I will attend to some of these changes, particularly in Chapter 6.

Supporting the claim that romantic understanding represents a predisposition for middle-school students is the third part of my aim, and forms the crux of the recapitulation argument. I will argue that students are predisposed to develop particular kinds of understanding in a particular sequence because of the logical and psychological forces that constrain and shape the process of acculturation. I will try to show that the same constraining and shaping forces operate both in cultural history and in individual students' educational development. Cultural history can thus provide us with important insights into how to construct a curriculum.

I realize that this may well seem a peculiar kind of argument and a very odd way of approaching how history or science should be organized and taught during the middle-school years. Even so, I will prepare this argument during the first seven chapters and elaborate it explicitly in Chapter 8. I will try to show that empirically we can observe a range of common features in the kind of understanding prominent during the Romantic period and prominent in students during their middle-school years today. Obviously this will not appear as an overall likeness between, say, Coleridge's mind and the minds of typical adolescents today in Putney, Peoria, and Perth. But if we focus quite precisely on the technical resources of thought, and the typical kind of understanding they entail, I think we will see a number of perhaps surprizing correlations. To proceed from a set of more or less interesting correlations in the direction of establishing causal relationships, and so the basis for the recapitulation theory, I will need to engage in the analytic work that will establish necessary relationships between particular technical resources of thought and particular cultural effects, such as kinds of understanding. If the relationship is necessary it will operate whenever and wherever these technical resources of thought are developed—whether in the process of cultural history or of student's education today. I will further try to show that not only are students predisposed towards romantic understanding during the middle-school years due to the influence of our cultural history on the nature and structure of the present cultural conditions into which they grow, but also that they both can and should attain romantic understanding on educational grounds.

The general shape of this book is a move from the rather abstract discussion of Romanticism and the attempt to characterize romantic understanding towards increasingly detailed observations of its features during the middle-school years and then to concrete implications for the curriculum in Chapter 9 and for teaching in Chapter 10. These two final chapters will describe the kind of curriculum and the kind of teaching that seem to me best able to evoke, stimulate, and develop romantic understanding. The curriculum chapter will include in outline a curriculum for the middle school years, moving from a year of transition to romantic understanding at about age eight to a year of transition at about age fifteen to a further distinctive kind of understanding. The chapter on teaching will include a framework for planning teaching to be engaging and stimulating to students during these years, and to make the curriculum content most meaningful and educationally useful.

It is fashionable today, perhaps it has always been fashionable, to bewail the failures of our educational institutions. We are constantly told that the schools are in crisis, that students seem to be learning next to nothing despite massive and growing expenditures. And indeed, particularly during the middle-school years, many students show little interest in learning the contents of typical school curricula. They commonly give little of their intellectual and emotional energy to the objectives of the school. Many seem to experience considerable difficulties in learning to think abstractly with any ease. Teaching is hard work, the schools pressure students to learn, and teachers and schools bear marks of the fatigue that applying constant pressure on reluctant learners exacts. It is salutary to keep in mind the anecdote reported in the front of the

British Newsom Report on Education (1963): "A boy who had just left school was asked by his former headmaster what he thought of the new buildings, "It could be all marble, sir," he replied, "but it would still be a bloody school."

There are, of course, the rewards of those students who learn well, who show imagination and creativity in their use of what they learn, and who come to understand and delight in their cultural inheritance. But why are these rewards for teaching effort, these educational successes, so relatively rare? Why do not all students, or many more, learn much more? The optimistic Enlightenment project to make the benefits of education available to all children is running aground against the apparent reluctance or inability of so many students to find point or meaning in significant parts of the typical middle-school curriculum. "What's the medieval papacy, or Hecuba, to me?" they ask, and the answers carry little conviction.

We find no shortage of diagnoses, and prescriptions for cures. It is, we hear, the nature of many children to learn ill and little; or, it is social conditions that make much knowledge meaningless, irrelevant, or even alienating; or, it is the incompetence of the school and its agents to educate effectively; and so on. Such diagnoses, and the different prescriptions they seem to imply, contribute to the sense of crisis concerning education. The diagnoses are so different in their identification of the causes and even the symptoms of the disease that it is hard to hold to any clear sense of what the organism should look like when it is well.

Some of the present difficulties seem to be due to considerable disagreement and some confusion about what schools are supported to do. We consider them primarily educational institutions, crucial parts of educational systems. But "education" is a label we put on a bag of ideas about how to treat the young which do not fit well together and which seem indeed in significant part to be mutually repelling. Let me mention briefly just three components of our idea of "education". (By "our" I mean most people in countries with large-scale state-overseen educational systems.)

In all societies children are initiated into the particular norms and conventions around them, and are encouraged to respect these cultural contingencies as though they are almost natural conditions. The more or less arbitrary forms of social life that have existed across the world, in time and space, have all been supported by strict sanctions. Human groups have developed powerful techniques for encouraging in their members strong emotional commitments to the group, and all use a range of punishments for members who transgress the conventions that maintain the groups' distinctive identities. In all oral cultures the norms and conventions that preserve the continuing identity of the group have to be sustained in the individual memories of their members. All oral cultures place considerable emphasis on the faithful transmission of the lore about appropriate social relationships, behaviors, economic status and activities, and so on, to the young. The techniques that aid reliable memorization are thus highly prized, and initiation into the lore of the social group tends to involve rhythmic chanting of vivid stories in a highly charged ritual context. The stories, or myths, carry the lore of the social group in coded forms (see, e.g.: Durkheim, 1965; Havelock, 1963; Lévi-Bruhl, 1985; Lévi-Strauss, 1966). In such societies the young are socialized to the norms and conventions of the group. A prominent feature of socialization is that it tends to make people more alike; it brings them to share beliefs, attitudes, norms of behavior and thought, and so on. This process of socializing children is one component of the general conception of education that informs our sense of the school's role. We do not today use the same techniques that were and are common in oral cultures throughout the world, but we share in an important sense the process of initiating the young into our social conventions and encouraging in them a commitment to those conventions.

A second component that survives in our general conception of education was first articulated after the relatively widespread use of the technology of writing in a society. Once one could write and so have ready visual access to records of various kinds, the social importance of memory, and of the techniques such as rhythm, meter, and story which helped maintain things in memory, was greatly reduced. With the reduced pressure to remember, and so to think in terms of story, proverb, and formula, the mind was in a sense freed for other tasks. This is to put it simplistically, of course, but the development of writing made possible new ways of thinking (see, e.g.: Goody, 1977; Goody, 1986; Goody and Watt, 1968; Havelock, 1986; Ong, 1982). One way of characterizing a part of Plato's immense achievement is to say that he worked out how to think once one could write. Perhaps he did not get it all correct, and one might see the history of Western philosophy as attempts to clarify and fill out how literate people should think. This odd way of looking at philosophy may appear less odd when we recognize rationality as one of the consequences of literacy (Goody and Watt, 1968), or, at least, as giving Western rationality its distinctive form, and a central task of philosophy as teasing out the nature of this rationality and its entailments. In working out this new form of thinking, Plato elaborated a new conception of education: knowledge was to be accumulated in particular sequences in order to form the mind to enable people to think rationally. The curriculum provided the logically organized forms of knowledge that carried the mind from conventional and confused beliefs to that clarity of reason that gives a privileged view of reality. The achievement of Plato's aim for education involved a constant critical reflection on the norms and conventions of social life.

Plato represented his conception of education as irreconcilably opposed to the older forms of initiation into prevailing conventions—to the point of waging a battle against the rhetoricians who preserved in their teaching many of the techniques developed in oral cultures. Plato argued incessantly that they seduced the mind away from the kind of abstract concepts through which alone the mind could gain access to what was real and true about the world and about experience. We, however, include both aims into our general conception of education. We expect the schools both to socialize children to the prevailing social conventions and develop commitments to those conventions, and also to make headway in the Platonic program of critical rationality which involves skepticism of all conventions and encourages intellectual contempt for the kinds of commitments socialization induces.

A third component of our general conception of education was given its most distinctive articulation by Rousseau. Gathering together ideas from a number of sources, including Plato and John Locke, Rousseau pointed out that if one thought of education largely in terms of the knowledge to be accumulated, one saw childhood and adolescence merely as incomplete forms of one's ideal end. Such a view, he argued, had a number of disadvantages that undermined one's ability to achieve that end. It blinded one to the fact that childhood and adolescence were not merely stages on a journey towards educated adulthood but also had their own distinctive forms. The aim of education was thus only in part some adult achievement; the aim was also the fullest achievement of each stage of life. So the aim of education is constantly and immediately to hand, whatever the age of the students with whom we are dealing. A range of pedagogical disadvantages thus followed from not recognizing the different natures of childhood and adolescence, and from not realizing that people are engaged by different kinds of knowledge and experience at different ages. The way to discover these differences and so increase pedagogical effectiveness was to study closely the *nature* of the developing child and adolescent, and arrange conditions so that that nature would be allowed optimal opportunity for development. Only when we have discovered the true nature of the learner will we be able to achieve our educational goals.

Rousseau agreed with Plato's general program for shaping the mind by means of carefully selected and organized knowledge and experiences. His eventual aim, no less than Plato's, was the making of what we might call a moral and cultured adult. But there are significant differences between the two. Plato made no distinction between the education of the individual and that of the citizen; society and individual were reflections of each other, at different scales of magnitude. For Rousseau, society was the source of potential corruption. It had to be kept at bay until the individual had grown, in concert with nature, sufficiently strong and self-reliant to be able to withstand its corruption. Plato and Rousseau also differ profoundly in locating the dynamic of the educational process. In Plato's scheme, knowledge drives the educational process, and its stages are recognized by the amount and kind of knowledge that has been accumulated. In Rousseau's scheme, the "internal" developing nature of the learner is critical, and the accumulation of knowledge and experience will further the educational process only if they cohere with the natural maturation of the individual.

Our general conception of education struggles to contain these conflicting components—along with a number of others, of course. But these three alone are enough to undermine any attempt at implementing this conception of education. If we try to implement one component rigorously, we conflict with requirements of the others. If we try to balance them, giving each proportionate importance, we can only reach flaccid compromises at a level that removes from each component its distinctive character and force. This I fear is the general condition of our attempts to implement our conception of education in state-run educational systems. We aim to socialize students, engaging their commitment to a range of attitudes, beliefs, values, and social conventions, and so make them more alike. We aim also to educate them in both the Platonic and Rousseauian senses, developing each individual's different potentials, making them more distinct, and also training them in the use of reason to dissolve beliefs and to be critical of social conventions. So we try to socialize students, but not so much that would risk accusations of indoctrination; we try to incorporate the Platonic program, but not so much that would risk accusations of élitism; and we try to develop the uniqueness of each student ensuring that the nature of the developing individual determines what learning and experience are most appropriate at any time, but not so much that would risk accusations of replacing education by entertainment or psychotherapy or solipsism. We allow each component inadequate scope for its proper implementation, and adequate scope only to undermine each other.

And yet we cannot dispense with the wisdom developed in oral cultures about socialization, nor can we dispense with Plato's and Rousseau's great insights about education. We cannot ignore socializing and its intellectual requirements, we cannot ignore the liberal tradition of teaching the best that has been thought and said, and we cannot ignore the distinctive nature of learners at different ages, nor the differences among them. At a sufficiently general level it seems we should be able to address all of these in educational institutions. But when we look at the implications of each of them, we seem to run into problems of mutual incompatibility. Our general conception of education that tries to embrace them all seems radically incoherent; its most prominent constituents seem discordant. The challenge for a curriculum that tries to implement such a conception of education is to make people more alike while making them more distinct, and to use knowledge to shape the nature of the individual while letting the nature of the individual determine what knowledge is relevant.

Now clearly I have characterized these components in a way that emphasizes their incompatibilities. And certainly some part of the problem is due to the way it is characterized. At the simplest level we can observe, for example, that having "to make people more alike while making them more distinct" is a tendentious way of putting it, suggesting mutual incompatibility. We could instead at least suggest the possibility of compatibility by saying that we aim to make people more alike in some respects and more distinct in other respects. As long as these "respects" do not conflict, we could hope to achieve both these aims in an educational program without necessary conflicts. So we might hope to encourage commitments to certain social conventions in a way not incompatible with the development of critical reasoning about them.

The challenge, then, is to give due weight to the various insights that are indispensible parts of our conception of education and to articulate them in a way that transcends the incoherences and incompatibilities that we have inherited. These incompatibilities are, I think, quite profound, and remain in the developments of the traditions derived from Plato and Rousseau and in the changing forms of the imperative to socialize children. They will not be resolved by world-play, or by some new facts about learning styles or development, but by new ways of conceiving of education. This is only to echo a conclusion reached by many others. The most comprehensive and energetic attempt to reconceive education and to find a coherence among its indispensible components was John Dewey's. Since then, with the conviction that Dewey's heroic achievement in the end gives too much weight to socialization and to Rousseau and too little weight to Plato's insight, there have been numerous further attempts. And this is another.

This is the second of a projected four volumes that attempt to elaborate a somewhat new conception of education. Each volume deals with how people at particular ages can best make sense of the world and of experience, with what things are educationally most valuable to learn, and with how one can meaningfully and engagingly teach those things at the appropriate ages. They are designed so that each volume can be read separately as an essay on the practice of education during the particular age range with which it deals. The first volume, *Primary Understanding,* characterized a kind of understanding that, implied by the recapitulation scheme, logically and psychologically precedes romantic understanding. I called the primary kind of understanding Mythic. I will give an abbreviated description of it in Chapter 3 while discussing the transition from it to romantic understanding. And in Chapter 7 I will give an abbreviated description of what I call philosophic understanding, which succeeds romantic. (The fourth kind I call Ironic.)

The conception of education I will elaborate in these volumes might best be seen as layered. I will describe the educational program as made up from four somewhat distinct layers, in each of which we develop a somewhat distinct kind of understanding. The educational program prescribes how these kinds of understanding can be acquired sequentially during an individual's formative years, yielding in their coalescence a modern educated consciousness.

Choosing labels is often a risky business. I hope you will accept these simply as attempts to suggest some central feature of each constituent layer of the educational process, allowing the characterizations of the layers to give meaning to the labels, rather than allowing other associations of the labels to color their meanings.

Having chosen to call this overall scheme Recapitulationist, I should perhaps take a few introductory paragraphs explaining what might seem the perverse move of associating this work with one of the few traditions in the history of educational inquiry that is generally assumed to have been convincingly undermined and repudiated. But, even so, this work outlines a recapitulation scheme; it argues that the individual's path to a modern educated consciousness follows in some significant ways the path of our culture's forging of that consciousness.

The plausibility of nineteenth- and early twentieth-century recapitulation schemes rested on the superficial similarities between the ways we can generally describe the historical development of a culture and individuals' initiation into that culture during their youth. The individual in becoming educated follows a path—recapitulates a process—which the culture itself forged. In a trivial sense, of course, all educational programs are recapitulationist. The term serves to distinguish a particular tradition when the historical description of the culture's development becomes a significant guide to the structuring of the curriculum.

The movement to develop distinctive recapitulationist curricula began in the latter part of the nineteenth century, as another expression of the immense influence of evolutionary theory. The movement, which had been prominent mainly in Germany and the United States, though influential throughout the western world, collapsed as a result of a number of problems. The initial formulations of recapitulation theory in education referred for support to the "ontogeny-recapitulates-phylogeny" doctrines of mid-century biology. The undermining of the simplistic version of that doctrine in biology was one blow to recapitulation schemes in education (Gould, 1977). They also tied themselves into a somewhat primitive developmental psychology, expounded in North America by G. S. Hall among others, and as the foundations of that recapitulationist psychology fell into disrepute so educational schemes based on it lost favor. Perhaps most important in their demise was their fundamental conflict with progressivism in North America and the modern education movement in Great Britain and Europe. The commonest form of recapitulation curriculum was the "culture-epoch" type. In this, children began by studying the primitive periods of human history and development, because children were taken to be psychological savages themselves. In such curricula the modern world did not appear until the end of schooling. A basic tenet of progressivism and modern education was that children must begin their exploration of the world with what is at hand and around them. By the mid-1920s the tide of progressivism and modernism had swept recapitulationist curricula away.

The recapitulationist dimension of my program will be developed through the first three volumes. It will be discussed explicitly in Chapter 8 of this volume. It differs from the recapitulationist schemes that were common at the beginning of this century in a number of ways. I make no attempt here to base the program on biology or psychology, though my argument does have a psychological dimension. It is different perhaps most significantly in what it claims is recapitulated. "Culture-epoch" theorists were imprisoned in the assumption that it was the knowledge or content of cultural history that had to be recapitulated through the curriculum or psychological processes from savagery to civilized reason. What is recapitulated, I will argue, are kinds of understanding.

The analysis of modern educated consciousness that undergirds this essay concludes that it is composed of four major, somewhat distinct, constituents. These were developed historically in the making of modern consciousness, in a complex but roughly distinguishable sequence. Mythic, romantic, philosophic, and ironic layers of modern consciousness may seem odd categories for characterizing an educational program. Certainly we are familiar with more technical sounding terms. But I will argue that education can be better grasped in terms of such forms of understanding. The romantic capacity to feel wonder at the particularity of the world, or the philosophic capacity to search for general patterns or recurrence in phenomena, and the extensive set of such sense-making capacities that I will outline in these volumes, seem to me the kind of terms from which we can construct a clear and coherent conception of the process of education. Any four-layer model, of course, must be simplistic and too schematic to catch the complexity of education adequately, but it can perhaps provide a general map and a sense of direction.

Perhaps a note of elaboration of this point is worth a further paragraph. In the early chapters of this book, our subject is in small part cultural history—features of Romanticism and romantic understanding—and in larger part students' intellectual lives. The forms and contents of thinking, the nature of ideas, are more complex than any language we have developed to refer to them. Ideas are protean things, sliding and changing constantly. The ways we normally refer to them are a little like the clear primary colored diagrams one sees in expensive biology texts, indicating the distinct elements of an organism. The neat pictures are so unlike the largely monochrome mess we encounter on first seeing the organism under a microscope. But the neat clear diagram helps the eye to discriminate the discriminable parts of the real thing. So, too, though much less reliably, the ways we represent ideas and students' thinking are terribly crude simplifications that strive after the shifting shapes of mental life. The theories and models we compose to represent some features of this immense complexity need to be seen as the crudest of diagrams. There is evidence occasionally in education that some tentative finding from research or some hesitant theory is taken as the whole truth about large areas of children's thinking, so this *caveat* is worth making here, and is intended to be borne in mind through what follows here as much as anywhere else. No doubt this is not a warning you need, but it serves the defensive purpose of clarifying a little my sense of what this scheme can offer.

My aim, then, is to describe as well as I can an ideal of education and a program for realizing it. This essay prescribes practical steps for educating children within the normal contexts of schools and homes in modern western societies, and it is coherent with what is logically and psychologically the case. The analysis of each layer of understanding yields principles from which I will compose a new curriculum and describe ways of planning teaching that will lead to more meaningful and engaging learning.

A few final words to a long introduction: My claim that romantic understanding is somehow appropriate in the middle-school years is not of course an original observation. It has been proposed by a number of people in different senses. Perhaps the best known is A.N. Whitehead's observation that during the process of education students should pass through a stage of romance. While much of my characterization of romantic understanding, and the "romantic" curriculum and teaching methods I propose, are quite unlike Whitehead's suggestions, they share and perhaps grow from his general insight. This sense of romance in learning is not a simple "motivator"; I will argue that it is an essential component of the educational process and an essential characteristic of an educated person.

Whitehead writes of these years in students' lives as the golden age for learning; a golden age over which in his time and social group "so often falls the shadow of the crammer" (Whitehead, 1967, p. 21). Today we are less concerned about the crammer than about a kind of aimless drift; the practical requirements of vocational training have not yet become urgent but no clear image of education provides direction and energy to the curriculum or teaching. But I think he was right to see a significant part of the solution in a sense of romance. And while such a notion might seem disproportionately trivial to the practical problems of education today, I will argue that romantic understanding is indeed a key that can help us get past at least some of the problems we are encountering.

Particularly in Chapter 2, I will discuss ways in which the invention of writing and printing have affected thinking and our cultural lives. We hear a lot at present about how electronic media are affecting current cultural life and thought. One theme of the next volume is the attempt, post-Romanticism, to establish an authoritative authorial voice that strove for a canonical fixity in texts. Authors tried to achieve what they saw as the authority of science, establishing a truth in their texts that would be relevant to all future times—not relevant only to the contemporary social environment and dissolving just a little more slowly than the voice in the ongoing social babble. One influence of electronic media seems to be the undercutting of this transcendent authorial ambition. I will conclude this Introduction with my electronic mail address, and invite readers to send their comments, criticisms, elaborations, emendations, questions, or whatever. I will reply to each message and also upload all the other messages and my responses to them. I will update these at irregular intervals for a few years. Thus this book becomes evidently not a canonical text in the old "philosophic" sense but more like the beginning of a conversation—in an older and newer sense—in which the readers become also the authors as our understanding of the text is elaborated and changed in the on-going discourse.

Please send your messages to:

USERKEGA@SFU (via BITNET)
USERKEGA@CC.SFU.CA (via Internet)
or
Kieran__Egan@CC.SFU.CA (via Internet)

1
Romanticism, romantic understanding, and education

Introduction

"Romanticism" is a twentieth-century term for a set of distinctive characteristics particularly evident in the work of a group of writers at the end of the eighteenth and the beginning of the nineteenth centuries. That their writings were received enthusiastically by a large part of the literate population at the time suggests that whatever attitude of mind is expressed in these writings was quite widely shared. Related characteristics are evident in contemporary paintings, sculptures, music, and in the enthusiastic responses of many to the French Revolution and then to the career of Napoleon. A part of Romanticism was the conviction that new and powerful ways of making sense of reality were combining with new ways of truly expressing that sense, that immensely complex problems about our place in the world were being in some new fashion addressed and resolved.

My interest in Romanticism here is due to its providing an unusually full expression of romantic understanding. I do not wish to suggest that romantic understanding is some discrete mode of thought and feeling. Rather, I will argue that it is a mode of sense-making that tends to emphasize certain features of the world and experience at the expense of others. It does not, except perhaps in some extraordinary cases, wholly dominate a person's manner of seeing and making sense, but during the historical periods of its greatest emphasis and during phases of individual's lives today, it can strongly condition the ways in which people make sense of the world and of their experience.

The characteristics I will briefly discuss below are not, however, unique to Romanticism. One of the reasons it is so difficult to provide a generally convincing account of Romanticism as a movement is that it is very difficult to identify anything that is unique to it. The more precisely one tries to describe some distinctive feature, the easier it becomes to point to examples of that feature in other times and places. Even if Romanticism is the fullest instantiation of romantic understanding, we find adumbrations of it throughout cultural history. The sense of romance is evident in much Greek classical writing, informing, for example, Herodotus's *Histories*—in which brave little Athens, on behalf of freedom and the democratic virtues, spearheaded the victorious battles against the vast and despotic Persian empire. The emphatic response of so many Europeans to the career of Napoleon is echoed precisely in Arrian's account of the career of that earlier lawless hero Alexander. If we note the characteristic fascination of romantic writers with dreams, we will be hard put to distinguish this from the similar fascination we see in Elizabethan/Jacobean writers such as Shakespeare.

It is common to try to highlight the distinct qualities of Romanticism by contrasting them with those of the preceding Enlightenment neoclassicism, which aimed to reintroduce classical rigor and reason into all areas of life. We are encouraged to see profound differences between succeeding generations here, to see, say, Wordsworth as representing a new freedom from the rigid conventions of neo-classical forms and a new incorporation of everyday language into poetry which achieves sublime effects. In part this real difference in style is exaggerated by the Romantics' own rhetoric, as when Coleridge insists on the new exploitation of the imagination and talks disparagingly of those

> who have been *rationally* educated, as it is styled. They were
> marked by a microscopic acuteness; but when they looked at
> great things, all became a blank & they saw nothing—and
> denied (very illogically) that anything could be seen (cited in
> Potter, 1933, p. 355).

Their rhetoric of a revolution in consciousness tends to suppress the continuities evident in their work with that of the neo-classical Enlightenment. Our use of categories which have been mainly deployed to define contrasts tends to hide the sense in which the Romantics' writings may be seen rather as the fulfilment of trends evident during the earlier period. As Marilyn Butler puts it:

> It is easy to miss Wordsworth's representativeness as it is to
> miss Blake's. Both are often taken to be initiating a new
> artistic tradition, rather than joining an established one. Yet the
> fact is that Wordsworth was brought up in the mainstream of
> Enlightenment culture, and he realized its potential better than

any poet anywhere, with the possible exception of Goethe
(Butler, 1981, p. 57).

One way of establishing a uniqueness for Romanticism is to establish
a canon of romantic writers and focus on their individual works. These
indeed are unique. But it quickly becomes clear that this merely moves
the problem a little, once we try to find common elements among the
works of the canon that are not present elsewhere. Then we are forced
to recognize Romanticism as a continuation of the neo-classical Enlightenment, which in turn continued and elaborated ideas and forms of
expression from the Renaissance. The Renaissance, the Enlightenment,
and Romanticism all contain significant features of romantic understanding, and my focus here is on Romanticism, not because it represents a
distinct kind of understanding from those evident in the earlier periods,
but because it represents some of its central features in a fuller form.
Lovejoy has also argued that:

> If . . . we recognize the shift from uniformitarian to the
> diversitarian preconception the most significant and distinctive
> feature of the romantic revolution, it is evident that there had
> always been present in the Platonic tradition a principle tending
> towards Romanticism, and that this had been enunciated with
> especial clarity and insistence by the philosophers and moralists
> and philosophic poets of the so-called Age of Reason (Lovejoy,
> 1936, p. 297).

So the differences among the cultural eras of modern Europe are of
less interest to me here than certain common features which develop
through the period, culminating in Romanticism. I realize that this might
seem a touch cavalier when so much scholarly effort—on which this
work is parasitic—goes to etch the differences among these periods,
particularly between the Enlightenment program of reason-guided re-
form and Romanticism's reaction against it. But it is a matter of the
level of the phenomena on which one focuses:

> At first sight nothing could be more sharply opposed to
> Romanticism [as neo-classicism], yet some of the most
> characteristic elements in the classical revival can just as easily
> be described as romantic—the attraction of the primitive and of
> simplicity, the appeal to the emotions in painting, the ecstatic
> language in which Winckelmann wrote about Greece, Piranesi's

exaggeration of the scale of Roman ruins, the admiration for the sublime (Bullock, 1985, p. 75).

It is also instructive to remember that James Macpherson's wildly romantic *Fingal*—"an ancient epic poem in six books" originally written by "Ossian, the son of Fingal, translated from the Galic language," as the title page avers—was published first in 1763, at the height of what we are accustomed to think of as the Enlightenment. This fraudulent invention was greeted with immense enthusiasm and translated within a short time into every European language (the Dutch translator, Nicholas Rupke, claiming to have ignored Macpherson and gone back to the Gaelic "original"). If our focus on the British Enlightenment strays from Pope and Addison and Hume we find endless cases of such "Romanticism within the Enlightenment" (Ashton, 1989, p. 302). We find them particularly among the largely female writers of "romance" novels, who also made and explored Gothic, ribald, fantastic, and philosophic forms, from as early as the time of Aphra Behn (1640–89).

Romanticism, suggested Baudelaire, was not to be defined by its choice of subject matter nor by any privileged vantage point on the truth, but rather by a distinctive manner of *feeling*. A feature of much romantic writing was the recognition of the absence of feeling in many expressions of the Enlightenment program; they were too coldly rational. In Romanticism one can see a coalescence of some of the developments of rationality that received particular emphasis during the Enlightenment with a reassertion of the importance of the emotions and of the imagination in making fuller sense of the world and of experience. Also, of course, there are a sufficient number of cases of Romantics who simply reversed the imbalance of their Enlightenment predecessors for many scholars to include an exaggerated emphasis on emotion and feelings as a characteristic of Romanticism. But the coalescence of the Enlightenment program with the liberating "feeling" Baudelaire recognized as central to Romanticism, led at its best to coordinating daring imaginativeness and subtle sensitivity with refined rationality in systematic pursuit of what the imagination grasped at. It also led to the deployment of highly developed powers of representation and expression in communicating the results of that systematic pursuit. The free—for modern tastes perhaps the over-free—expression of feeling, the scientific rigor, and the mastery of literary technique coalesce perhaps most notably in Goethe. But technical sophistication, as well as imaginative exhuberance, mark all the major figures of Romanticism. Coleridge's contempt for the kind of education which is styled rational is sharpened by his own appreciation of rationality as the combination of imagination and systematic method working together.

It may seem a little crude to crawl under the glittering surface of Romanticism searching for techniques that support the kind of understanding evident in its literary and artistic achievements; it smacks of trying to explain the magic of the theatre by exposing stage props, two-dimensional scenery, machines, and the techniques of the actors. The emphasis on techniques, particularly in the following chapter, is not a product of mechanistic reductionism, but is motivated by the desire to grasp some of the cultural prerequisites of romantic understanding—to grasp some of the capacities that needed to be in place for that kind of understanding to become prominent and to be sustained.

In trying to account for the unusual number of writers of the first rank working around the turn of the century, and in giving the sense of a genuine romantic *movement,* it is common to note the considerable increase in the kind and number of books circulating in the later eighteenth century in most of Europe. My interest, however, will be also on the technical changes one might observe in those books, changes that subtly but profoundly affect the relationship of the reader and the text, changes, indeed, that affect the kind of thought and understanding that texts can encourage, and changes that lead to quite new kinds of texts, such as dictionaries and encyclopaedias. Technical developments that made the thought coded in texts more easily accessible to readers had continued from the Middle Ages. These had gradually transformed the appearance of the page, making visual access constantly easier and faster. The innovations of the early Middle Ages, such as spaces between the words, paragraphs, notes separated from the main text, and so on, led to the revolutionary change of enabling almost any literate person to master the great art of silent reading. When there were no spaces between words, it was necessary to sound out the letters in order to interpret even what the words were. Reading was a noisy business. The increasingly accessible text not only affected reading, but also the kind of thinking that could go on while reading. Being able to read easily meant that one did not have to invest considerable intellectual energy at the lexical level, but one could shift that energy and focus it instead on the semantic level. Print, and the further developments in designing accessible pages, continued these changes in the kind of thinking possible while reading. Ong sees the late eighteenth century as the time when "writing and print matured;" in his terms, "typography was interiorized in the Western psyche definitively at the moment in Western history known as the Romantic Movement" (Ong, 1977, p. 283).

Other larger scale technical developments affected consciousness at this time, of course. As the French Revolution and the career of Napoleon transformed people's consciousness of what was politically possible, so the early Industrial Revolution was transforming in perhaps some deeper sense what was conceived as possible. The changing face of parts of Europe, the force of King Steam, and King Cotton, and King Iron were creating a conception of the future as something unknowable in a new sense. One could project all kinds of hopes and fears into it. The imaginative artist exploring this new consciousness was seen as a kind of prophet; the artist was no longer holding, as it were, a mirror up to nature, but rather shone light into the hidden recesses of present consciousness and into future possibilities (Abrams, 1953). The romantic reaction against the dehumanizing machine and factory system, against the dark satanic mills, was only one face of this consciousness; the romantic sense of a better and quite different future was another. But we might be cautious of attending too insistently to the vast industrial, economic, and political changes of the time and so underestimating the influence on all these changes of the organization of printed text on a page.

Without a large number of technical achievements, which constitute Western cultural history and which have had profound influences on how and what people think, what I am calling romantic understanding could be achieved only fitfully and could not be systematically sustained. Within Romanticism, in a remarkably prodigal production of artistic and other imaginative intellectual work, was generated a range of further technical achievements which make the capacity to attain this romantic understanding relatively easy for anyone who lives after that movement. The poetry of Wordsworth, for example, involves and expresses a romantic understanding of the world and of experience (among much else, of course.) The poetry of Wordsworth can evoke, stimulate, and develop our capacity to grasp the world and experience in that romantic way; it enables us more easily to achieve and sustain that romantic view, that kind of feeling, that kind of understanding. The recapitulation of that kind of understanding during the middle-school years, and of the capacities and technical achievements that undergird and sustain it, is, I will argue, educationally desirable. An incidental benefit of this recapitulationary approach is the kind of justification provided for the inclusion of—to stay with the present example—Wordsworth's poetry in the curriculum. At present such poetry, and what tend to be called the Fine Arts, are justified by rather effete claims that carry very little weight against utilitarian arguments for mathematics or science or "the basics." In this scheme, their justification turns on their ability to stimulate a set of intellectual capacities that empower the mind to deal more adequately with the world and with experience. I hope a set of much better arguments will emerge from the first seven chapters to justify a prominent place in the middle-school curriculum for the arts, along with some insights about how to make them meaningful and engaging to students.

The task for this chapter then is to begin with a brief characterization of Romanticism and so prepare for an inquiry in Chapter 2 into the capacities and technical achievements that undergird and sustain it. In both chapters I will elaborate on what I mean by romantic understanding. I will also indicate briefly in this chapter why any of this might have anything at all to do with education today. Despite this lengthy introduction, I do not intend to make an extensive exploration of Romanticism, and have no ambition at all to try to contribute to the continuing intense debates about its nature. What I want to do is take an overlapping set of characteristics that are fairly generally agreed to be central to Romanticism and indicate how one might use those towards building a sense of romantic understanding.

Some aspects of Romanticism

The diffuseness of Romanticism makes it hospitable to quite disparate characterizations, and allows those who identify its "essence" in some particular qualities plenty of material in which to find supporting texts. My aim here is to work at a relatively superficial level gathering a set of characteristics which seem to be very generally accepted as reflecting some prominent aspects of Romanticism; in as far as it is a distinguishable movement, that is, these are some of the things most commonly pointed to in distinguishing it.

One of the key achievements claimed for the principal Romantics is that they saw through the conventions of an increasingly ossified neoclassicism and forged a new and purer vision of reality. Conformity to artificial social conventions was connectedly seen, not as the necessary framework of social life, but as getting in the way of more natural and sensible human relationships; rigid political structures were seen, not as reflecting God's preferences, but as getting in the way of more generally effective political arrangements; conventions of painting, sculpting, and writing were seen, not as given forms which were to be refined and elaborated, but as getting in the way of art's proper job of expressing new visions of the world and of human experience.

By seeing political, social, and artistic life in terms of the same metaphor of overthrowing conventions which get in the way of more natural contacts among people, and between people and Nature, we make, or recognize, connections among some aspects of Beethoven's music, Frances (*quondam* Fanny) Burney's diaries, the French Revolution, William Wordsworth's poetry, changing social *mores,* Jane Austen's novels, Napoleon's career, Artemisia Gentillesci's paintings, Rude's sculpture, and so on. The "fit" of the metaphor to disparate events and forms of expression during the late eighteenth and early nineteenth centuries is what sustains the sense of a *movement* with a graspable, if diffuse, character.

A somewhat paradoxical aspect of Romanticism, at least as a literary movement, is that its breaking of neo-classical conventions and its revolt in favor of the kind of "enthusiasm" so deprecated by eighteenth century rationalists did not only, or even most characteristically, lead to fantastic invention. The main discovery of Romanticism, to the Romantics, was reality. The excitement of Romanticism was not simply a sense of imagination being freed, but its freedom being to explore afresh the reality of human experience and of the world. Blake expressed it in terms of the need to cleanse the gates of perception; Shelley, as lifting the veil from the hidden beauty of the world, making familiar objects seem as if they were not familiar. So it is the everyday *details* of experience and of the world, often at a purely descriptive level, that fills much of the most distinctively romantic art and literature: "The greater part of their poetry was the record of observation, whether of their own souls or of the world outside. The accuracy is sometimes painful and the detail excessive. . . . Romantic art, then, is not 'romantic' in the vulgar sense, but 'realistic' in the sense of concrete, full of particulars" (Barzun, 1961, p. 25–26).

This drive to record detail in all its diversity is seen by Lovejoy as an expression of one of the most profound shifts in the history of thought. From the neo-classical impulse to conform to universal and uniform standards supposedly inherent in nature, Romanticism turned instead to celebrate diversity, to strive for "the fullest possible expression of the abundance of differentness that there is, actually or potentially, in nature and human nature" (Lovejoy, 1936, p. 293). What most distinguished Romanticism, according to Lovejoy, was its expressing this radically new spirit of "diversitarianism," along with what he calls "organicism" and "dynamism." The shift from a Platonic search for the paradigm of things to a focus on the things for their own sake seems generally accepted as signalling Romanticism: "A cardinal axiom of Romanticism was that of the uniqueness, singleness and particularity of everything in the universe" (Morse, 1982, p. 2): An axiom given a precise form in Austen's novels and an almost tangible vividness in the Journals of Dorothy Wordsworth.

The authority commonly appealed to in challenging the conventions of neo-classicism was the freshly perceived Nature. An inspiration of this appeal, an earlier dramatic challenge to social, political, and educational conventions made in the name of Nature, was available in the writings of Rousseau. He held the conventional ideas of social and political life up to ridicule by contrasting them with his vision of Nature's preferred processes, passionately denouncing the unnecessary constraints that keep us all in chains though we were born free children of Nature: "Fix your eyes on nature; follow the path traced by her" (Rousseau, 1974, p. 14).

The purity, consistency, reliability of the natural world is commonly represented in romantic writing in contrast with the distress or frenzy or corruption that cities and society entail. Interiorizing the admirable qualities of nature, however, can help to sustain the mind through the distress of social life:

> Nature never did betray
> The heart that loved her; 'tis her privilege,
> Through all the years of this our life, to lead
> From joy to joy: for she can so inform
> The mind that is within us, so impress
> With quietness and beauty, and so feed
> With lofty thoughts, that neither evil tongues,
> Rash judgements, nor the sneers of selfish men,
> Nor greetings where no kindness is, nor all
> The dreary intercourse of daily life,
> Shall e'er prevail against us, or disturb
> Our cheerful faith, that all which we behold
> Is full of blessings.
> (Wordsworth, "Tintern Abbey" ll. 122–134)

The lofty thoughts that ensue from reverent attention to Nature provide a basis of authority, a sense of truth, that is for the Romantics close to the voice of God:

> so shalt thou see and hear
> The lovely shapes and sounds intelligible
> Of that eternal language which thy God
> Utters . . .
> (Coleridge, "Frost at Midnight," ll. 58–61)

This sense of Nature contrasted sharply with the Nature of eighteenth-century rationalism. Eighteenth-century scientists and theologians "shared a common starting-point. Both parties accepted [the] Order of Nature as the fundamental datum, assuming that the material world in all its aspects conformed to certain fixed laws" (Toulmin and Goodfield, 1965, p. 101). Along with a universe of fixed laws and ignorance of the earth's and species' mutability, went an influential, informing package of mechanical metaphors. Another of Lovejoy's indices of the revolution involved in Romanticism was what he called "organicism." The Romantics spun from their new conception of nature a web of organic rather than mechanical metaphors with which to attain some grasp on experience and on the world. Organic growth is more natural than machine making, and a God who was sensed through the infinite diversity of the natural world seemed more worthy of worship than "the Supreme watch-maker" who constructed the complex mechanism of the universe. Organic metaphors also caught at the sense of mystery, of the strange and secret, that was a common feature of the Romantics' response to Nature (Abrams, 1953).

The focusing of imaginative energy on the details of the natural world seemed to lead (in contrast again to neo-classicism) to a new appreciation of a range of experience neglected or depreciated earlier. The natural rural scene—not the park carefully domesticated by a Capability Brown but the wild mountain top or unspoiled river side—became aesthetically valued, as the earthy wisdom of the peasant became valued in contrast to sophisticated town society and its polished wit. The aesthetic response to undomesticated nature involved a sense of mystery in the fact of its existence, of awe before its purity and beauty, and a sense of the self as the appreciator and experiencer. What is also characteristic of the Romantics' responses to Nature is their self-consciousness in their role as responders.

Another feature of Romanticism, then, to quote a rather stark summation of it, is that "Western European men and women came to believe in experience as something that goes on in the head, not as a drama in the world external to the self" (Harold Bloom, cited in Butler, 1981, p. 9). Wordsworth exemplified this shift when he claimed to find the old sources of external drama no longer the arena in which the most powerful emotions can be found or represented:

> Not chaos, not
> The darkest pit of lowest Erebus,
> Nor aught of blinder vacancy, scooped out
> By help of dreams—can breed such fear and awe
> As fall upon us often when we look
> Into our Minds, into the Mind of Man—
> My haunt, and the main region of my song.
> (Wordsworth, 1814 Preface to "The Excursion" ll. 35–41)

This identification of the inner self as the haunt to be explored for knowledge about experience apparently caused Blake, on reading these lines, severe physical distress (Darbishire, 1958, p. 139). One of Wordsworth's great achievements was to transform the details of his private experience into a form which was widely taken as expressing universal human experience. That may be too crude a way of putting it, but Marilyn Butler describes a part of his development this way:

> he felt that there had been a period in which his eye,
> dwelling on external things, had meant too much.
> Gradually his vision internalized itself: he perceived that
> significance lay not in the simple object in the world of
> Nature but in the power of his imagination to work upon
> the impression he retained, fully to appropriate to his own
> thought the 'spots in time' (Butler, 1981, p. 67).

Wordsworth's technique of seeking public significance in the details of private experience led logically to his great autobiographical poem, *The Prelude*. But this kind and degree of controlled self-consciousness seems to be something new in European culture: "Self-awareness of the intensity found in Rousseau and Wordsworth either did not exist before them, or for good reason was defined as a mode of madness" (Bloom, 1971, p. 461). The new kind of discovery of the self within, the conceptualizing of a central identity somehow tied up with nature—our natural self—led to the proliferation of autobiography as a literary *genre* during the Romantic period and after. It remains a *genre* in which close analysis of the details of private experience is expected to yield publically significant, and even universally valid, truths (S. Egan, 1984). Romanticism opened up the world within for detailed exploration and forged the techniques and much of the language that have been used in its exploration ever since. The haunt of our minds as explored by Freud and Jung is very much a discovery, perhaps invention, of Romanticism.

G.H. Mead considered Romanticism not simply a discovery of the self, but crucially a separation of the sense of self from the role played in the world. The "invention" of the self involved also the invention of quite new roles for people to "play" or to be. Peckham has identified new roles that appear within Romanticism—the Byronic hero, the visionary artist, the bohemian, the virtuoso, the dandy, the historian (Peckham, 1970, pp. 41–47); and, one might add, the compassionate humanitarian and the feminine creatrix. One might add, too, the new roles for women which male poets dwelt on, such as woman as nature, as mad mother, as enchantress, and so on.

Common to many of these roles, and vividly a part of much Romanticist writing and art, is the hero. (Butler notes: "The writers who achieved the greatest popular success in the late eighteenth and early nineteenth century were those who created simpler, more colourful imaginative worlds, dominated by heroes of superhuman effectiveness" (Butler, 1981, p. 2). The Byronic hero represented just one rather dramatic instance of heroism—one owing much to such Walter Scott characters as Marmion and drawing not a little, furtively, from the French cult of Napoleon. The ideal image of such heroism is caught in the supernaturally masterful Napoleon in Géricault's painting, calmly mounted on a wild horse, leading his army over the storm-tossed Alps. But each of the roles Peckham identifies has its own form of heroism in acting out in reality an artistic representation of aspects of one's personality. Not least among the heroes of romantic literature were the literary artists themselves. They partook in heroic action: this romantic view is caught in Ezra Pound's claim that "The history of an art is the history of masterworks. . . . The study of literature is hero-worship" (Pound, 1929, p. 7).

As in the earlier outburst of romantic energy during the Renaissance, which in part involved a revolt against the ossified scholasticism of the late Middle Ages, so the movers of Romanticism looked back to the earlier liberation of spirit they saw in, or projected into, myth and popular fantasy. The resistance to "classical" reason and Apollonian order led many to a fascination with the exotic and mysterious, to fantasy and the "irrational" myths of the ancient world and of modern "savages." The hearts of darkness that enticed new expeditions were attractive, we can see from diaries of the time, not only because of the promise of great financial profits—as resulted from taking beaver pelts from Nootka to China, for example—but also because of the lure of the strange and the unknown.

In Romanticism, then, we see (at least) one powerful ambivalence: attraction to the imaginative freedom of myth and fantasy, coupled with reverence for the particular details of everyday reality. Clearly these two impulses would be felt in different proportions in different people at different times. Nevertheless, in as far as certain general ideas had influence over how people made sense of the world and of their experience, this ambivalence seems inescapably characteristic of that distinctive sense-making movement we call Romanticism. It was a movement which sought to transcend reality in the spirit of myth and fantasy, while also being constrained within reality by its reverence for the diverse particularity of the world. It is, of course, out of attempts to forge coherence from such apparent ambivalences that great art seems often to come.

The hero particularly exemplifies this ambivalence. A hero is someone who is natural, who lives within the constraints of reality, yet who also transcends the normal bounds of human behavior and achievement. A touchstone of Romanticism is reverence for "genius." In the transcendent power, compassion, energy, ability, will, or whatever, of the genius lay the means to transform the world to something new and different, closer to the heart's desire, perhaps closer to an earthly paradise.

Thus Beethoven, Goethe, Byron, Scott, and so many others, almost worshipped the immense romantic spirit of Napoleon. It was not that the great figures of Romanticism always or consistently approved of Napoleon. To some of them, indeed, he was seen as a great evil. But he embodied, in awe-inspiring degree, force of will, energy, ingenuity, power, and an absolute recklessness about long-standing political, social, and legal conventions. What he did was breathtaking even to fervent Romantics, and beyond the bounds of what conventional politicians could begin to imagine. He seemed like some demonic force loosed upon the world, and yet he was a real flesh and blood person. The excitement of Napoleon was in part that he pushed further outward the sense of what was possible. His career provided a great sense of discovery, a discovery about the limits of the possible. It is harder for us with our more ironic view to share the Romantics' enthusiasm for Napoleon; we tend to see the corpses and count the cost. And while we may consider Napoleon, and Alexander, bandits who merit no admiration, and the French Revolution a regrettable excess, an understanding of Romanticism requires that we see what it was about them that filled people's throats with overflowing emotion and made their heads light with excitement:

> Bliss was it in that dawn to be alive,
> But to be young was very heaven!
> (Wordsworth, *The Prelude*, XI, l. 108–109)

The romantic hero was also typically a rebel. Romantic literature brims with sympathetic rebels assailing unjust authority figures. As in reality Kings Louis and George were seen by many to represent unjust authority and were revolted against, so Shelley's Jupiter and the God in Byron's *Cain* and Blake's Nobodaddy and Urizen justified revolt by those subject to them. A more subtle rebellion against an ingrained paternalism is evident in the work of some women writers which constitutes a quality of Romanticism only recently being adequately recognized. The novels of Anne Radcliffe, for example, portray female heroines, noble but beleaguered—a role allowing energy and ingenuity and transcendence over the constraints most commonly felt by women.

The hero exemplifies a further ambivalence in Romanticism. If the hero is a projection of our desire to transcend the constraints of everyday reality, that leaves our everyday selves somehow still fettered by reality. A commonplace of romantic literature that recurs throughout the century is the Doppelgänger, the double, who may represent one part of the self not adequately able to inhabit our role. The relationship between Frankenstein and his designedly transcendent monster catches this ambivalence, which we find also in *Wuthering Heights, Jane Eyre, Villette,* Jekyll and Hyde, *Moby Dick,* and eventually in crudest form in Clarke Kent and Superman, to name only a few sources. All express in some dramatic fashion the ambivalent conception of the self developed within Romanticism.

The ambivalence involved in wishing to transcend a reality whose constraints at the same time we recognize leads not only to the romantic hero, but also to an ambivalence in our relationship with nature. The reverence for detail and particularity lives in strained cohabitation with the desire for transcendence, but we can try to satisfy both impulses by seeing universes in grains of sands or forests in a handful of seeds. The everyday detail is thereby seen afresh, but still the mind strains outward to the limits, which somehow help to define and give meaning to the particulars. After Herschel's 1781 discovery of Uranus, it was considered the most distant planet in the solar system. Blake's *Book of Urizen* spans from Creation to the Last Day, exemplifying the imagination striving after the limits that are connected to, and give context and meaning to, the immediate details of everyday life.

Another side of the ambivalence about nature is evident in its representation as mute and immutable but also as able to express emotional states to us. This lakewater scene, these daffodils, can inject something of their hypostatized serenity and joy into the mind of their beholder. Romanticism invented a way of seeing the world which involved a sense of the world looking back at us. This may be self-consciously recognized as an invention even while being used, as in Emerson's "The ruin or the blank that we see when we look at nature, is in our own eye" (Emerson cited in Bloom, 1973, p. 157). Or it can give bliss to the inward eye that can call it forth in later solitude. Its implacable constancy can help us transcend our too easy mutability, its purity can help us transcend our corruption, its ever-renewed beauty can help us transcend our individual decay. This sense of spiritual transcendence finds physical analogues in romantic literature in the discovery of the mountain, as a place where a kind of transcendence is at least physically achievable. Such places give sight over, perhaps insight into, the world below. At a physical level it is exemplified by the rapid rise in mountain walking and mountain climbing. In literature it is perhaps best captured by Wordsworth's meditations after his climbs of Snowdon, Helvellyn, Black Comb, and so forth.

Central to Romanticism is the imagination. Shakespeare's worldly-wise Theseus might scoffingly claim that

> imagination bodies forth
> The forms of things unknown, the poet's pen
> Turns them to shapes, and gives to airy nothing
> A local habitation, and a name.
> (*A Midsummer Night's Dream,* Act V, Scene i.)

But the Romantics were convinced that the imagination could indeed give a local habitation and a name to much about the world and experience that had not before been rightly seen and which, though central to our lives, had remained unknown or unrecognized. Romantic literature is rich in what sometimes seem extravagant tributes to the importance of the imagination. The "inward eye," the "visionary gleam" suggest imagination's value to us. The Romantics complete a development in Western intellectual history wherein the mind is conceived as a kind of inward theatre or cinema in which we can project images and actions and ideas quite cut off from reality. In this inward theatre anything is possible that we can imagine, and, from our imagining, new ideas or plans or whatever may come. The same Greek root for "theatre" and "theory" indicates the early consciousness of this development. The romantic sense of the importance of the imagination is an expression of the full realization and exploitation of a mental capacity whose development got underway, I will argue in the next chapter, with the invention of the alphabet. This new power was seen by many of the Romantics as immensely beneficial: "The great instrument of moral good is the imagination" (Shelley 1960, p. 14).

Traditionally the canon of romantic writers has been dominated by men, and is, in some counts, entirely, male. Many of these male writers have tended to glorify masculine qualities and to deprecate or patronize the feminine. Even Blake, who overtly in his philosophical poems conceives of male and female as equal and interdependent, nevertheless constantly associates weakness with femininity and any assertiveness by females with a kind of unnatural power-hunger. As Susan Fox puts it: "He admired women, but not enough to imagine them autonomous human beings" (Fox, 1977, p. 508). "Blake's philosophical principle of mutuality is thus undermined by stereotypical metaphors of femaleness which I believe he adopted automatically in his early poems and then tried to redress but found himself trapped by in his late works" (Fox, 1977, pp. 507–8). Blake certainly came to recognize the destructive effects of received attitudes towards women but, while these attitudes may be representative of the society in which he was educated and for which he wrote, this aspect of his work cannot but arouse some discomfort in modern readers. The fact of the received canon being largely male and even its more sensitive writers harboring patronizing attitudes, or worse, towards women has persuaded some modern feminists to see Romanticism as a whole as "masculinist." If they are right, they would damage my argument, because I want to claim that the characteristics of romantic understanding which we find most fully developed in Romanticism are properly to be acquired by both males and females in their education today.

Fortunately for my argument, another energetic current of feminist writing has been concerned to show that much of the problem is due to the "masculinist" bias in modern scholarship that has tended to neglect the many female writers and artists who should be recognized as significant in the romantic movement. During the last couple of decades, critics have both acknowledged the importance of women writers and painters whose work prominently embodies romantic characteristics, and reinterpreted and reevaluated the familiar but depreciated work of some women. So, for example, the chatty diarist Fanny Burney is seen differently as the experimental novelist Frances Burney; the precocious girl whose conversation delighted Dr. Johnson becomes the more potent, and less easily patronized, woman who shared drugs with de Quincey and Coleridge (cf. Doody, 1989). Dorothy Wordsworth has emerged from her brother's shadow as a considerable romantic writer, not simply the fair-copyist of William's poems, and Christina is seen as the more considerable of the Rossetti poets, and so on.

That is, the persistence of patronizing attitudes towards women among some males prominent in the romantic movement does not mean that the intellectual capacities that Romanticism stimulated and developed are somehow therefore "masculinist." The recent recovery and reevaluation of much work by women romantic writers and painters has helped to make clear that Romanticism is not simply a male movement, and has helped also to enrich our sense of Romanticism, by emphasizing the kinds of sensitivity, compassion, and nurturing that we find prominently in the work of some of these women.

The above, then, are some commonly recognized constituents of the rather diffuse movement we call Romanticism. They are particularly prominent in the works of a group of major writers and artists, and in what seems the general educated taste, of the period around 1800. They do not disappear thereafter, of course; they become rather devices of style or techniques used to achieve recognized effects on readers, audience, or viewers, but devices incorporated with others. What is unusual about Romanticism is the number of major artists who used these devices in heightened form. While the high notes of Romanticism are rarely heard again so clearly and purely, they recur consistently through the nineteenth century and up to the present day. Unfortunately perhaps for the reputation of "romance," they seem particularly vulnerable to degeneration into a kind of sentimental whimsy. But they are evident also in some of the finest later artistic work, though often transformed by coalescence with other devices and techniques. The constituents of Romanticism, however, are not historical curiosities; they are a part of the ways we now see, hear, and make sense of the world:

> 'Romanticism' is inchoate because it is not a single intellectual movement but a complex of responses to certain conditions which Western society has experienced and continues to experience since the middle of the eighteenth century (Butler, 1981, p. 184).

Romantic understanding

My reason for plunging thus briefly into Romanticism has been to get some help in describing what I mean by romantic understanding. In Romanticism one can see both a range of powerful expressions of romantic understanding and also the invention or discovery of the techniques that make romantic understanding relatively easy to attain for succeeding generations. I will explore this latter point in Chapter 8: here I would like to begin moving from the particulars of Romanticism as an historical movement identified through the unique works of particular individuals towards abstracting from those a set of characteristics of the kind of understanding that they exemplify.

The leading romantic figures did not use, nor would have used, such a term to describe themselves. It was not till the 1860s that people looking back recognized those individuals as embodying certain common features that seemed well labeled as "romantic." To the Romantics themselves this would likely have seemed a quite peculiar label. A "romance" to them denoted primarily a medieval story in verse which combined chivalry, a love interest, and commonly a patina of mysticism. "Romance" derives from the Romanic, what we more often call the Romance, languages—the vernaculars that developed in southern Europe largely from the decay of Latin. By extension it became the term used to describe the most distinctive form of literature that survived in those languages. "Romances" continued developing, achieving a further distinctive prose form in sixteenth century Spain. These later "romances" typically involved extravagant and sentimental adventures, with a free-wheeling imaginative narrative line—parodying which was a part of the success of *Don Quixote*. Central to the meaning of "romance" in these sources, and persisting in our meaning, are adventure, marvels, surprise, coincidence, characters who are lost, wandering, enchanted, searching for their somewhat mysterious Holy Grail (they usually can't describe it but are confident they will recognize it when they meet it)—parodying which in our time is a part of the success of some of David Lodge's novels (see, Lodge, 1975, 1984). Freudians characterize this as a libido seeking for a fulfilment that will deliver us from the anxieties of reality. It is our state on leaving Eden or childhood: wanderers in a dangerously attractive but fundamentally alien world yearning for the security of home.

While the Romantics would not readily have associated their work with knightly quests full of wonderful deeds in mysterious places on behalf of transcendent ideals, we make connections, looking back, that enable us to use the same root word for the literary forms of both periods. What connects them are characteristics of what I am calling romantic understanding. Although the works of medieval bards and romantic artists are different in many ways, yet they have significant common features. We can see a sustained development of technical devices from medieval romance to Romanticism, which makes the latter a fuller exemplification of romantic understanding, and so more useful for my present purposes.

Constituents of Romanticism touched on above, then, include a new sense of reality or a sense of being able to find a way to a new, purer, uncluttered view of reality, an engagement with the details of reality and their diversity, an attraction to the extremes of reality, to the exotic, strange and mysterious, an appreciation of "unspoiled" nature and a sense of awe before it and of the numinous in it, a rebellious contempt for the artificial, the conventional, and unjust paternalism, a self-conscious sense of the self as set off from nature and from social roles, a central ambiguity in the desire to transcend the bounds of everyday reality while recognizing their constraining power—an ambiguity caught in the distinctive role of the hero—and the conception of the mind as an internal theatre directed by the free imagination.

From these characteristics of Romanticism I want to begin building an image of romantic understanding. The move from Romanticism is already begun in the abbreviated and abstracted list in the previous paragraph. While the characteristic of, say, "attraction to the exotic" has been arrived at by considering a lot of romantic literature and art and finding instances of it in many individual works, once abstracted and made into a category it becomes a candidate for recognition as a constituent of romantic understanding—one to which I will try to give further definition by considering how it is exemplified in children of middle-school age today. As the topic is so vast, I will focus on just a few such characteristics; trying to develop all of the constituents of Romanticism touched on above, and the many others I have simply ignored would result in an unwieldy volume. So I will take a small set of what seem to me crucial constituents of Romanticism and central features of romantic understanding, and try to make clear connections between them and middle-school education today.

What then is the initial sense of romantic understanding that I am proposing? It is a way of making sense of the world and of experience that highlights certain features and suppresses others. It serves as a kind of mental lens that brings particularly into focus—to take the limited set of characteristics that I will emphasize in the following chapters—a sense of reality and nature as vividly present to the senses and rich in meaning; the extremes of reality and its more exotic, strange, and mysterious features; a sense of the self as located within the head, distinct from the natural world and from social roles, and as director of the imagination; and an ambiguous, partly rebellious, desire to transcend everyday reality but also to recognize its bounds.

And education

Why should romantic understanding be accepted as having anything to do with students of middle-school age, and why should it be accepted as a useful educational category? I hope I need do no more to answer the first part of the question, at least initially, then point at a number of the characteristics I have sketched above as constituents of romantic understanding and show similar characteristics prominent in the mental lives of typical children of this age. Indeed, I hope you will already have made a number of such connections yourself. To take just a few of the more simply made: the fascination with the extremes of the natural world and with its exotic and strange features noted in Romanticism and taken as exemplifying a significant constituent of romantic understanding is evident in students' ready engagement with the contents of, say, *The Guinness Book of Records;* the discovery of a distinct sense of self and an absorbed exploration of it is a common feature of middle-school age students no less than the leading Romantics; the attraction to heroes, to those who could transcend the everyday world, is equally a feature common to both, whether the attraction is to Napoleon or to a pop-star or a football team; the eager rebellion against unjust authority figures and against the styles and conventions of the authorities is similarly common.

Now, such connections may seem rather facile, more a matter of describing quite dissimilar phenomena using similar words to imply a common element that will disappear once one delves below the surface level of the verbal description. I will try to show that quite the opposite is the case, that the further we delve below the surface, the more strikingly similar are the connection between the Romantics and modern middle-school age students. The modern forms of romantic understanding, I will try to show, are profoundly like their romantic predecessors, even though superficially they may look quite dissimilar, because they are expressions in different times and circumstances of the same kind of understanding.

To make such connections, however, is not to argue that the minds of the Wordsworths, Austen, and Goethe and typical modern students are alike in all kinds of ways. It is, however, to argue that they do share a considerable range of mental capacities and inclinations, aesthetic impulses, and so on. This does not, of course, mean that each does the same with these capacities, but I think it is fair to say that they share, or can easily share, a kind of stance before the world, similar procedures to make sense of it, dispositions to be engaged by particular features of it, and a range of other characteristics to be explored below.

I will try to show, furthermore, that these connections are not just more or less interesting correlations but that they are causally related in a rather complex way. That is, modern students growing into our culture make sense of the world and of their experience in particular ways as a consequence of the history of our culture. I mean this not just in the obvious sense in which cultural history provides the content of what the initiate learns, but that the process of individual intellectual development is a recapitulation of the layers of achievement of cultural history.

Even if I can show that these are predisposed to make sense of the world and of experience in terms of romantic understanding, I still need to show that evoking, stimulating, and developing this predisposition is educationally desirable. The working out of that argument will occupy the following chapters, but at least I can sketch here how one can derive an educationally desirable quality from a characteristic of Romanticism. If we take, for example, the enthusiastic admiration of Napoleon or some other hero figure as a characteristic of the historical movement of Romanticism, we can recast this more abstractly as a constituent of romantic understanding, as, say, the enthusiastic admiration of heroic achievements. This in turn can be recast directly into a desirable educational quality, as the capacity to enthusiastically admire expressions of human energy, intelligence, ingenuity, or whatever, along with the wish to emulate these. To take another example, the more direct and colloquial language that was characteristic of romantic poetry, can be recast as a constituent of romantic understanding. In that more abstract form it would appear as an impatience with conventions that constrain our ability to express clearly what we understand about the world and about experience. This can be recast again as the desirable educational quality of being able to recognize worn-out conventions and artificial expressions and being able to re-form them to express better one's understanding. Each of the characteristics of Romanticism can be similarly recast into desirable educational qualities. Again, as we go along, I will try to show that this is not merely a matter of superficial verbal connections, but results from the causal consequences of cultural history on educational development.

So while we may not wish to teach our students to admire Napoleon, or Genghis Kahn, we surely recognize as desirable the ability to admire enthusiastically and associate with examples of human energy. While we may not want to teach students to copy the new artistic and literary forms of Romanticism, we surely recognize as desirable the ability to remake conventional forms the better to express their vision. While we may not want to teach students to reject particular eighteenth century social *mores*, we surely recognize as desirable the daring and courage required to reassess the value of inherited conventions in the light of changing circumstances. Perhaps the most overarching characteristics of Romanticism and romantic understanding are enthusiasm and wonder in exploring the world and experience. They are also vital educational capacities. Without them one can, of course, continue to learn and indeed one can become a renowned scholar. But we would want to observe that such scholars have a serious educational deficiency. We recognize their work as possibly valuable, but dessicated and devoid of energy and life. Those who are deficient in the educational qualities of enthusiasm and wonder may have life, but they tend to have it less abundantly.

Conclusion

Because of some of the prominent polarities that have affected educational discourse during this century, talk of wonder, enthusiasm, the imagination, and other characteristics of Romanticism and romantic understanding, may encourage the notion that accumulating knowledge, rationality, and academic skills are in for short shrift in what follows. As this is one of the dichotomies that I hope to transcend in this essay, I will turn now from considering the most visible expressions of Romanticism to exploring their technical substratum. In the process I will try to show why it makes sense to see romantic understanding as an early product of the evocation, stimulation, and development of the techniques of rationality.

2
The transition to literacy

Introduction

My choice of title for this chapter might appear a little odd, in that it is conventionally supposed that the transition to literacy will already have taken place before the middle-school years begin. An alternative title that might initially seem more straightforward in signalling the contents of the chapter is "The consequences of literacy." This echoes the title of a celebrated essay by Jack Goody and Ian Watt (1968), on which I will indeed draw, (which title Goody in retrospect would revise as "the implications of writing" (Goody, 1987, p. xvii)). In that essay Goody and Watt indicate a number of changes in Western cultural history that seem to result from the development of writing—such as historical consciousness, logic, skepticism, and in general the distinctive set of intellectual activities shaped in ancient Greece which are commonly bundled into that rather vague notion we label "rationality."

I will, then, suggest a more comprehensive conception of literacy than is currently common, one that sees literacy as properly tied up with the acquisition of the intellectual capacities that support rationality. I also will argue that the conventional sense of literacy in education, which sees it as a somewhat discrete set of encoding and decoding skills acquired during the early school years, is seriously inadequate. The transition to literacy will be represented here as a complex and relatively lengthy intellectual process in cultural history and in children's education. I want to try to sketch a richer sense of what being "lettered" properly entails, and then in later chapters go on to discuss how we can bring this about.

This chapter is divided into four rather uneven sections. I will begin by briefly distinguishing some conceptions of literacy, indicating some of the general features of the comprehensive sense I want to develop. In the second, rather bulky, section I will try to characterize the comprehensive sense in some detail and to lay out support for its appropriateness—indicating why it makes sense to think about literacy "in cultural history and in children's education" together. In the third section I will consider the persistence within literate Western culture of elements that previously sustained oral cultures, and the form they take within what is generally called rhetoric. I will try to show the connection between rhetoric and romantic understanding. Children in Western culture become literate very largely in a print environment, and print has effects, both in cultural history and in education, on the way literacy can affect thinking. So in the fourth section I will consider some of the effects of print, and particularly how its technology affected Romanticism and how it can affect romantic understanding. I will try to show how literacy reaches one kind of culmination during the romantic period, and indicate why, even though the distinctive note of romance appears throughout the period of literacy in Western culture, there is a sudden flood of romantic feeling, and the distinctive intellectual characteristics of romance are exemplified so emphatically at the turn of the nineteenth century. Following Walter Ong, I will argue that Romanticism was not a passing movement but rather that particular characteristics of romance then became permanent features of Western cultural experience—features to which, I will argue, students are culturally predisposed, and for educational purposes, ought to develop during the middle-school years.

This is rather a long chapter which tries to pull together what might at times seem like a kaleidoscopic array of diverse bits and pieces. I hope they will, like the kaleidoscope's bits and pieces, come together into a clear pattern. My aim is to set in place a number of elements that will help to clarify what I mean by romantic understanding and also prepare for the recapitulation argument.

Conceptions of literacy

I will distinguish three conceptions of literacy. The first I will call Conventional; it is the sense of literacy that has been dominant for half a century or so in North America and for somewhat less time and with less pervasiveness in Australia and Europe. The second I will call Emergent; it has become prominent within the 1980s as a result of energetic research and practice. And the third I will call Comprehensive. (I would have been tempted to call it cultural literacy, except that that title has been pre-empted By E.D. Hirsh Jr. [1987], who uses it in a different sense from that which follows.)

In the Conventional view, literacy is seen as a relatively narrow set of decoding and encoding skills, in which the skills are taken as distinct from any curriculum content. Once proficiency is attained, literacy is mastered. In Conventional practice, greater emphasis is put on reading than on writing, and reading skills are assumed properly to precede writing skills. Instruction in reading is designed to achieve the sequential attainment of sets of subskills, whose successful mastery leads to successful decoding. The ability to write involves its own encoding skills and sequential sets of sub-skills, some of which follow by a kind of inversion from those already acquired in learning to decode. Literacy *is* successful decoding and encoding. These skills are considered of unquestionable educational importance. They are prerequisites to further educational achievements, and so instruction in them is considered free from the kind of value controversies that surround some curriculum areas. The attainment of literacy in the Conventional view is not seen as tied up with "transformations of consciousness" or with "critical thinking" or with other more general cognitive activities; it is held to be a set of largely distinct skills that are instrumental in achieving or engaging in these more general cognitive activities.

A number of the characteristics of the Conventional conception of literacy are evident in the following quotation:

> Reading is first of all and essentially the mechanical skill of decoding, of turning the printed symbols into the sounds which are language. . . . We are intensely concerned that our children understand what they read, but the mechanical decoding skill must come first if we are to get them started properly. In the earliest stages of learning to read there is very little need for thinking and reasoning on the part of the child. What he needs is a little practice in mastering a decoding skill and the thinking will come along quite some time later (Walcutt, in N. Hall, 1987, p. 2).

From the mid-1970s, many of the most basic assumptions of the Conventional view have been increasingly persuasively challenged. One significant set of challenges has come from what I am calling the Emergent conception of literacy. This has grown largely from within the field of educational research on literacy. The results of particular empirical studies have carried challenges to the Conventional view, while at the same time conceptual research has supported interpretations of literacy that do not fit easily with the rather mechanistic view that has held sway for so long. (For a clear survey of this movement and its supporting research see N. Hall, 1987.) The Emergent conception has been influenced by its strong reaction against the Conventional conception.

The term "Emergent" is appropriate because it catches something of how literacy is seen properly to "emerge" in the child's experience. Literacy, in this view, is not something children acquire as a simple product of instruction (involving a pseudo-science of instructional sequences and the artificial panoply of skills and sub-skills, and invariant stages and substages, as articulated within the Conventional conception). Literacy is seen, rather, to emerge in children as a fairly straightforward product of their everyday sense-making being focused on a literate environment. The Emergent view sees a number of clear and precise links between the emergence of oral language use in early childhood and the emergence of literacy rather later. In the Conventional view these have been considered quite distinct attainments, the former being a natural development whereas literacy is a learned skill and as such requires scientifically determined schedules of instruction. In the Emergent view, the social context which so easily supports the development of orality in children by relating sounds to purposes, hopes, fears, pleasures, and anxieties that are meaningful to them, is not to be sharply distinguished from the kinds of contexts which can support children in constructing relationships between written symbols and their purposes, hopes, fears, pleasures, and anxieties.

The Emergent view involves a more coherent connection between the child as learner in home and street and in the classroom, and brings into its conception of literacy a range of features of children's language, thought, and behavior that have tended to be neglected in Conventional practice—the stories, games, rhymes, metaphoric play, jokes, puns, riddles, T.V. experience, etc., of the oral culture of childhood.

Also, in the Emergent view, writing and reading are not seen as rather distinct sets of skills needing separate attention. They are seen instead as intimately connected. In a trivial sense, it is logically necessary that in cultural history writing preceded reading. (Until someone wrote a symbol, there was nothing to read, or "decode," though obviously there were gestural codes, etc. (Kendon, 1989).) This simple logical point is taken as having something suggestive to say about young children's acquisition of literacy. The conceptual point has spurred much empirical research that has supported the possibility and the pedagogical efficiency of encouraging early writing activity as a precursor to reading, an activity, indeed, out of which literacy emerges (N. Hall, 1987, Ch. 4).

The Emergent view has been developing largely independently of the research in those disciplines that have been laying the grounding for what I am calling the Comprehensive view. "Comprehensive" is not a particularly descriptive, or elegant, (or unpretentious) title, but I have chosen it simply to indicate that this conception of literacy takes into its view a range of considerations little attended to in either of the other two positions. From the confluence of findings about literacy in classics, anthropology, social-psychology, cultural history, and other areas of research, a distinct new conception is forming of what is properly involved in the transition to literacy. It has enlarged the conception of "literacy" into the semantic space traditionally inhabited by "rationality" and it sees literacy as a more complex cultural and cognitive change than is imagined in the Conventional view.

The Emergent conception and the Comprehensive conception are not distinct positions yielding different doctrines about literacy teaching. Rather, the Emergent conception might be seen as dealing with some of the pedagogical problems that have resulted from the long dominance of the Conventional conception. The Comprehensive conception might be seen as embodying in significant part the Emergent conception, but combining it with implications from the range of recent research on literacy outside of education. One result may be to extend the practical implications of the Emergent conception more widely through children's education than its current focus on the early years.

Important to the development of the Comprehensive view is the new understanding of orality produced by the study of emerging literacy in ancient Greece and in Medieval Europe. In exposing something of the cultural and cognitive effects of literacy this research has exposed also something of the cultural and cognitive effects of orality. In particular this research has made clear that orality is not well understood if considered merely the absence of literacy. Orality entails a complex of positive techniques—more or less well developed by particular individuals—for making sense of the world and of experience that are different in significant ways from those encouraged by literacy. This is true both for oral cultures around the world and also, perhaps less commonly noted, for young preliterate children in Western cultures. The Conventional view has tended to take little or no account of young children's orality, seeing the pedagogical task as simply to equip them with literacy skills and seeing this as a straightforward addition of new capacities. Even the little literacy that some children acquire is considered so much to the good. Literacy instruction in the Conventional view is thus risk-free. In the Comprehensive view this comfortable assumption is removed; an inadequate transition to literacy can involve significant losses to the young child's positive orality. In the Comprehensive view and also, though less explicitly recognized, in the Emergent view, the transition is seen not as from illiteracy or pre-literacy to literacy but from orality to orality-and-literacy. That is, important cultural and cognitive capacities are developed in children's attainment of the techniques of orality, and the most effective transition to literacy needs to build on these and further develop them. So "literacy" in the Comprehensive view does not displace orality, but rather encourages its further development, in part, as I will argue, by stimulating and developing the techniques of rhetoric. Insensitivity to the positive features of orality can, and too often does, lead to their suppression by Conventional instruction in the skills of literacy—which has the effect of impoverishing whatever literacy is attained. (How one might develop orality while teaching early literacy is discussed in the previous volume (Egan, 1988) and how both might continue to be stimulated and developed is a prominent subject of this volume.)

The focus on literacy encouraged by the Comprehensive view encourages us to see it always as a social/cultural/political tradition, rather than as a set of skills. The decoding and encoding skills themselves may be useful or useless or even damaging in particular times and places for particular individuals. In modern Western educational systems they might most usefully be seen as parts of a cumulative tradition of sense-making capacities. So initiation into—or each child's re-creation of—literacy might be seen, Comprehensively, as initiation into, or re-creation of, a particular cultural tradition: "the intellectual advantages of literacy come not simply from reading and writing but from the construction of and participation in a literate culture" (Olson, 1987, p. 3). Relatedly, the Comprehensive view is sensitive to the relationships of power and politics that are tied up with literacy; literacy cannot be treated as a causal variable which operates regardless of the particular social and political circumstances within which it has a role (Luke, 1988; Lankshear and Lawler, 1988).

A part of what is at issue among these conceptions of literacy is their practical pedagogical implications. One cannot, of course, run empirical studies to see which conception yields the best results because they conceive of successful literacy differently. At base these conceptions no doubt derive from different metaphors. It seems fair to say that the undergirding metaphor of the Conventional view has a somewhat mechanistic component. The image of how things are made to work in education seems to be projected from how one might best build a machine. To make something most efficiently one makes all the parts separately according to precise specifications and then one brings them together using particular skills. In the best romantic tradition, the Comprehensive conception wants to replace this with a more organic metaphor. These different metaphors are not simply equivalents between which we can casually choose without hazard. The metaphors make competing claims about how adequately they grasp and represent the phenomena. The implicit argument here is that the Conventional conception grasps and represents the phenomena of literacy inadequately. What is at stake is that in applying an inadequate conception, derived form an inappropriate metaphor, one will achieve inadequate literacy in students, and the more determinedly one applies the conception, with ever more intricate and "scientifically" sequenced kits for reading instruction, the less adequate the ensuing literacy will inevitably be.

A couple of additional points before going on: I have mentioned that the Comprehensive conception of literacy overlaps with what has traditionally been considered rationality. Rationality, however, is not to be considered—as "critical thinking" or "problem solving" commonly are—as a set of generic intellectual procedures. Rather it is tied up with learning about history, geography, science, mathematics, logic, and so on. One of the stranger, and I think educationally destructive, currents in educational discourse during the later twentieth century has been the suggestion that one can achieve some of the finest fruits of learning without actually having to do the learning. This is often connected with the claim that knowledge is doubling every x number of years and so it is pointless to try to teach a great deal of particular knowledge, especially as we can easily observe that some of those who seem to have packed in the greatest quantities of knowledge show little ability to use it flexibly or wisely or to understand the world with any greater insight than some less informed people. These observations then commonly lead to the conclusion that we should rather focus on teaching generic thinking skills. Thus instead of students tediously learning a great deal of factual material, they can instead acquire the skills that will enable them to recognize problems and know where to go to find whatever particular knowledge they need to solve them. A rather acerbic response to this movement towards procedural skills and away from knowledge acquisition is given by John Bayley:

As a substitute for knowledge it can appear highly effective, working as it does on the premiss that knowing things is obsolete. There was far too much *stuff* there. Replace the great mass of it, which used to weigh on the memories and desires of youth, with a streamlined apparatus, crafted by professionals, and excitingly accessible to students once they have mastered the magic formulae (Bayley, 1988, p. 167).

The separation of knowledge and skills in curriculum documents and taxonomies seems to have persuaded many people that they are indeed distinct things with independent existences. Certainly it seems that one can accumulate knowledge without it enriching one's life in any evident way, remaining "inert" and dessicated. And we are uncomfortably familiar with the newer skilled problem-solving critical thinker whose ignorance sets one's teeth on edge: all froth and enthusiasm with no substance, usually proposing schemes of teaching or curricula which will prove immensely effective for little effort. The separate pursuit of knowledge and procedural skills is of course vacuous. The educational problem is how to ensure that knowledge is learned in such a way that it is meaningful to students and enhances their capacities to make sense of the world and of experience and to deal effectively with them. The answer for students of middle-school age, I will argue in this book, is tied up in the idea of romance.

The second additional point concerns the danger of trying to simplify diverse ideas into a few seemingly discrete categories—as I have done in sketching three conceptions of literacy. The danger is that one will seriously falsify what one is trying to describe. I do think it fair to describe a dominant Conventional view of literacy which has the general features indicated above. While there has obviously been diversity within that view, particularly concerning the competing doctrines, and their supporting research, for different schemes of literacy instruction, I think there has been very general acceptance of the main assumptions outlined above.

The related danger of setting out the introduction for the subsequent discussion this way is that one clearly signals a villain of the piece and trumpets the white-hatted Comprehensive view hero, who comes with promises of revolutionary and millenial improvements in literacy achievements. There are many social and psychological conditions that affect students' attainments of literacy—however narrowly or broadly literacy is defined. These include students' home background and all kinds of other cultural conditions. I think the comprehensive view offers a better grasp on what developing literacy properly *is*. Clarity—as philosophers constantly remind us of their stock-in-trade—is only a limited virtue. In matters of education, however, clarity is not easily come by—and perhaps certain delusive forms are too easily come by— but what is currently being clarified about the nature and implications of literacy seems centrally important to education and worth exploring even if the millenium will not follow directly.

Potential consequences of literacy

In this quite lengthy section I want to survey a fairly extensive range of work, perhaps trying to tie together too much in too short a space for coherence, so we might benefit from some internal signposts. I want to consider the bases for the Comprehensive conception of literacy and to show how they can give us a better grasp on what is properly involved in becoming literate in the Western cultural tradition. This will lead us to consider, in the next section, the cumulative influences of print technology on Western culture, and particularly on Romanticism, which ties the discussion in this chapter to that of the previous one, setting up the foundation for a richer conception of what is involved in romantic understanding.

The literacy hypothesis

The "literacy hypothesis" as it currently stands—and is challenged— is sustained by the confluence of research in a number of discipline areas. The basic hypothesis is that the invention of writing, particularly with the alphabet, provided a technical enhancement to certain kinds of thinking, that these have had an enormous transforming effect on the minds and on the cultures that have taken advantage of them, and also that they have the potential to bring about this transformation in any individual who masters literacy in appropriate circumstances. What constitute "appropriate circumstances" is a focus for much current research, and for this book, as is the nature of the "transformation" of the mind which literacy can bring about.

Well, would that anything were so straightforward! There are, in a sense, two main literacy hypotheses: A psychological one, with neurophysiological undertones, about the cognitive effects of alphabetic literacy, and a historical one about the way literacy in ancient Greece and, somewhat parasitically and somewhat distinctly, in medieval Europe had cumulative cultural effects. A lot of the interest in "the literacy hypothesis," especially among educationalists, is due to these two kinds of effects of literacy constantly overlapping and interweaving. But these overlappings and interweavings also generate complexities and confusions and some ideological edge, none of which can be easily avoided. The ideological edge is, as always, the least easy part to touch, and very dangerous to ignore, without some damage to oneself. Some people (e.g., Street, 1984) argue that the literacy hypothesis is just another, perhaps more subtle, form of asserting that most non-Westerners' minds are different (not transformed by alphabetic literacy) and so, given the enhancements that follow from literacy, inferior. It is merely a new guise for old cultural imperialism: "lesser breeds" are now characterized more neutrally as members of oral cultures, and literacy is used to explain what are taken as vastly superior uses of the mind in modern Western societies. Instead of "civilized" and "savage" the literacy hypothesizers employ "literate" and "oral," but mean much the same things. This perspective on "the literacy hypothesis" is enough for some to see it as generally disreputable, infected inescapably with all the faults of cultural imperialism, and enables them to dismiss it out of hand as "decisively discredited." (This is a perspective that an extended essay on cultural recapitulation in education has to be somewhat sensitive to! I will attend to the argument in detail in Volume 4, but here will try simply to be sensitive to the undoubted danger of using the literacy hypothesis as a code for culturally imperialistic intentions. I might add that I find the ideological argument naive in its inability to perceive any alternatives between cultural imperialism on the one hand and a disabling cultural relativism on the other—but this is an argument for later. I want here only to indicate that I am aware that some people consider the whole literacy hypothesis as somehow undermined, and that I am not insensitive to their reasons for so consider it, but that I think the good argument against potential abuses of the literacy hypothesis is quite inadequate when generalized against the literacy hypothesis holus-bolus.)

The research that has led to the development of the literacy hypothesis includes prominently that of Milman Parry and Eric Havelock in classics, Jack Goody in anthropology, and Walter Ong and Brian Stock in cultural history. The form of the hypothesis has been significantly affected by the work of Harold Innis and the pyrotechnical Marshall McLuhan, and has been intensively elaborated and qualified by the scholarly and organizational work of the co-directors of the McLuhan program in Toronto, David Olson and Derrick de Kerckhove. Because I am writing during a period of significant developments and accommodations of the literacy hypothesis, because much research on its educational implications is underway, because there are a number of excellent and extensive accounts of the hypothesis available (notably Ong, 1982; the entire issue of the journal *Interchange* 18, 1987; and a clear "popular" introduction, Cayley, 1988), and because my interest in the hypothesis for the purposes of this book is somewhat restricted, I will give here only a brief account of it, focusing on features of particular interest to my argument.

Between about 750 B.C.E. and 700 B.C.E. the Greeks borrowed, adapted, or invented a fully phonetic alphabet, whose Latinized descendant I am now writing. (Most of you are no doubt reading the S.I.S. [Shavian Intergalactic Standard] derivative.) Writing systems that preceded the alphabet, such as the syllabaries, provided symbols for the main sound chunks of speech. They commonly ran to hundreds of symbols, getting caught between the Scylla of proliferating symbols to represent the variety of sounds adequately to avoid ambiguity and the Charybdis of having so many symbols as to make the system too complex to learn. The Greek unintuitive and analytic achievement was the generation of separate symbols for consonants and vowels. This allowed the alphabet to be restricted to twenty-two symbols, which could relatively unambiguously represent to sight the sound and meaning of speech.

Derrick de Kerckhove thinks that the invention of the "vocalic" alphabet converted much knowledge acquisition and communication in a quite new way into a visual task. He draws on Innis' (1951) ideas about how forms of communication *bias* the mind, and he elaborates these ideas by bringing them together with suggestive neurophysiological data and with studies of the changing styles and directionality of writing systems in the ancient Near East and in Greece. The product is an argument that the invention of the alphabet and the consequent dominance of the eye in gathering information has *biased* thought connected with reading and writing into an activity dominated by the left hemisphere of the brain (de Kerckhove, 1986; McLuhan & McLuhan, 1989). He likens the effect of alphabetic literacy on people to changing the program in a computer (de Kerckhove, 1988).

The alphabet is composed of entirely meaningless bits, which in combination can carry whatever meanings we are able to express. De Kerckhove argues for the program-like effects of the alphabet on the human mind, trying to expose various indices of such effects. Cross-cultural study of brain lesions, for example, has shown that alphabet users are inhibited from being able to read and write by certain kinds of damage to the left hemisphere which seem not to inhibit ideograph users in the same way. He gathers further data that show that ideograph and "consonantal" alphabet users seem to process writing as visual patterns, which are more easily processed by the brain if scanned from right to left. The vocalic alphabet, on the other hand, as a purely disembedded code, is more easily processed from left to right. De Kerckhove correlates these neurophysiological data most suggestively with directionality in writing systems and the changes from the various Near Eastern pre-alphabetic systems to the left to right direction of the Greek and all subsequent alphabetic systems. He further correlates the left to right pattern of alphabetic writing in ancient Greece with the rapid development of the analytic forms of thought associated with left hemisphere dominance. The rich sensorium of oral cultures—in which sound, touch, and smell all play roles in communication—is replaced by a "decontextualized" code which can yield its meaning up to sight alone. The more proficient one becomes with alphabetic script, the more it invades aspects of one's cultural life, then the further is the mind *biased* towards left-hemisphere, analytic, activity.

For de Kerckhove, then, the invention of the alphabet is a great divide in human cultural history. Whatever we make of the kind of explanations he gives of this divide, it is clear that literacy has long been recognized as bringing with it distinctive forms of thought. Even though this recognition has often involved no explicit theory about literacy, it is evident in the way Western literates have found the forms of thought common in oral cultures, expressed in uninterpretable myths, puzzling rituals and "irrational" beliefs, very hard to understand. Most of those responsible for the literacy hypothesis share de Kerckhove's sense of a great divide: "the history of the human mind . . . falls into roughly two epochs, the pre-alphabetic and the post-alphabetic" (Havelock, 1980, p. 96).

The literacy hypothesis is an attempt to account for the differences evident between the kind of changing cultural forms and cumulative disciplines of knowledge that seem to be connected with alphabetic literacy and the more homeostatic-in-intent oral cultures of the world, whether contemporary or prehistoric.[1] The connection between Western cumulative culture and the alphabet is identified with the alphabet's making speech visible, transportable, and independent of speakers, changing the patterns of sound into visible objects which can be inspected

---

[1] I should note in passing that this common way of indicating a difference between modern Western and oral cultures is, like all others, problematic. "Homeostatic-in-intent" refers to the mechanisms evident in oral cultures to preserve stability over time. But it is far from clear that such cultures do not change quite as much as Western cultures, though, perhaps not in the kind of lineal accumulation of knowledge and technology on which we tend to focus. Ironically one of the effects of writing has been to "freeze" some of the forms of cultural life in which literacy developed ["writing petrifies the tradition it covers" (Detienne, 1986, p. 126)] and then to elaborate those over centuries; similarly print "froze" a particular cultural movement and has developed its particular forms (Eisenstein, 1979). We tend to see the somewhat arbitrary cultural forms captured and developed by writing and print as somehow natural or inevitable.

and reinspected, compared with others, and so on. "Writing, commitment of the Word to space, enlarges the potentiality of language almost beyond measure [; it] restructures thought" (Ong, 1982, p. 8). It is this sense of the technology of writing *restructuring* (or programming) thought that is at the heart of the literacy hypothesis. Ong points out, as a circumstantial support for the hypothesis, that a typical oral language has available at best a few thousand words. Literate languages accumulate refinements, qualifications, and variants over centuries, so that English, for example, now has a vocabulary resource of around a million and a half words. The ability to see one's text, and to reflect on it, and to refer to dictionaries and thesauruses for help in more precisely expressing what one thinks, supports a different kind of discourse than is possible in relatively word-limited languages without such resources.

Some qualifications

In his reading of Plato as the first to understand the implications of literacy for thinking, Havelock characterizes the Platonic revolution in a number of ways. To take two examples: "and it is fair to say that Platonism at bottom is an appeal to substitute a conceptual discourse for an imagistic one" (Havelock, 1963, p. 261); "What Plato is pleading for could be shortly put as the invention of an abstract language of descriptive science to replace a concrete language of oral memory" (Havelock, 1963, p. 236). In the details of a complex argument one can see how Havelock can consistently see orality as involving both a "concrete language" and an "imagistic discourse," but such diversity of characterization suggests a degree of imprecision in the literacy hypothesis about the nature of orality. And this is mirrored in what Brian Stock calls the "imprecision of the idea of literacy" itself (Stock 1983, p. 6). The imprecision of the idea of literacy is compounded when one considers its status as both a historical hypothesis and a psychological one.

The difficulty here concerns the degree to which the literacy hypothesis is taken as a straightforward causal explanation of cultural or psychological changes. If certain "transforming" consequences of literacy follow by necessity, then such effects will occur in cultures over time and in individuals during their development.

Drawing on Luria's work in remote areas of the Soviet Union in the early 1930s, Ong reinterprets his results as demonstrating the effects of even small acquaintance with literacy. Luria found that illiterate peasants had great difficulty dealing with the simplest formal logical tasks, while those with some schooling performed dramatically better. The latter clearly understood the grammar, as it were, of the formal logical problems; they could "disembed" their thinking from the practical details of the world and deal with problems abstractly to some degree. Ong sees these results as due straightforwardly to the degree of literacy or illiteracy of the participants in Luria's studies. He concludes that "it takes only a moderate degree of literacy to make a tremendous difference in thought processes" (Ong, 1982, p. 50).

Such conclusions are at one level psychological claims, but are used also in forming the historical claims of the literacy hypothesis. The reverse occurs too. When Goody concludes that "writing helped to develop new types of formal logical operations" (Goody, 1986, p. 182), this product of historical research can be easily read as a psychological claim. Indeed, one reason for the literacy hypothesis being so interesting to educationalists, is that it seems to provide a different kind of explanation of some prominent data bout typical psychological development than has hitherto been available. Piaget's theory, for example, has explained certain features of psychological development as due to some spontaneous process which his theory tries to characterize in detail. The literacy hypothesis suggests that such changes in the process of development are due, not to the kind of process Piaget characterizes, but rather to stages in the "internalization" of literacy—and claims about the historical "internalization" in ancient Greece are put in a language that seems applicable to the psychological effects literacy will have in any circumstances.

The literacy hypothesis when taken as a simple causal account of a technology transforming mental structures or *biasing* or reprogramming the mind, runs into some difficulties. Jerome Bruner, for example, has pointed out (Bruner, 1988, p. 5) that an hypothesis of such a direct causal kind is clearly inadequate; what is needed is also an account of why particular technologies influence thought in particular ways at particular times in particular circumstances. Carol Feldman (Feldman 1988, p. 6) similarly criticizes the notion of writing being interpreted as the sole cause of the transformations claimed for it, pointing out that some of the effects claimed for literacy are evident in some oral cultures. She refers particularly to the Ilongot people of the Philippines who have developed a special form of language which is rich in "reflexive" terms, of a kind that the literacy hypothesis suggests were first made possible by writing and which are taken in the hypothesis as crucial to the development of a cumulative Western culture.

Sylvia Scribner and Michael Cole have studied the effects of literacy in newly literate societies (Scribner and Cole, 1981; see also Cole and

Scribner, 1974); they were interested to see whether the cognitive effects on individuals are invariably like those claimed by the literacy hypothesis for the introduction of alphabetic writing in the West, and whether the effects on the social group as a whole reflect anything of the pattern encapsulated in the literacy hypothesis. Their conclusions suggest that many more social factors and schooling practices need to be considered in accounting for whatever cognitive changes writing is taken to be responsible for in the literacy hypothesis. That is, rather as Feldman argues, a much wider set of intellectual and social conditions effect cognition than are incorporated into the literacy hypothesis. Cole and Griffin also argue that the effects of literacy are narrower than notions about transformation or reprogramming suggest: "there is more than a little evidence to suggest that while cognitive changes arising from literacy or schooling are not completely specific to literate or school tasks, they certainly do not represent general changes in the way people processes information" (Cole and Griffin, 1980, p. 358).

Heath has further shown that within Western societies the effects of literacy are profoundly influenced by a range of social and cultural conditions. Literacy, she shows, is shaped and used by other more powerful social norms rather than being itself the potent causal force implied by the simple form of the literacy hypothesis (Heath, 1983). From her study of the uses of literacy in different communities in the U.S.A., she concludes that people in those different communities "had grown accustomed to participating in literary events in ways appropriate to the community's norms" (Heath, 1982, p. 95), and that, in the least "literate" community, "written information almost never stood alone . . . it was reshaped and reworked into oral modes" (Heath, 1982, pp. 99–100).

These are salutary qualifications to the literacy hypothesis, though, and one should add, it is not clear that anyone has ever held the simple causal notion of literacy that they qualify. Goody, for example, has warned against any simple division between the thinking of people in oral and literate societies: "I have never experienced the kinds of hiatus in communication that would be the case if I and they were approaching the physical world from opposite ends" (Goody, 1977, p. 8). Havelock observes that "Literacy when it came did not create a culture; it transmuted one which it inherited" (Havelock, 1980, p. 91). Consistently it has been pointed out that literacy is better viewed as catalyst rather than cause:

> Literacy is for the most part an enabling rather than a causal
> factor, making possible the development of complex political
> structure, syllogistic reasoning, scientific enquiry, linear
> conceptions of reality, scholarly specialization, artistic

elaboration, and perhaps certain kinds of individualism and of alienation. Whether, and to what extent, these will in fact develop depends apparently on concomitant factors of ecology, intersocietal relations, and internal ideological and social structural responses to these. (Gough, 1968, p. 153)

The most commonly accepted qualification of the literacy hypothesis is that the potential for literacy to lead to the cultural and cognitive consequences evident in Western science and "high" culture is indeed merely a potential, and one dependent on a number of other cultural, political, and cognitive conditions being met: "Literacy unlocked a variety of doors, but it did not necessarily secure admission" (Cressy, 1980, p. 189) or in Stock's phrase, texts "promised, if they did not always deliver, a new technology of the mind" (Stock, 1983, p. 10). These observations about historical conditions seem to apply equally to individuals and to different classes or sub-cultures in modern Western societies. So to see literacy as purely causal is obviously simplistic. It clearly played a catalystic role in Western cultural history, furthering characteristics of Greek intellectual life that were already developing. The appearance of alphabetic literacy is hardly an uncaused cause; the generation of the alphabet required analytic capacities which cannot then be seen purely as products of literacy.

The other main area of qualification concerns how profoundly or superficially literacy affects the mind. Some authorities argue that literacy and its potential consequences are "not . . . linked to innate mental ability, but to the tools, concepts and programs available for intellectual activity" (Goody, 1986, p. 140). Writing as a technology that transforms thought is to be understood, then, when it is situated very precisely in the institutions and social contexts that support such forms of thought and in which such thinking is productive. We tend casually to note clear differences between the intellectual activity of the average modern inhabitant of any great Western city and that of the average adult in an oral culture. But the evident differences seem very largely tied in with the technologies of such societies and with the forms of thought required by participation in particular writing-based activities in such societies. It is less evident that any difference exists between modern Westerners and members of oral cultures when we think about our emotional engagements, our personal relationships, or our range of feelings about everyday life. Indeed, in as far as there is a "carry-over" effect from our technology-sustained thinking to our everyday lives, it is far from clear that this works to Westerners' advantage. It seems that a product of this carry-over may be the alienation Westerners commonly feel from their emotional security, their social role, and the natural world. Indeed, Romanticism was, in part, a reaction against symptoms of such inappropriate carry-over.

What remains vivid about literacy is its actual role in Western cultural history and its potential role in education. We are clearly some way from decoding and coding skills, but the Comprehensive conception of literacy is one that involves mastery of such skills and the "transformation" of thinking, but in contexts in which such literacy is appropriate and productive. It might be useful to sketch, however briefly, just what the potential consequences or implications of literacy that students may hope to "internalize" are supposed to be. I will try to survey the main claims of the literacy literature about the cultural effects of literacy and then later see how these might be "ontogenized" in individuals' education. Literacy in the Conventional sense has largely disentangled itself from these historical processes and in such a sense there is no reason to expect the acquisition of decoding and encoding skills by themselves to lead to any particularly complex psychological or cultural consequences for students. But if we re-entangle our conception of literacy with its cultural-historical consequences we may be able to see ways to recapitulate some of these in individuals' education.

Cultural-historical consequences of literacy: what literacy makes easier and possible

Initially, writing was a technique for recording what had previously been expressed orally and remembered. It made certain records and transactions easier, especially more complex ones. As with any effective tool designed to achieve particular ends more efficiently, its existence allows us to conceive of new ends that can now be achieved. Literacy seems to have this quality in spades, so to speak. It had implications that gradually unfolded layer on layer through our cultural history. Whatever we make of theorizing about mental *biases,* or the reprogramming or transformation of intellectual processes, we can observe differences in, as it were, the uses of mental labor that were consequent upon the introduction of this mental tool.

Written records had cultural implications that went beyond their function as written mnemonics. Once one could visually inspect accumulated records, they invited organization, which in turn invited reflection on how best to organize them. This can produce practical problems of classification, as in whether one should put tomatoes in the vegetable or fruit category—which in turn can stimulate inquiry into the nature of the categories and their components, and the nature of tomatoes. When accumulated records are seen to disagree or to be inconsistent, whether records about the lineages of prominent families or even collected accounts of gods and their powers, then the task of organization can lead to systematic skepticism, and to logical processes for working out how to test conflicting claims made in written records.

One can try to give an account of the research that describes cultural-historical consequences of literacy in the West by setting them out in a list. There is something uncomfortably artificial about this as they are not a set of somewhat discrete consequences. Rather, there is a single diffuse consequence that finds various outlets in the social activities, interests, and institutions into which literacy slid and uncurled. Perhaps one way of indicating some consequences of literacy is to take a couple of general areas and consider how those implicate numerous others. I will, then, briefly survey, in a condensed form, some implications of writing—on how people made sense of the past and how they made sense of themselves.

Goody and Watt consider a sense of history, lacking in oral cultures, is a consequence of literacy, or an implication of writing (Goody and Watt, 1968). References to the past in oral cultures are a part of what Goody and Watt call the "mnemonics of social relationships" (Goody and Watt, 1968, p. 309). Genealogies, for example, are not fixed and endlessly accumulating series of names. They serve the pragmatic function of authorizing present patterns of property entitlements, social status, economic activities, and so on. As current power relationships and economic activities shift, so do the genealogical accounts and so do myths of origin (Malinowski, 1954): "oral societies live very much in the present which keeps itself in equilibrium or homeostasis by sloughing off memories which no longer have present relevance" (Ong, 1982, p. 46). Once written records accumulate they can be referred to as not subject to the plasticity and decay of human memory. Also "writing certainly promoted incipient interpretation and comparison of various versions of the same account" (Detienne, 1986, p. 32). From a practical point of view, such fixity as writing gives—though subject to forgery and other forms of unclarity—has potential disadvantages as well as potential advantages. One disadvantage concerns the sheer accumulation which, without some form of "structural amnesia," can become like a dead weight on the present. (Some other disadvantages, ways in which history can fail to "serve life," are given in Nietzsche's vivid *The Use and Abuse of History*, [1873/1949].)

The need to coordinate diverse activities in an increasingly complex society tends to lead to forms of time measurement that are "disembed-ded" from the activities themselves. Once diverse written pasts[2] of various families and cities became available for inspection, such as were produced in Greece and Asia Minor during the early sixth century (Drews, 1973; Pearson, 1939; Vernant, 1982), the need to coordinate them similarly led to a disembedding of the past from the particular accounts. Family genealogies that traced ancestry to gods in four genera-tions needed coordinating with those that claimed seven mortal genera-tions since the time of the gods. And these in turn required more radical coordination with the experience of travellers like Herodotus who encountered in Egypt long lists of mortal generations of high priests stretching far back into a past which the Greeks' accounts had populated only with gods.

Coordinating different pasts led toward history, toward the attempt to record, in Ranke's celebrated phrase, *Wie es Eigentlich Gewesen war*—what actually happened, regardless of one's present interests. This is something that remains notoriously difficult even for the most austere historian. But the disembedding of the past from the self-glorifying of interest-justifying stories of particular families and cities, created a temporal extension of experience. Trying to coordinate what records and claims were available led to logical procedures for assessing the truth-value of such records and claims, and consequently to a skeptical stance before them. The mental stance is well expressed in the opening fragment from the *Genealogies* of Hecateus of Miletus: "The stories of the Greeks are many and, in my opinion, ridiculous." (In another fragment, Heca-teus seems to have calculated that there were sixteen mortal generations between his sixth century present and the time the gods "mingled" with people—but, then, I suppose this might just have been a joke.)

A consequence of a past filled with accounts of what actually happened is the troubling recognition that the forms of one's current social exis-tence are simply a set among what is an indeterminably large kaleido-scope of variations possible for human beings and human societies. Without the reconstructed coordination of diverse pasts, one can assert—as do most uncoordinated pasts of oral societies—that one's own society with its current conventions is divinely ordained and that it is made up of people who are special and privileged while others are the product of some evil chance. This kind of ethnocentrism is hard to shake off, of course. History is one of its most effective cures, but unfortunately in

---

[2]I am using J. H. Plumb's distinction between "past" and "history" in which the "past" is an account whose purpose is to serve someone's present interest rather than record the truth of what happened; history is the reverse (Plumb, 1971).

modern nation-states students still tend to be fed a past of their nation that is very poorly coordinated with the pasts of other nations. "Social Studies" and "History" typically do very little at present to encourage an historical consciousness in students; but this is something to be pursued in Chapter 9.

Accumulating records also expose a past made up of constant change. In oral cultures, due to "structural amnesia" and the "obliteration of history" by connecting present conditions directly to mythic origins (Eliade, 1959), the past is not a story of changes leading to present conditions that point to an unknowable and different future. Historical consciousness does not only create a past full of change but also a future full of possibilities. That is, the sense of the future as a time of potential changes which we have some power to make is a consequence of historical understanding. A sense of history, then, is what Philip Rahv calls "the powerhouse" of change, only historical understanding can properly equip one to make adequate sense of a changing world. The alternative to history is myth and "stagnation" and "the fear of history" which "is at bottom the fear of the hazards of freedom" (Rahv, 1966, p. 20).

Well, we are running into some complex claims at rather high speed here. But I have tried to sketch, however sketchily, the connection between the development of writing and historical understanding and to indicate some ways in which historical understanding is crucial to important social values. I have sketched these connections to show something of what I see as involved in the transition to literacy. That is, in the Comprehensive conception of literacy, the attainment of these consequences or implications or, I would prefer to call them constituents, is vital. Conventional "literacy" without historical understanding, for example, is largely meaningless; it destroys the positive features of orality while putting no equivalent sense-making techniques in their place. It provides "skills" of marginal utility that tie one tightly into the technology that requires them, but provides no empowerment to make sense of that technology nor to control it.

As with all the implications of writing, historical thinking is not something entirely new. The effect of writing, rather, is to change a form of thinking common in oral cultures, and develop it in a particular way: "Logical, explicit, definitional, written text does not so much *add* new functions to language or thought as it specializes some functions present in early language while presumably inhibiting certain others" (Bruner and Olson, 1977/78, p. 12).

Let us, again too briefly, consider another implication of the transition to literacy: that of the conscious self. The inward self becomes a focus of particular interest during Romanticism, and commonly becomes a matter of intense absorption during early adolescence. The "self" with its unique "mind" or "soul" appears in a form we recognize, because it is one we have inherited, in Plato's writings, where *"psyche"* gathered meanings that remain problematic even today.

In seeking to make his conception of philosophy central to any educational curriculum, and especially to replace the practices of rhetorical training, Plato developed most forcefully the notion of "ideas" as the proper objects of contemplation: "For Plato, rationality was ultimately associated with certain 'ideas' external to the human mind, whose validity was independent of our individual opinions, but which we could— so to say—come to 'see' with the 'eye' of the mind" (Toulmin, 1972, p. 44). But such abstract or disembedded ideas were largely invented or disembedded during the early years of Greek alphabetic literacy. In the earlier Homeric world it is indeed, as Havelock argues, concrete particularities that are used to build up images of events and people. One can trace—or at least one can if, like Bruno Snell, one has spent much of one's life with classical texts—the development from Homer's conception of *psyche* to that of Plato.

Snell points out that Homer's vocabulary is short on general terms while being immensely rich in particulars. Even at a gross level, Snell points out that Homer lacks a term for the human body as a whole. Even further, "To be precise, Homer does not even have any word for the arms and the legs; he speaks of hands, lower arms, upper arms, feet, calves and thighs. Nor is there a comprehensive word for the trunk. . . . [Also] Homer has no term for a whole of a man's mental equipment, for the mind or soul in our sense" (Snell, 1960, p. 310). In Homer's vocabulary the *psyche* is what leaves the body at death, breathed out through the mouth or through a wound, and flutters about in Hades. But the *psyche* seems to have no clear function in the living body, though it leaves it during unconsciousness and it is risked in battle. After death it is a spectre looking like the deceased, dissolving like smoke to the touch and able to live and recall the events of its life only after drinking blood. But, significantly, "the predicates of the soul remain completely within the bounds set for the physical organs" (Snell, 1960, p. 19).

An effect of writing is to make one's words into objects that one can see. In an oral culture words are a part of one's physical activity which immediately pass away once uttered. The recording of a part of our bodily functioning in an alien medium is so common in our experience that we find it hard to recapture a sense of its peculiarity. What is it that came out of oneself that one can see when written down? "With writing the earlier noetic state undergoes a kind of cleavage, separating the knower from the external universe and then from himself" (Ong, 1977, p. 18). In Havelock's words: "As language became separated visually from the person who uttered it, so also the person, the source of the language, came into sharper focus and the concept of selfhood was born" (Havelock, 1986, p. 114). Once one can see a record of one's thought and reflect on it and can record one's experience and reflect on it, and revise the records to better express one's thought or describe one's experience, allowing a new kind of "editing, so to speak, of experience" (Stock, 1983, p. 4), then the sense of a thinking, observing self that is somehow separable from one's experience seems inescapable.

With the development of writing in ancient Greece we find evidence of precisely this process of the separation of a distinct sense of the self and its elaboration in what Solmsen calls "the new psychology" of the late fifth century (Solmsen, 1975), until we find the familiar sense of self with its rational and emotional and generative mind or soul in Plato's writing. Havelock calls this "an invention of Socratic vocabulary" (Havelock, 1986, p. 114).

Chronologically and logically central in this story is the literate Heraclitus, who lived in the Ionian city of Ephesus probably around the turn of the 6th century. He conceived of the *psyche* in terms quite distinct from those of Homer. It has its own dimension, quite different from any connected with our physical body: "You would not find [its] ends . . . though you travelled every way, so deep is its *logos*" (Diels, fragment 45, cited in Snell, 1960, p. 17). In addition Heraclitus claims that the *psyche* "has a *logos* which increases itself" (Diels, fragment 115, cited in Snell, 1960, p. 19). That is, the *psyche* is subject to development, and there is the suggestion that within us we have some way of learning. He makes the apparently revolutionary assertion "I searched within myself" (Diels, fragment 80, cited in Cornford, 1957, p. 186); for "it is open to all men to know themselves and to be wise" (Diels, fragment 106, cited in Cornford, 1957, p. 186).[3] Reflection on the *psyche* which is within reveals a source of knowledge, with which what we learn from without will have to come to terms: "Heraclitus was perhaps the first Greek speculative philosopher to raise the question of the validity of sense perception" (Stokes, 1967, p. 479).

Homer's way of seeing the world as flashing with bright
particulars has yielded now to a complexer, more mental vision

---

[3]It is interesting to compare this with Wordsworth's revolutionary move of making what he found within to be "My haunt, and the main region of my song."

to which the world forever presents similarities and hints at underlying laws" (Finley, 1966, p. 45).

Among the bright particulars which moved Homer's stories along were the Olympian gods. Homer does not have a psychology; he has an Olympian pantheon. The *psyche* is not a source of decision or strife within Homer's individuals. A hero in difficulty does not search within himself for the stimulation to renewed effort. The stimulation comes from the action of a god. What we would describe in terms of psychological forces, Homer describes in terms of the regular intervention of the gods. In the early years of Greek literacy, the gods, while maintaining their divine appearances on the one hand, were on the other converted into the mental language of psychological forces and abstract concepts: "In the generation of Thucydides [late fifth century] realistic analysis took possession of a subject, in which formerly divine operations had been allotted a large share" (Solmsen, 1975, p. 172). During the next century, culminating in Plato's writing, the bloodless fluttering *eidolon* that was Homer's *psyche* has become the essential, conscious self with its tri-partite soul.

A consequence of the transition to literacy seems to be a sense of a conscious self that is distinct from the world and that can observe and make sense of the world and its own experience as objects. Ong describes this distinction as enabling a "detached" analysis of the world and of experience but "at the price of splitting up the original unity of consciousness" (Ong, 1977, p. 18). In Western cultures this particular form of self-consciousness is so common that it seems often to be taken as a part of the process of development, a constituent of the stage of adolescence. It seems to be considered a "natural" development, rather than a cultural artifact. I take it to be a cultural artifact consequent to becoming literate in what I am calling the Comprehensive sense.

With the splitting of the knower from the known, and the development of detached observation and analysis, came the gradual removal or diminution of personal interests from various kinds of inquiry and so the transmutation of astrology into astronomy, alchemy into chemistry, magic into physics and medicine, and myth into philosophy. These are reflected in the moves "from verse to prose, from shape to concept, from story to analysis, from mythological to conceptual ways of thinking" (Finley, 1966, p. 58). At least, these are consequences of literacy in the particular social and cultural conditions of ancient Greece. They led on to Aristotle's conspicuous enterprise, whose results are evident in the structure of the present day school curriculum and the administrative organization of colleges and universities throughout the world. Whether such consequences of literacy are inevitable is largely irrelevant to this work; they are consequences which are inescapable given our present cultural conditions. We are involved in the accumulation of knowledge, treating the world and our experience as objects knowable by our "selves," much as the enterprise was formulated in ancient Greece. We can, indeed, as a part of the accumulation, revise and reformulate our accounts to reflect reality better: "Cultural inheritance is distinctly Lamarckian; acquired traits can indeed be transmitted" (Simon, 1983, p. 56).

One of the inheritances that has come with "the conceptual ways of thinking" is Plato's insistent claims that reality can be grasped only by means of the procedures of rationality. But the conception of the *psyche* that Plato inherited, shaped, and passed on was that "new psychology" of the turn of the 5th century whose "core" was "the opposition between reason and the irrational emotions" (Solmsen, 1974, p. 171). Despite numerous attempts to resolve this opposition within philosophy (see, e.g., de Sousa, 1988), it remains overwhelmingly influential in conceptions of what is worth pursuing in an educational curriculum. Those things to do with rationality are given the highest status, reflecting Plato's belief that only the rational part of the *psyche* is immortal. The continuing influence of this opposition between reason and emotion in alphabetically literate cultures and in their educational systems was considered in the previous volume, and its relevance persists in this one. There is still a strong belief that the emotions somehow interfere with rationality, and their place in an educational curriculum is uncertain and unclear. The transition to literacy will involve dealing with this particular historical consequence of literacy in Greece when considering the curriculum.

These historical consequences of literacy are not some natural or logical unfolding of implications. Their appearance at all and their particular character require further historical accounts of the conditions which determined that those consequences, and not others, occurred at those times in those places. They are not inevitable consequences, such that we can expect their appearance today in anyone who masters conventional reading and writing skills. To illustrate this point, one might consider one of the consequences of literacy in ancient Greece touched on above. While systematic skepticism is an historical consequence that numerous scholars identify, this does not mean that all individual literate ancient Greeks were systematically skeptical, but rather that the élite achievements commonly exhibited this characteristic. Nor does this mean that skepticism is not common in oral cultures, but rather that its elaboration into a systematic principle undergirding and disciplining inquiries is much easier in a literate environment. As Goody notes, "skepticism is not unusual in oral societies but when predictions are written down it is more difficult to escape the intellectual consequences of their non-fulfillment. . . . [T]he accumulation of skepticism in writing leads to the establishment of a critical tradition that rejects 'magic' side by side with a more orally based one that accepts it" (Goody, 1986, p. 37). The difference between oral and literate skepticism is that the latter is much more easily able to accumulate into systematic principles: "There is no accumulation of non-conforming ideas" in oral societies (Goody, 1986, p. 121).

So skepticism is not a necessary consequence of conventional literacy—as the circulation of papers such as the *National Inquirer* in North America testifies. It is however a constituent of the Comprehensive conception of literacy; that is, the individual *can* recapitulate the "skeptical" consequence of literacy if he or she becomes literate in the Comprehensive way which this essay seeks to characterize. Such skepticism is a central ingredient in all academic disciplines. It is encouraged particularly in tertiary educational institutions, as is exemplified in the celebrated and no doubt apocryphal graduation address by a college president, in which she announced that "Half of what we have taught you is false. Unfortunately we don't know which half."

Memory, prose, rhetoric and romance

In this and the following section I want to touch on two disparate strands that lead into the particular forms of Romanticism and romantic understanding developed in Western cultural history. In this one I want to identify some features of what Ong has called the "overwhelmingly massive oral residue" (Ong, 1982, p. 36) that persisted with the developing literacy of the West until the period of Romanticism. In the next section I want to consider some effects of the printing press on this oral residue. I will focus largely on rhetoric, as the most prominent and organized form in which intellectual elements important for sustaining oral cultures were used in literate cultures.

The *"bias"* of the mind in oral cultures is influenced by the great emphasis placed on memorizing sound patterns. In an oral culture, to repeat an obvious point, one knows only what one can remember, and the lore of the tribe—its social relationships, economic activities, culinary practices, and so on—must be transmitted orally from generation to generation and must be retained clearly by the young members of the tribe. It must be retained also in such a way that the hearers will feel emotionally committed to the lore. The relatively stable preservation of the social group's identity relies heavily on the memory techniques developed to achieve these goals. Prominent among these techniques, to make memorizing easy, are rhyme, rhythm, meter, formulae, and vivid images. Also, in order to encourage commitment to the lore so communicated, conditions of heightened emotional intensity and the story are deployed. Myth stories carry the lore of the tribe in coded forms, and these forms include the mnemonic device of vivid images. These have among their effects the stimulation and development of the imagination.

The introduction of writing reduces the social pressure to memorize and so reduces the social importance of the techniques developed to preserve and communicate the lore of the tribe in a memorable way. It also reduces the social usefulness of the psychological conditions which those techniques generated in hearers to ensure receptivity to the tribal lore. Though we can describe a reduction in the social importance and use of these techniques over the first alphabetically literate generations, they did not just wither away. They persisted and still persist in a variety of forms, but some of them underwent a new kind of development in the form of rhetoric. The long historical development of rhetoric is seen by Ong as persisting until the advent of Romanticism (Ong, 1971). I will later suggest that this view might reasonably be modified, but his observation about the transformation of orality within rhetoric is important:

> when we say that Western culture until recently was rhetorical,
> we are saying something more specific than that it was oral.
> We mean also that Western culture, after the invention of
> writing and before the industrial revolution, made a science or
> "art" of its orality (Ong, 1971, p. 3).

Rhetoric is that body of knowledge and practical skills that may be employed in persuading others to see and feel about something in a particular way. Plato, rhetoric's greatest enemy, calls it, in the *Phaedrus,* "a universal art of enchanting the mind by arguments" (Jowett, 1937, p. 264). Not, note, persuading the mind by reasons, but enchanting the mind by the way arguments are organized and well presented. The difference, from Plato's point of view, between rhetorical training and his own kind of philosophic education is that in the former one persuades people to believe something is true, in the latter one enables people to know that something is true. While rhetoric became the most organized part of the "massive oral residue" that persisted into literate times, literacy entailed a *bias* that was antipathetic even to this residue.

Plato was indeed "the most extreme and implacable enemy 'the art of persuasion' has ever had" (Nehamas, 1988, p. 771). In developing and elaborating the new "conceptual ways of thinking," Plato articulated a curriculum, in *The Republic,* and examples of the best procedures for learning the new philosophy, in the Dialogues in general. He set these up explicitly in opposition to the systems of education offered by the rhetoricians, whom he represented as dealing only with the appearances of things, with cosmetics, and with superficial tricks or knacks of persuasion. Rhetorical language, as Kenneth Burke put it, is inducement to action (K. Burke, 1969), but action resulting from an emotional response rather than conceptual analysis. The *Georgias* is one of Plato's more powerful attacks on the rhetoricians' claims to knowledge and on the value of the kind of education they offered. This dialogue seems aimed directly at Isocrates, the most famous of the rhetor-educators, who opened a school of 'philosophy' around 388 B.C.E. The training offered in Isocrates' school would have seemed to Plato "no more than a thorough soaking in untested opinions and prejudices, combined with a training in speech-making which in the absence of a sound educational grounding amounted to putting a powerful weapon in the hands of the irresponsible" (Melling, 1987, p. 31). (In the *Phaedrus,* however, a rather more mellow view of the place of rhetoric is offered, in which Plato suggests that the rhetor's skills may be of some value if their user already has genuine knowledge of a subject.)

Aspects of rhetoric are evident in a number of intellectual forms developed in classical Greece. To take Herodotus, "the father of history," again as an example: he wrote to be heard primarily, and read secondarily. He told a complex story sure to be pleasing to his Athenian audiences' ears. But one effect of writing is to reduce the anxiety of forgetting, which thus allows the introduction of any detail that might charm one's audience, as long as it can be coherently fitted into the overarching story. Though things were to change quite quickly, Herodotus' Athens constituted "a world in which oral discourse is not devalued in relation to written discourse—a world of orality, or still largely so" (Hartog, 1988, p. 273). Indeed Herodotus, we know, received a prize of ten talents from the Athenians for the recitation of his work (Hartog, 1988, pp. 274–275).

So the fact that the Egyptians shaved off their eyebrows at the death of their cats is interesting to one's audience and can be included in one's narrative if it can be slotted into the account of the Persians and the nature of their previous enemies. The effect is a little like trying to put the contents of the *Guinness Book of Records* into one's story. The hearer is kept alert and fascinated by the exotic detail bound within an epic true story which glorifies the hearers and the heroic city with which they identify. Such a narrative clearly embodies a number of the characteristics of romance—reality, heroism, the exotic, etc.

Most noticeably the ability to write reduced the need for the "poetic" elements of oral composition and easier memorization, and so prose became the predominant form for keeping records and presenting accounts of events. The early Greek recorders who preceded or were contemporary with Herodotus have been called *logographoi*—writers of prose. Dionysius of Halicarnassus was later able to describe them as follows:

> some of them wrote Hellenic histories, and some barbarian
> histories. They did not write connected accounts, but broke
> them up instead according to peoples and cities, treating each
> separately, but with one aim in view—to make generally
> known whatever local records had survived, whether of peoples
> or cities, and whether lying about in temple precincts or
> anywhere else, without adding anything to what they found, or
> leaving anything out. Mythological material, acceptable
> because of its antiquity, was included, and also some dramatic
> tales, quite silly from a modern point of view. For the most
> part, writers who choose this kind of speech have much the
> same style, clear, ordinary, pure, succinct, and appropriate to
> the matter at hand, but showing no pains of composition. In
> varying degrees their works do have a certain freshness and
> charm, and that is why they have survived (cited in Brown,
> 1954, p. 829).

From such as these to the highly "literately" organized composition of Herodotus is a considerable step. But Thucydides, who—so goes the legend—wept as a boy on hearing Herodotus recite his history, was later scornful of Herodotus' inclusion of "entertaining" elements. Thucydides wrote to be read forever, he tells us, not to delight a particular audience. Despite his fanatical concern to track down and record the facts of the Peloponnesian war, it is clear that the particular facts are not Thucydides' primary concern. Rather he wants to study that one war to show what *happens* in history, to expose general truths about historical events. (Though even he was not immune from the tug of romance, arguing that his subject was the greatest of all wars that had ever occurred and that he wanted to keep it from "sliding over into myth" as the Trojan war had when left to poets.) By Plato's time, the general truth, the idea, is what matters and particular events are seen as sources of illusion, and of no account by themselves. Aristotle does not even include history among the fields for rational inquiry.

While this move towards the general and abstract is one of the historical consequences of literacy, my interest here is on a particular phase of it—that in which rhetoric becomes prominent and at which, relatedly, romantic elements become vivid. Whitehead observes that "romantic emotion is essentially the excitement consequent on the transition from the bare facts to the first realizations of the import of their unexplored relationships" (Whitehead, 1967, p. 18). I think we can recapitulate the move from mythic to rational forms of understanding, but to do it while maximizing the intellectual benefits of this move and minimizing its losses, we need to be sensitive to some of its crucial stages. I have dwelt on Herodotus because he most clearly represents the crucial stage I am trying to distinguish under the label of romance. He exemplifies one of the fullest exploitations in ancient Greece of the possibility literacy opened up for recording events. He did so at a time when "the transition from the bare facts to the first realizations of the import of their unexplored relationships" was hinting at the potential for a Thucydidean systematic inquiry but Herodotus was more caught up with the sheer excitement, and fun, of laying out the exotic variety of the world. Released from the anxiety of remembering, drawing on the story-form of the epic, and recording whatever seemed worthy of note, Herodotus used both literate and oral techniques, creating a new and mixed form of inquiry—whose epistemological status still remains a matter of scholarly debate: is it an art or a science, and so forth?

The oral, rhetorical elements mixed with the "prosaic" concern with what particular things happened have also produced lip-pursing disapproval down the ages:

> The kindly Herodotus, without portraits, without maxims, yet flowing, simple, full of details calculated to delight and interest in the highest degree, would be perhaps the best historian [for youth to read] if these very details did not often degenerate into childish folly, better adopted to spoil the taste of youth than to form it. (Rousseau, 1974, p. 201)

Now this might seem an excessive scruple in an age like ours in which it would be considered the wildest optimism to expect youths to read Herodotus. Rousseau's is not a view of Herodotus that is common among historians today, but the regret about something unreliable in the "oral" elements of such history writing was common in classical Greece and later. Strabo noted that "one might more readily believe Hesiod and Homer, with their stories of heroic times, and the tragic poets, than Ctesias and Herodotus and Hellanicus and the rest of them" (cited in Pearson, 1939, p. 8). Admirers of Thucydides' austere style—who himself gave his highest praise to Pericles because he alone of orators never spoke with a view to pleasing his audience—deprecated Herodotus and his ilk because their work demonstrated the oral desire of the epic to tell a story and to beguile an audience's ears: in short, to generate a psychological condition that was inimical to the new conceptual kind of thinking.

In the long battle between rhetoric and philosophy, and their seemingly competing, somewhat overlapping, claims on truth, the battle lines were set by Plato. Indeed he gave not only the arguments on behalf of philosophy, but also those on behalf of rhetoric, and nothing much has been added since (Vickers, 1988). Plato's was not an easy case to make in a city in which "The art of politics became essentially the management of language" (Vernant, 1982, p. 50). The rhetoricians offered an education in which the individual was equipped with the skills to deal with a form of public life in which mastery of language was an important means to power and success: "The system of the *polis* implied . . . the extraordinary preeminence of speech [over] all other instruments of power. Speech became the political tool *par excellence,* the key to all authority in the state, the means of commanding and dominating others" (Vernant, 1982, p. 49). That is, in terms of today's pressures on the schools to teach socially relevant skills, and to justify the contents of the curriculum in terms of social utility, Plato's position was one of implacable hostility and scorn. Education for him involved learning those things that enabled one to see the good, the true, and the beautiful; from such understanding one could see better how society might be improved. Education was debased if it was merely a fitting to the conventions and fashions of the time. Plato's was *par excellence* the system of education that exploited the consequences of literacy; it was abstract and aimed towards a conception of knowledge and truth that was beyond the conventions of any time or place. Like writing, Plato's forms of knowledge contained a conception of permanence, of something that transcended particulars of time and place.

Plato has Menexenus say in *Ion,* "You are always making fun of the rhetoricians, Socrates" (cited in Jowett, 1937, p. 776). And indeed Plato and Socrates keep up the attack on rhetoric throughout the dialogues, sometimes earnestly and fiercely as in the *Georgias,* sometimes more playfully as in the *Phaedrus.* In his friendly mockery of Phaedrus' admiration of Lycias' rhetorical skills, Socrates tries to expose the hollowness of what Phaedrus admires by copying it: "I appear to be in a divine fury, for already I am getting into dithyrambics" (cited in Jowett, 1937, p. 243). Socrates analyzes the speech he extemporizes in competition with that of Lycias:

> There was . . . a simplicity about them which was refreshing; having no truth or honesty in them, nevertheless they pretended to something, hoping to succeed in deceiving the manikins of earth and gain celebrity among them. Wherefore I must have a purgation. And I bethink me of an ancient purgation of mythological error which was divised, not by Homer, for he never had the wit to discover why he was blind, but by Stesichorus, who was a philosopher and knew the reason why (cited in Jowett, 1973, p. 247).

Socrates goes dazzlingly on, using with consummate skill the tools of rhetoric in order to damn them in Phaedrus' eyes and those of the readers of the carefully composed dialogue. What is at issue is the truth and how to know it and tell it. The seducers of the ear were a prominent enemy in Plato's battle to make his conception of philosophy the dominant method of inquiry and the proper aim of education. (It should be noted also that those who looked for truth in the appearance of things were also enemies. The empirical scientist, who studied the stars or earth in order to discover what was the case about them, was equally deceived. The kind of objective truth sought by empirical science was trivial in Plato's eyes, tied as it was to the impermanent, changing world. This conception of objective truth available to empirical research also had a root in a prime arena of rhetoric: "legal proceedings brought into operation a whole technique of proof . . . and judicial activity contributed to the development of the notion of objective truth" (Vernant, 1982, p. 81).)

But rhetoric survived Plato, who was ironically one of its greatest exponents while promoting an ideal of education that was hostile to it. One reason for its survival, apart from its obvious social uses, was the realization, as Goody puts it, that "writing is no mere phonograph recording of speech . . . it encourages special forms of linguistic activity associated with developments in particular kinds of problem-raising and problem-solving" (Goody, 1977, p. 162). Oral techniques had been refined so that messages of special importance would have a particularly powerful impact on their hearers. Many of these techniques were incorporated into rhetoric, but their form and uses changed as a result of literacy. In addition, however, rhetoric involved the development of techniques appropriate to writing so that its impact on readers might be made most powerful. The more forceful the impression we want our speech or writing to have, the more we call on the art of rhetoric. So, while we may see a powerful movement in Greece which is tempting to characterize as from poetry to prose, from story to analysis, etc., it is important to note that poetry and story do not fade away, but undergo accommodations of their own and find new social uses. The change in Greece, as in medieval Europe, "was not so much from oral *to* written as from an earlier state, predominantly oral, to various combinations of oral *and* written" (Stock, 1983, p. 9). In the classical and medieval worlds the persistence and prominence of rhetoric testified to the fact that "ways of thinking associated with orality . . . survived in a textual environment" (Stock, 1983, p. 12).

In rhetoric, then, the logic of the message, the knowledge to be communicated, has to accommodate to the logic of the audience's heart. The rhetorician cannot attend purely to the hard factuality of his content; he has constantly to be sensitive to shaping it, altering it, to make it most engaging.[4] Plato's attempt to hijack philosophy from rhetoric did not succeed completely, and the still popular meaning of "philosophical" as tied in with wisdom and a concern with the human heart, reflects the influence of rhetoric within philosophy up until early modern times. But what Plato failed to attain Newton and Descartes managed, at least for a time. What they achieved was a sense that one could establish truths about the world and our experience certainly and absolutely. As this sense fades in our culture, we can perhaps see their achievement more clearly. But formal training in rhetoric, as a central pillar of education in Europe, went into a decline from which it still has not recovered after the work of Descartes and Newton became internalized in Western cultural life. Descartes represented the mind as an inner theatre in which one could, by careful observation, establish absolute certainty. His work represented

the triumph of the quest for certainty over the quest for wisdom. From that time forward, the way was open for philosophers either to attain the rigors of the mathematician or the mathematical physicist, or to explain the appearance of

---

[4]I should add, by way of an educational aside, that the use of "he" here is quite appropriate. Rhetoric, especially from the European Middle Ages to the period of Romanticism, was very much a male preserve. Rhetoric was tied in this period to the strange history of Latin. Cicero provided both the main textbook of rhetoric and the ideal to be emulated. Ong, more than wittily, describes the learning of Latin in this period as a male puberty rite (Ong, 1971). For more than a thousand years Latin was no one's mother tongue, yet it was the indispensable medium for scholarly discourse.

rigor of these fields, rather than to help people attain peace of mind. Science, rather than living, became philosophy's subject, and epistemology its center. (Rorty, 1979, p. 61).

We are at a point today when a number of philosophers, Rorty notably among them, are questioning whether the triumph of a Platonic or Cartesian conception of philosophy that rigorously excludes rhetorical elements has been the progressive achievement commonly assumed. Certainly it is becoming clear that the triumphs of modern science and technology which allow us increasingly to see into the nature of things and have pragmatic control over an increasing range of them, do not increase our joy, nor love, nor peace of mind, nor help for pain—to echo Matthew Arnold. And it is becoming clear that the enormous investment of human energy and ingenuity into science and forms of philosophy and even literary criticism that doggedly follow the Platonic and Cartesian program and neglect rhetoric and our emotional lives is imbalanced in an undesirable way. Petrarch's famous comment that "It is better to will the good than to know the truth," is at the heart of rhetoric's challenge to the Platonic or Cartesian program for knowing the truth. (Plato, of course, believed that knowing the truth would automatically lead to willing the good.) Central to willing the good, Vickers argues, is the appropriate stimulation of the *affectus,* the source of feeling, that the orator, poet, painter, musician draws on and arouses in others (Vickers, 1988).

Well, we do not need to take sides in this ancient and continuing quarrel. Rather, we can seek a way of transcending the opposition which the dialectics of argument help to generate. What I want to bring forward with this discussion, however, is that the consequences of literacy do not only carry us in the direction of abstraction, logic, and modern science, but that there is also an important tradition in which significant features of orality found an accommodation with literacy. Rhetoric is also a consequence of literacy, and one we may wish to attend to in an educational program intent on recapitulating forms of understanding.

The fate of rhetoric in European educational systems during the eighteenth century can perhaps be better dealt with after we add the other significant development in the technology of literacy, the printing press.

Print, technology, and romance

We cannot accept too easy comparisons between historical transitions to alphabetic literacy, whether in ancient Greece or medieval Europe, and individual students' transition today, however suggestive such comparisons can seem. One complicating factor is that students today become literate in a heavily print-dominated environment. The character of the literacy that students reconstruct today is a kind affected by the proliferation of print. Increasingly, with easy access to word processors that produce their writing via dot-matrix, daisywheel, or laser printers, students do not recapitulate the kind of literacy which was the only kind known in the ancient world and in medieval Europe.

One of the difficulties in tracing the consequences of print on our cognition is that "It is difficult to observe processes that enter so intimately into our own observations" (Eisenstein, 1983, p. 6). Print enters into our observations by its cumulative effects over the centuries since we entered the Gutenberg galaxy. The cumulative effects were such that "typography was interiorized in the Western psyche definitively at the moment in Western history known as the romantic movement" (Ong, 1977, p. 283). Not only was Romanticism a product of printing in this view but so was the whole Industrial Revolution—and the co-incidence of the two was far from coincidental: "Mechanical technology [emerged] from our alphabet and the printing press" (McLuhan, 1962, p. 278).

These are large claims not always clearly spelled out and, in McLuhan's pyrotechnic expositions, we are occasionally too dazzled to be able to make out exactly what is going on at ground level. But McLuhan and Ong both draw on the Innis notion of mental *biases:*

> If a technology is introduced from within or from without a
> culture, and if it gives new stress or ascendancy to one or
> another of our senses, the ratio among all our senses is altered.
> We no longer feel the same, nor do our eyes and ears and other
> senses remain the same. (McLuhan, 1962, p. 24)

As Baudelaire identified Romanticism as a new feeling, so those who argue for the profound effects on our consciousness of our modes of knowledge acquisition and communication identify the cause of this new feeling as one of the longer term consequences of the alphabet and the printing press. How can this be? What basis is there for such vast generalizations? And what does it have to do with middle-school education anyway? The relevance to the topic of this book is due to the predisposing effects of literacy and print on cognition. It is useful to get as good a grasp as possible on what seem to be causes of these predispositions, so that one can see what of value needs to be encouraged and what problems might be associated with them. The hypotheses and arguments we have about the implications of print are such that we might be sensibly cautious, but they are also now spelled out sufficiently that they should not, at the very least, be ignored, and we might learn something of practical value from them.

When we read the literature on the move from orality to literacy, and the consequences of literacy, all the characteristics of Western rationality seem to be dealt with, leaving little else for which print can to take responsibility. And, indeed, writing and print seem to claim some responsibility for a number of recurring elements. This familiarity of topics, and causal echoes, is reasonable, given that one of the effects claimed for print is an intensification of some of the consequences of writing. The focus now is on a shift from one kind of literacy to another, to borrow a phrase from Eisenstein's two volume study of the process (1979).

Certain consequences of print are relatively easy to observe—though sometimes effects of those consequences are rather more difficult to grasp. Perhaps the most obvious consequence was the number and variety of books in circulation. During the half-century after Gutenberg's press began operating early in the 1450s, more books were produced than from all the scriptoria of Europe and the Roman Empire since the first centuries of the Common Era. While the first printed books often looked very like scribal products, there was a revolution in scale. Eisenstein shows that, in 1483, the Ripoli Press charged 3 florins per quinterno for setting up and printing Fincino's translation of Plato's *Dialogues*. The going scribal rate for the same work was 1 florin per quinterno. At the end of their work the scribe produced 1 copy, the press 1,025 copies.

One consequence of this revolution in productivity, evident early in the next century, is the possession of libraries. Erasmus and Montaigne both had at hand a range of works the likes of which no medieval scholar could have hoped to encounter. The medieval scholar who hoped to consult a variety of books had to be ready to travel (Waddell, 1954). This "novelty of being able to assemble diverse records and reference guides and of being able to study them without having to transcribe them" (Eisenstein, 1983, p. 255) had profound effects, according to Eisenstein. She argues persuasively that the revolutionary ideas of the century following this remarkable proliferation of printed material, such as those of Copernicus and Galileo, were not so much a product of new data being discovered as of scholars suddenly having access to a wide range of data and diverse commentaries on them.

Such discoveries were a part of "the ferment engendered by access to more books" (Eisenstein, 1983, p. 43), a ferment which we perhaps cannot easily recapture because we take access to huge data resources so much for granted. (A little while back I was unsure of the date of Gutenberg's first published book, unsure, that is, whether there was a precise date known. Within seconds I was able to "access" an encyclo- paedia via my computer and consult an authoritative source.) Printing standardized texts like maps of earth and stars, allowed for gradual revisions, and led to reliable bases for mariners', travellers', and astrono- mers' activities. The increasingly accurate texts of ancient scholarly works were only a small part of the flood of religious books and pam- phlets (orthodox, heterodox, and mystical), and endless "how-to" books—the book trade's continuing reliable money-makers. The presses produced quantities of material that intensified religious and secular beliefs and controversy at the same time.

In an oral culture, much intellectual effort has to go to the preservation of the society's horde of knowledge. A scribal culture, too, is subject to constant transformation and decay of knowledge. The materials on which writing was done were perishable, subject to worm and fire (and, as Umberto Eco suggests, eating) and the less dramatic wear of time and use. And, significantly, texts were subject to copyists' corruptions and imagination, whether by a scholar copying a work he was studying and interpolating ideas of his own, or replacing sections, or the inevitable errors of scriptoria where a tired copyist only half-heard what was read. While print initially, and in abundance, reproduced the corrupted texts it inherited from scriptoria, and added its own, what it ensured, particularly through the print-shops as competitive centres of entrepreneurial activity and scholarly concourse, was the beginning of the reversal of the process of corruption. Texts quickly appeared with "errata" slips which were sent to subscribers across Europe. New and improved editions appeared, outpacing the worm. The apparatus of editorial and textual scholarship, that reached a peak of immense refinement by the late nineteenth century, began its career.

The improvements made during the twelfth century in the accessibility of the ms. page to the eye were also intensified by print. Initially the typical printed page looked very like a good scribal page. But printing in the West was tied up with an emerging capitalist, competitive business world, and in a short time the conventions of scribal forms began to yield to the interests of the book market. By experiment encouraged by competition, pages and typefaces were made more accessible while the flood of books increased. The old Roman letters were increasingly found to be cleaner and easier to read than the common scribal Gothic.

Rather less easily observed, or grasped, are the kinds of cognitive consequences McLuhan has claimed result from scanning lines of print. The general claim, elaborated by Ong, is that print intensifies the "visual *bias*" of people who become "immersed" in it. Seeing words in print encourages us to experience them as objects in space, and no longer as sounds. It is a common experience for a literate person to be entirely familiar visually with certain words while never speaking them. Indeed the shock of hearing an unfamiliar sound for a word one was familiar with is also common. (I would be embarrassed to admit how old I was before I recognized the familiar name "Goethe" in the appropriate sound. Catherine Egan and her friends were constantly inventing "shems," which turned out, on bewildered parents' inquiries, to be spelled "schemes.")

The increase in private collections of books further intensified the sense of the individual eye, alone, observing knowledge. Increasingly people did not come together to hear addresses delivered—they might more readily read a pamphlet or broadsheet. There was an increasing ease in acquiring knowledge privately, alone and in silence. The printed page, increasingly accessible, even lacked the marginal glosses, interpolations, and notes from diverse hands that made so many medieval books a kind of communal conversational activity. Printing silenced this kind of discourse—a marginal comment on one's private copy had no impact on the thousands of others. Even today the, usually irritating, marginalia lack any authority compared to the printed page. On a manuscript page, the marginalia and the text were in a similar medium (Eisenstein, 1979, p. 129). But as a writer of a to-be-printed text, one's conception of the discourse one was engaged in with perhaps thousands of readers around Europe must have been unprecedented. Certain consequences are evident, others are more shadowy.

Despite the silence of the writer's and readers' private studies, or because of it, the writer could affect a new kind of individual intimacy with readers. One of the first to realize this was Montaigne, who developed what is to us the familiar, in more senses than one, essay style. It allowed him to engage in a kind of conversation with his readers: "I speake unto paper as to the first man I meete" (cited in Willinsky, 1987, p. 149). Though Montaigne uses this oral metaphor for his essay writing, it is significantly unlike the form of narratives we have from, say, Aristotle or Cicero. Despite that "speake," what is written is not expected ever to be spoken. It may be an entirely silent discourse (Olson, 1977).

The intensified reliance on sight for communication and knowledge acquisition, encourages that distancing and discrimination of the knower from the known which Ong describes. The essay form seems to encourage the writer's sense of being, to echo Graham Good's title, "the observing self" (Good, 1988); the sense of "I" as a place to view from. We do seem in this literature to be constantly discovering "the self."

Havelock describes it as a product of Socratic vocabulary, Stock characterizes the new scribal literacy of the Middle Ages involving a change "in the means by which one established personal identity, both with respect to the inner self and external forces" (Stock, 1983, p. 4). And we have seen in the previous chapter the claim that a symptom of Romanticism was a new discovery of the self. Perhaps we may see these all as part of a single lengthy process, in which print intensifies the sense of self generated by writing, and Romanticism establishes this particular kind of self-consciousness as a central feature of Western cultural consciousness (Hanson, 1986).

More tangibly, print results in the conception of originality, which is one aspect of this self-consciousness. With the fixity of print and the possibilities of proof-reading and correcting, with the date of an edition, the publisher's and author's names set on a front sheet, claims to originality and to inventions and discoveries became clearly establishable. In a scribal culture, a text might be copied by a dozen hands, each making emendations, corrections, and additions, or it might have started from an oration copied by students with more or less accuracy before setting forth on a career of unknowable and uncontrollable changes. After printed texts, the individual's contribution was much clearer. Again, we may see this as a long process, emerging from the collectivity of myth, to the authorship of written texts, to the incorporation of the significance of individual originality in Western cultural consciousness during Romanticism.

The process of scribal corruption which was reduced, then reversed, by the printing press gave way not just to less corrupt editions but also to a process of increasing security and accessibility of knowledge. This process continued through the establishment of reliable maps of earth and heavens, to more reliable ancient texts available in abundance and to new departures in European scholarship, to the "scientific revolution" and the founding of the Royal Society, and so on. It reached one culmination in what we still call, though no longer without a tincture of irony, the Enlightenment, and most visibly in that great Enlightenment project, the *Encyclopédie* of Diderot and d'Alembert. All knowledge was to be brought together, arranged alphabetically, and made accessible to anyone.

The *Encyclopédie* both exemplified and supported a kind of confidence and sense of security in knowledge. This had two sides, at least. On the one side was a proto-positivist confidence in the advance of knowledge, vividly expressed by d'Alembert's pupil, Condorcet. While in hiding from the arrest decree of the Republican Convention in 1793, Condorcet wrote an outline for a vast historical survey of human cultural development, the *Esquisse d'un tableau historique des progrès de l'esprit humain*. He sketches the growth and progress of reason, projecting its irresistible advance as the spread of knowledge through education would lead the whole human race into a condition of liberty, equality, fraternity, peace, and long-lived happiness. On the other side, represented well by Diderot's own particular genius, was the confidence to doubt. McLuhan and Ong argue that the security of knowledge storage exemplified by the *Encyclopédie* and later similar compilations represented a culmination of another long process. In Ong's words: "the store of knowledge accumulated in print was no longer managed by repetitive, oral techniques, but by visual means, through print, tables of content, and indices" (Ong, 1977, p. 297). Never before had the store of knowledge been held so securely and so accessibly. Not only could one afford to be more confidently skeptical, but one could more steadily contemplate precisely the areas one did not know about, the mysterious, strange, and exotic. When there was anxiety about preserving the knowledge one had, the security and leisure to explore the mysterious could be only a flickering impulse. By the end of the eighteenth century it became a central feature of Romanticism.

While at one level the fascination with the mysterious was somewhat trivial, echoed today in the "Bermuda Triangle" kind of literature, there was also a level, represented by the leading romantic poets, which was concerned with pointing out that the advance of knowledge was confident only in very limited areas. The most important parts of our lives, the day to day sense we make of them, were left largely untouched and unenlightened. Indeed, the confidence of propagandists for the Enlightenment and the irresistible progress of reason was seen as quite misplaced.

McLuhan and Ong see Romanticism as the intellectual partner of the Industrial revolution. This may appear a surprizing partnership, as we tend to think of Romanticism as a kind of reaction against the "satanic mills" of the new industries. But together they exemplified confidence in the conquest of nature, practically and theoretically:

> Romanticism appears as a result of man's noetic control over
> nature, a counterpart of technology, which matures in the same
> regions in the West as Romanticism and at about the same
> . time, and which likewise derives from control over nature
> made possible by writing and even more by print as means of
> knowledge storage and retrieval (Ong, 1971, p. 20).

What is reduced to near-invisibility by print is the tincture of anxiety attached to the retention and accumulation of knowledge in scribal and oral cultures. One might get a sense of it by imagining a catastrophe that destroys our cities, libraries, and data-storage facilities. If you are one of the few survivors, how much of the accumulated knowledge of Western culture will you be able to pass on, and how would that be stored? The anxiety attached to the insecure hold on knowledge did not allow the confidence and intellectual leisure to play with knowledge, such as we find in books of trivia and exotica. These too become elements of Romanticism. In oral or book-poor cultures much of one's mental energy went into retaining and repeating formulae, tags, and what we would consider clichés. The late medieval student would organize much of his understanding under a set of formulae he would carry around in his head—*"nihil in intellectu quod non prius in sensu"; "entia non sunt multiplicanda praeter necessitatem,"* and so on. With the security provided by print, the cliché, far from being an important mnemonic, becomes disreputable, and the function of literary art is not to mimic classical paradigms but to venture into the unknown and report to us its discoveries.

These identifying features of Romanticism all signal a decisive break from the residue of orality. Mnemosyne, the rememberer, was the Muse whom the epic poets asked to sing through them. But Mnemosyne was not so important to literate writers. The literary form that reaches maturity after print had become commonplace was the novel:

What distinguishes the novel from the story (and from the epic in the narrower sense) is its essential dependence on the book. The dissemination of the novel became possible only with the invention of printing. . . . What differentiates the novel from all other forms of prose literature . . . is that it neither comes from oral tradition nor goes into it. . . . The birthplace of the novel is the solitary individual (Benjamin, 1969, p. 87).

The "observing self" wrote novels as well as essays. The problem entailed in this retreat from orality is, to put it in Ong's terms, the ever-increasing dominance of the eye, and its accompanying mental *bias* in knowledge acquisition and communication. The problem with *this* is that it "divorces knowledge from understanding and subjectivity" (Ong, 1977, p. 122). That is, the danger of a visually biased mode of acquisition of knowledge is that the knowledge will largely remain in the form of its visual codes and will not become a part of one's *"unbiased"* or balanced or harmonious understanding. The result is to "rob knowledge of its interiority" (Ong, 1977, p. 122).

I think this is an important observation, made often in education in a variety of ways. It is usually made very vaguely, by suggesting a profound distinction between "knowledge" and "understanding" that the suggester can rarely spell out. Ong's manner of making the distinction, in the context he has elaborated, enables us better to grasp what is so inadequate about, say, conceptions of learning that measure it by tests that require only the exteriority of knowledge to be reflected back. One might also observe, however, in possible qualification of Ong's point, that it was only after print had secured knowledge storage that meaningful learning demanded more than memorization of formulae, or that it became clear that memorization as evidence of meaningful learning was empty. Print could remember for us; our task was meaning and doing things with it.

Perhaps we might pick up a thread from the story of rhetoric here. Ong represents rhetoric as finally killed off by the "internalization of print," which, in his account, is represented by Romanticism. I think we might see the fate of rhetoric rather differently; at least, we can if we see rhetoric as the attempt to reach an accommodation between features of orality and consequences of literacy. In this view, during the early centuries of print, rhetoric got lost, committed suicide, and was triumphantly reborn. It got lost by increasingly losing touch with its living oral resources. It became, most emphatically in neo-classicism, artificial, cut off from the oral culture of the time, harking back to Cicero and classical Roman times. Its effects on the vernacular were to try to Latinize it as much as possible. Like most cultural movements, even in this suicidal separation from the living oral culture of its time, these artificial rhetorical forms lived on powerfully in education. Wordsworth's own education involved stultifying hours of memorizing Latin verse, and composing to formulae, and training to imitate paradigms which had genuine vitality only more than a millenium and a half previously.

By the mid-eighteenth century the uselessness of this kind of education was being vividly pointed out. Pope satirized Dr. Bushy of Westminster school in *The Dunciad* as declaring:

. . . Since Man from beast by Words is known,

. . . . . .

Words are Man's province, Words we teach alone.
(Pope, *The Dunciad*, Bk. IV, ll., 49,56)

This is echoed in Rousseau's (echoing Hamlet) contemptuous dismissal of the typical education of his time and place as "Words! Words! Words!" or, Pope again:

As Fancy opens the quick springs of Sense,
We ply the Memory, we load the brain,
Blind rebel Wit, and double chain on chain,
Confine the thought, to exercise the breath;
And keep them in the pale of Words till death.
Whate'er the talents, or howe'er designed,
We hang one jingling padlock on the mind.
                    (Pope, *The Dunciad*, Bk. IV, ll., 56–62)

Let me also pick up one other thread here. Undergirding the educational practice of the eighteenth century was another, now familiar inheritance. That is the "new psychology" of the late fifth century B.C.E. in which reason is seen as in conflict with the irrational passions and emotions. We have added or incorporated into this psychology the residue of the medieval soul/body conflict. Given this, an urgent principle for the eighteenth century educationalist was to ensure that "the animal appetite be retarded as long as possible in both sexes" (Kames, 1782, p. 249). The educational literature of the time overflows with references to "unusual fervour in the blood" of youth, "impetuous conflagration, through the whole extent of their faculties," and such like. Hannah More wrote: "In the warm season of youth hardly anything is seen in the true point of vision" (cited in Spacks, 1981, p. 109; see especially Ch. 4). Many of these educationalists considered one of nature's cruellest tragedies that "passions reached highest intensity before reason has developed" (Spacks, 1931, p. 109). One of the dangers of youth, it was commonly assumed, is "the special dominance of the inner life during the teen-age years, and the resultant difficulty for the young of coming to terms with the social world they necessarily inhabit, a difficulty compounded by their relative ignorance of that world" (Spacks, 1981, p. 107). That inner life seemed tied so readily to the animal appetites and both were likely to be dangerously inflamed by imaginative literature. Dr. Johnson, too, was disturbed by the imagination's "unhealthy" power to recreate the world, unrealistically, to its better liking. Any power of fancy over reason is a degree of insanity, was how he put it in *Rasselas*.

One great achievement of Romanticism, confident with dictionaries of clarified meaning and encyclopaedias of accessibly stored knowledge, was not to enlist in the progressive Enlightenment crusade to secure the victory of reason. Rather, Romanticism embodied the insight that the "springs of fancy" were the key to making reason serve human life. The purified, and, we might now say, extreme print-literate conception of reason was seen as representing an imbalance in the mind of which

Romanticism was the cure. Romanticism was a kind of cure for the alienation from nature and from ourselves which seemed involved in the Enlightenment glorification of reason. Within Romanticism we see the constant insistence that it is only by energetic use of the *imagination* that the dessication and alienation of excessive rationality can be overcome. The educated imagination can, in Innis' and McLuhan's sense, harmonize the ratio of the senses. Reason, in the neo-classicist sense, is no solution by itself; indeed, it becomes the problem:

> The Spectre is the Reasoning Power in Man, & when separated
> From Imagination and closing itself as in steel in a Ratio
> Of the Things of Memory, it thence frames Laws and Moralities
> To destroy Imagination, the Divine Body, by Martyrdoms & Wars
>   (Blake, *Jerusalem*, 74, ll. 10–14)

While rhetoric committed suicide by losing contact with the oral life of its time, the reassertion of the value of what Ong generally calls orality is central to Romanticism. Romanticism, rather than being, as Ong suggests, the final internalization of print in Western culture, seems better understood as the rebirth of the original and proper aim of rhetoric: to forge an accommodation between the forms of thought evident in ancient and in modern oral cultures—whether those of travellers' tales or those of the European peasantries—and the rationality and print based, visually-*biased* literacy which dominated intellectual life during the eighteenth century. And the prophets of this romantic accommodation were self-consciously clear what they were about:

> Hear the voice of the Bard!
> Who present, past, and future sees;
> Whose ears have heard
> The Holy Word
> That walked among the ancient trees
>   (Blake, "Hear the Voice of the Bard")

And, most acutely, Wordsworth hammered at the alienation that eighteenth century neo-classical, high-literate culture had encouraged: "Little we see in Nature that is ours;/We have given our hearts away, a sordid boon!" The imaginative participation in nature common in oral cultures is what he feels cut off from:

> Great God! I'd rather be
> A Pagan suckled in a creed outword;
> So might I, standing on this pleasant lea,
> Have glimpses that would make me less forlorn;
> Have sight of Proteus rising from the sea;
> Or hear old Triton blow his wreathèd horn.
> (Wordsworth, Sonnet, XXXIII)

The achievement of Romanticism, then, lies in the degree of its success in discovering a key to harmony and balance in our cultural lives. A prime instrument is the vivified imagination and an important agent is the natural world to which the imagination can give proper access. In the terms I have been using in this chapter, Romanticism relies on the security of knowledge storage provided by print in order to point to some of the deficiencies of the kind of knowledge that can thus be stored, and to some of the dangers of relying too confidently on that knowledge and the forms of thought it evokes, stimulates, and develops. Literacy, if relied on excessively, is a sordid boon, but it need not be so if we can engage it and use it in such a way that it does not erode our orality; that orality we know as children (when the "world lies/More justly balanced" [Wordsworth, "Personal Talk," II]). Romanticism does not, then, mark, as Ong seems to suggest, the final capitulation of rhetoric to literacy. Rather it embodies the reassertion of central features of orality within a literate world.

I have suggested that Romanticism is better seen as a decisive cultural achievement, rather than as a movement that came and went. That is, it fixed certain features of romance, which I have sketched above, as permanent characteristics of Western culture. This is a very general and vague way of putting it, of course. I do not mean to suggest that these features are automatically "internalized" by anyone who attends the normal kind of educational institutions that are supposed to initiate the young into the Western cultural tradition. Rather, they have become pervasive features of our culture, such that it is relatively easy for people to recreate for themselves what required rare individual geniuses to generate. Romanticism has become a permanent constituent of Western culture in the sense that the characteristics of romance that flickered into life intermittently after literacy became common, were given so powerful, compelling, and satisfying instantiation that they remain almost inescapable for anyone becoming literate today. While almost inescapable, we do need to be very much clearer about these characteristics of romance. It is indeed far from automatic that students will recreate them in their richest forms. Our failure to escape them may mean only that we engage their debased or trivialized forms, such as we see commonly in T.V. shows and other popular media. But this is a topic to be picked up later, as is an account of how we can devise a curriculum that will encourage students to recreate characteristics of Romanticism and romance, and so create for themselves what I am calling romantic understanding.

Conclusion

Well, we have travelled quite a journey in this chapter, and I hope the twists and turns and jumps and skips have not put too much strain on your mental leg muscles or my credibility. We have skated, twisting and turning, over a dozen issues that properly require book-length treatment. My aim has been to try to indicate something of the cultural stuff that is, it seems to me, inevitably entailed in making the transition to the best uses of literacy in our culture. One can indeed become literate merely in the conventional sense, and use that literacy to perform a useful job but little else. One can also become literate in the positivist sense, first bruited by Francis Bacon and the neo-classicists of the Enlightenment; this is a kind of "high literacy" and refined rationality, that nevertheless can easily lead to dessication and sterility. (And that dessication can, as it did in the later nineteenth century, become itself romanticized.) Becoming literate in the Comprehensive sense I am trying to characterize here means incorporating the rationalizing consequences of literacy sketched above with the inheritance left to us by Romanticism.

Among the too general and vague topics skipped across in this chapter are the meanings of literacy and orality, especially when used ambiguously to refer to forms of culture on the one hand and cognitive conditions on the other. Perhaps a few lines on the latter would be useful here. The two terms become hopeless when used as though standing for two quite distinct kinds of mind. A similar hopelessness comes from trying to suggest that no cognitive differences are signified by the terms. I am using them with the assumption that all people have pretty much the same range of cognitive capacities and that the different social and cultural conditions in which we are reared evoke, stimulate, and develop that range of capacities differentially. Oral cultures seem in general to evoke, stimulate, and develop some capacities more than others, as do literate cultures. "Oral" and "literate" indicate what seem to be among the more significant of the differential stimulators of the range of cognitive capacities; it seems also obvious, however, that some individuals in one of these kinds of culture may indeed be cognitively more like some individuals in the other than they are like other individuals in their own. Indeed this seems likely the case for whole sub-cultures, too. The crude visual metaphor that comes to mind is of a band of variously colored more or less magnetized metallic filings on a line. As a magnet is placed above them, it attracts particular segments of the line of metal filings upwards. If the magnet is placed at a different point, other slightly different configurations of filings sit up from the line. If the magnet is a particular cultural environment and the band of filings our range of cognitive capacities, we might consider "literate" and "oral" as distinct positions at which the magnet might be held. (And if one can, as it were, move the magnets a fair distance over the "literate" areas and the "oral" areas, we might consider the positions of the magnets representing Conventional and Comprehensive literacy as not necessarily less distant from each other than some "oral" and "literate" positions.) (This is the kind of metaphor that can get out of hand, a case of the interpreter being the more difficult to understand of the two.)

Literacy has tended to be seen as an unqualified good, which, if widespread in a population, will cure the nation of unemployment, poverty and ill-health, among much else. David Olson has pointed out that "It is difficult to overstate the significance of literacy to a modern society . . . [but] politicians, educators and newsmen have succeeded in overstating it" (Olson, 1988, p. A7). Part of the problem, he argues, is due to the failure to distinguish different kinds of literacy. But, as Olson has also argued powerfully, literacy, especially in what I have called the Conventional sense, can be a major problem, partially skilling students for some job but at a considerable cost. In describing the successes claimed for the great national drives to increase literacy rates over the previous century, Enzensberger notes:

> Our joy over this triumph has certain limits. The news is too
> good to be true. The people did not learn to read and write
> because they felt like it, but because they were forced to do so.
> Their emancipation was controlled by disenfranchisement.
> From then on learning went hand in hand with their state and
> its agencies: the school, the army, the legal administration. The
> goal pursued in making the populace literate had nothing to do
> with enlightenment. The friends of mankind and the priests of
> culture, who stood up for the people, were merely the
> henchmen of a capitalist industry that pressed the state to
> provide it with a qualified work force. It was not a matter of
> paving the way for the "writing culture," let alone liberating

mankind from its shackles. Quite a different kind of progress was in question. It consisted in taming the illiterates, this "lowest class of men," in stamping out their will and their fantasy, and in exploiting not only their muscle power and skill in handwork t t their brains as well. (Enzensberger, 1987, p. 13)

This is, of course, a somewhat jaundiced account, but the history leads in to the discovery that "today we find that the illiteracy we smoked out has returned. . . . This new species is the second-order illiterate" (Enzensberger, 1987, p. 13). This second-order illiterate looks very like what I have described as the Conventional literate. Enzensberger's analysis leads to the conclusion that "the project of the Enlightenment has failed" (Enzenberger, 1987, p. 13). That project was the confident progressive program to provide "culture for all." I'm not sure that we should give up on it completely. The problem, I think, has been that those educationalists not committed only to their states' agenda, who truly believed in the Enlightenment project, seemed generally to forget the Romantics' project. I want to suggest that if the transition to literacy is conceived of as entailing the development of romantic understanding, we can go some way both towards satisfying the states' needs and making the Enlightenment project richer and more realistic.

3
Reality and its limits

Introduction

The reality referred to in this chapter's title is the kind that seems commonly to impact on people's consciousness around the age of eight in Western culture. This is not to suggest that younger children have any special problem in distinguishing between what is real and what is fictional, pretend, or fantastic, but rather that reality and its limits seem to gain a new kind of intellectual importance about age eight.

We may see an aspect of this in a prominent difference between the kinds of stories that engage the typical five-year-old and those that engage the typical nine-year-old. In the earlier years, children readily accept magical or fantastic elements, being unperturbed by the processes whereby Cinderella's Fairy Godmother turns the mice into footmen and a pumpkin into a coach. Nor do they typically inquire where the Fairy Godmother comes from nor about her means of locomotion. By about age nine, however, while stories may obviously contain impossible elements, the impossible has to conform with a kind of realistic plausibility. Superman's powers, for example, cannot simply be asserted as are the Fairy Godmother's. We need to be told about his birth on the dying planet Krypton and his escape to Earth into the care of Mr. and Mrs. Kent. His great powers are explained, I uncertainly recall, by the different molecular structure of our sun compared with that of his home planet Krypton. Similarly, other superheroes and superheroines require an aetiology that establishes a kind of plausible toe-hold within reality for them. The Hulk—again my memory is imprecise and a better scholar would no doubt do further research to establish the facts—gains his distinguishing capacities as a result of a nuclear experiment that goes somewhat awry.

The systematic structure of the world generated in what I will call a romantic story is realistic in a way that is not the case for the fantasy stories of early childhood. Even if the protagonists of our stories are rabbits, we can recognize that Peter Rabbit's world is not systematically realistic in the same way as the world of Hazel and Bigwig in Richard Adams's *Watership Down*. The structure of Peter's world is driven as much by the needs of the narrative, playing on themes of security and fear, cultivation and wilderness, life and death, as by the constraints of reality. Although Adams requires us to suspend disbelief in his anthropomorphized rabbits, his narrative moves within the constraints of the real world. "What distinguishes the fantastic narrative . . . is the fact that its possible world is structurally different from the real one. I use the term 'structural' in a very wide sense: to refer to cosmological structure as much as social" (Eco, 1984, p. 1257). One wouldn't expect Bigwig to bring Hazel a nice cup of camomile tea. In both kinds of story we require internal consistencies, but in the romantic stories we also require a more elaborate consistency with the world outside the story.

Certainly there is no clearly agreed distinction between fantasy and romance. Some people use the terms vaguely as synonyms, others mix them up in various ways, as does Bloom in discussing "a particular kind of romance invention . . . that we have agreed to call fantasy" (Bloom, 1982, p. 1), or as Siebers does in his discussion of "The Romantic Fantastic" (Siebers, 1984). Still, the distinction I am suggesting here seems to cohere with much common usage. The crucial distinguishing mark is a sense of an autonomous reality central to romance and only slackly acknowledged in fantasy. So Mary Shelley's *Frankenstein*, while incorporating an impossible element, explores its action within the constraints of everyday reality, and so, in this view, is a romance rather than a fantasy.

In the previous volume I examined the prominence of binary opposites in young children's understanding and the process of mediation between opposites that enables children to make sense of a variety of phenomena. Thus the content of much of the world that children perceive is commonly made sense of in terms of binary opposites (such as hot and cold) and these are then mediated to provide new categories (such as warm). When this procedure is applied to discrete phenomena such as life and death, for example, the mediating category of ghosts is generated. (As warm is to hot and cold, so ghosts are to life and death.) When it is applied to such "opposites" as nature and culture, it generates such creatures as talking middle-class bears or rabbits. These are the result of mixing the discrete categories of nature and culture, as warm is what we get from mixing hot and cold. When applied to human and animal, it yields such mediations as yetis and sasquatches. Fantasy in this view is that realm created by mediating between what are really discrete categories. There are no things that are both alive and dead, cultural and natural, human and animal, at the same time. The sense of reality to which this chapter's title refers is that which results from "realizing" that the mediating categories generated between discrete oppositions do not exist. We give up at about the same time the belief in Tooth Fairies, Santa Claus, ghosts, and so on. With this realization comes a sense of an autonomous reality and "nature" unaffected by our hopes and fears about it and independent of our thinking about it.

In part, this change seems simply a matter of experience: it takes some time to grasp the conditions of reality that exclude Jack Frost and the Tooth Fairy and include telephone hygienists and university professors. It is not immediately obvious to most young children which are the more plausible; certainly there tends to be rather more evidence for the former set. But experience alone cannot account for the loss of faith in fantasy worlds and fantasy creatures. A number of psychological theories attempt to account for this significant change in mental life that commonly occurs around eight years of age. These competing theories are well known and I will touch them only in passing here. I will focus primarily on what seem to be the cultural causes that affect it. The principle cause I want to consider is the schooling and literacy induction that evoke, stimulate, and develop the techniques of thinking that support what I am calling romantic understanding.

The distinction between fantasy and romance in stories is not one we can make with great clarity for a number of reasons. The theory being developed here about layers of understanding is not a stage theory in which we move *from* one stage *to* another. Rather, we accumulate layers one on top of the other. The new layers significantly interfere and coalesce with parts of the older layers, but they do not displace them, nor, I should note, do they coalesce with them completely. Romance, then, does not simply displace fantasy; rather, the capacity for fantasy will ideally be preserved within romantic understanding, though the attitude towards it will be significantly changed. One may then incorporate fantastic elements into "realistic" romantic stories. Indeed one may construct stories that look entirely like fantasies, the only difference being the author's and the informed readers' understanding of the story. An uninformed reader might understand such a story purely as a fantasy. So Lewis Caroll's Alice adventures are read somewhat differently by a child and by a sophisticated adult logician. Also, while we may say that the young child does not know the conditions of reality that prevent Tooth Fairies from existing, we need to acknowledge that we never completely know the conditions of reality that define what is possible.

We might catch a sense of how our early use of fantasy persists into later kinds of understanding by relating it to Freud's sense of "the omnipotence of thought" in the early years. While we might develop forms of understanding more attentive to the constraints of reality as we grow older, "Nevertheless, in our reliance upon the power of the human spirit which copes with the laws of reality, there still lives on a fragment of this primitive belief in the omnipotence of thought" (Freud, 1938, p. 875). An element of the fantastic belief that the limits of reality can be transcended lives on in romance, or perhaps we might better say that there is an ambivalence between acknowledging the constraining limits of reality and the fantastic desire to transcend them. "Humankind cannot bear very much reality," T.S. Eliot pointed out, but romance is a way of making reality bearable, of domesticating it. We can put the worst experience into a romantic story we tell ourselves and conclude it "Is only romantic, i.e., bearable," as Czeslaw Milosz puts it.

Reality, then, is the constraint within which we live. We have access to reality only by means of tacit or explicit interpretative schemes or theories; our access is mediated by our minds' ways of making sense. I don't want to explore such murky philosophical issues except to observe that the general interpretative schemes through which we access reality seem to vary somewhat from time to time and place to place. Romantic understanding, I am suggesting, is such a very general interpretative scheme, and if we look at the world and experience through its route of access to reality, we will see reality configured and colored in a particular way. It is some characteristics of this particular romantic reality that I want to explore. One prominent characteristic of romantic understanding is that it is self-consciously interested in reality, in a way not common in fantasy or in the kind of understanding evident before the sense of romance develops.

"Self-consciously interested in reality" is an apt phrase, I think because it brings out the fact that it is the developing focus on "external" reality that begins to bring the self into focus. The developing sense of an autonomous reality, in other words, also brings into focus what the world is autonomous from, that is the observing self. So both the self and reality become prominent features of the intellectual landscape of romantic understanding.

And what are "the limits" of reality doing in this chapter's title? Whitehead described a central feature of romance as the excitement about the unexplored possibilities opened up by contact with new experience or with new information about the world. Romantic understanding is a kind of general case of this. The realization of an autonomous world opens up that world for exploration. The initial romantic exploration seems constantly attracted to discovering the limits of reality. It is the exotic, the strange, the weird, the extreme that romantic understanding first grasps.

The next five chapters, then, will deal with aspects of the romantic exploration of this autonomous reality and its limits. I will begin, in this chapter, by providing an abbreviated account of the previous kind of understanding, which I call mythic, and of the merging of mythic with romantic understanding at about eight years. In the body of the chapter I will begin elaborating characteristics of romantic understanding as they are commonly exemplified in modern students. I will consider these first constituents of romantic understanding as particularly important in the transition from mythic understanding. In Chapter 9, I will suggest that year four should have a somewhat distinctive curriculum designed deliberately to stimulate and develop the techniques that support the new layer of understanding. I will make occasional comparisons with the discussions of Romanticism and the technologies of literacy in the previous two chapters.

It may be worth mentioning briefly here, what is to be argued at length in Chapter 8, that I am not trying in these chapters to describe what is invariably the case in students' development. This is not a theory like Piaget's that aims to describe what developments necessarily occur in what sequence and thereby explain certain observable changes in cognition. This is not, then, a theory that is open to falsification on the grounds that there are a lot of students who do not during their middle-school years develop a sense of awe or associations with transcendent qualities. Nor is it a theory of the kind that I could support by showing that x number of students in y conditions have developed these capacities. People familiar with students at these ages will recognize that such developments are not uncommon. The empirical claim I need to establish goes no further than that such developments are possible during this period of life, and this I take to be uncontentious. I will later argue further that there is in Western cultures a predisposition to develop these capacities during the middle-school years, because of our cultural history and the present social and cultural environment which that singular history has generated. I will also support the claim that the development of these various romantic capacities is educationally desirable.

Mythic and romantic understanding

"When rag dolls cease to talk, when imaginary friends are no longer real, when fairies and Santa Claus cease to visit in the night, the modern child, too, is preparing for more substantial knowledge; he is learning to lose Eden" (S. Egan, 1984, p. 69). Jacques Barzun described the task of romantic consciousness as having to create a new world on the ruins of the old (Barzun, 1961). Ong has described the acquisition of literacy as involving a restructuring of thought. One could go on and on with the various dramatic ways in which the "romantic" changes in human cognition in our culture have been characterized. While we do not commonly see the development of more realistic thinking at around age eight as like the catastrophic expulsion from the joy of Eden to earn bread by the sweat of our brows, or as having to create a new intellectual world on the ruins of the old, or even as having our thought restructured, certainly in retrospect, many people find such metaphors best for catching and expressing that experience (Coe, 1984). In this chapter I will be focusing on just a few characteristics of this common experience, and even though I will be trying to address what may seem a crude technical level, it would be useful to keep in mind that the diffuse impact of these techniques of thinking reverberates deep and wide through the rest of our lives.

The process of education is commonly described in terms of developments from *x* to *y:* from concrete to formal operations, from the simple to the complex, from ignorance to knowledge, "from a social and human center towards a more objective intellectual scheme of organization" (Dewey, 1938, p. 83), and so on. The pervasiveness, and indeed usefulness, of the "from-to" schema, particularly in developmental theories, is such that I will no doubt slip into it now and then, but I want to resist it when dealing with the development of new layers of understanding. These layers, mythic and romantic, are not best grasped if seen as stages, *from* one of which we "develop" *to* another. An underlying principle of this scheme is that ideally we leave nothing behind. Perhaps it is too much to hope that we can take Eden with us, but Wordsworth's insistent claim that the imagination can enable us to carry much of it in our minds retains some credibility, even as the light of common day breaks around us in the autonomous world, dissipating the radiance of Eden. This is a consciously romantic way of putting it, of course. My point is that in developing romantic understanding we do not properly thereby displace the sense-making capacities, the techniques of thinking, that were developed in the earlier period. Indeed, romantic understanding will involve the further development of many of them, though in a somewhat changed form.

Romantic understanding, then, should be seen as largely comprising mythic understanding. In some areas mythic understanding provides a kind of template for romantic understanding, as, for example, we can see in the fantasy binary opposites of giants and dwarfs giving way to the romantic interest in who were the biggest and the smallest people *really*. In the romantic layer we find students using similar underlying forms of thought, but applying them now to the autonomous external reality.

As this is a cultural recapitulation scheme, and as I have begun this volume by looking at a prominent example of romantic understanding in cultural history, so I began to characterize mythic understanding in the previous volume by looking at examples of it in cultural history. In that case the historical instantiation I discussed was that of oral cultures and the techniques developed within them to make sense of the world and of experience. I called the earlier layer of understanding Mythic because of a number of the prominent features of the form of understanding that seemed to be mostly fully evoked, stimulated, and developed in Western young children today, were also evident in the ubiquitous mythic stories of oral cultures.

A couple of times already in this book I have noted some of the sense-making techniques encouraged in societies that do not use writing. The need to preserve knowledge in living memories places a high social value on those techniques that make memorization easy and reliable. And so we find sacred myth stories full of vivid images generated by metaphoric coding of the knowledge to be preserved. Their telling used such techniques as rhyme and rhythm, and the story form helped to generate in their hearers the appropriate affective commitments to the knowledge so narrated; myth stories, in other words, also told their hearers how to think and how to feel about their contents.

Young children today also live in an oral culture. We may fairly easily sketch, as with Romanticism and early adolescents, a number of perhaps surprising correlations between the sense-making techniques prominent in oral cultures and in the oral culture of young children in Western societies today. In the previous volume I considered at length the use of the story form, of narrative shaping, which is so common in the way young children make sense of the world and of experience. Vivid images, particularly those generated from mediation between discrete binary opposite categories, readily engage children, and provide the stuff of the fantasy worlds in which their imaginations can find sustenance and growth. Knowledge is most readily engaged when children can get an affective grasp on it, and this seems most easily achieved by constructing the knowledge within a story structure using binary opposites that are both profoundly abstract and affectively engaging, such as good/bad, brave/cowardly, security/fear, and so on. The rhymes and rhythms, the jokes and ghost stories of the oral culture of childhood exemplify very similar techniques as are employed for memorizing and sense-making in oral cultures throughout the world. Children, too, very readily and flexibly understand and use metaphor (for example, "Mom killed that idea").

The practical task of the earlier volume was to build from these, and from some other characteristics, a curriculum that would stimulate and develop the sense-making techniques of orality, rather than displace and suppress them while inducing a conventional literacy as so often is the case in schools. I tried to show that the development of such oral techniques was not at all inconsistent with teaching reading and writing and, indeed, that the development of a rich literacy required rich orality. The latter was not so much a prerequisite as a *constituent* of rich literacy. Children's orality was to be developed by a curriculum rich in the content of history, logic and mathematics, language, science, and arts. These were to be learned as the great stories of our culture, and I outlined a planning framework, with examples, that would encourage teachers to see lessons and units as good stories to be told rather than as sets of objectives to be attained.

The techniques of sense-making, the kind of understanding, that young children seem able to develop most powerfully are those we often call poetic. They are the techniques that have long been used in poetry to grasp the world and experience. We begin as poets, was a conclusion of the earlier volume, echoing Vico's insight about oral cultures. The educational job, I argued, is to stimulate and develop that poetic grasp while beginning to introduce the techniques that allow what I called a more *literal* sense of the world and experience. These two were not seen as alternatives, but rather as coalescing layers that properly enrich and extend the power and grasp of each other. This literal sense is what is to be stimulated and developed in the romantic layer. We might wish to see the oral characteristics of children's mental lives in modern Western cultures as examples of a Vygotskian psychological interiorizing of the techniques developed in earlier phases of our cultural history for socialization and memorization.

The most notable changes to be introduced to mythic understanding by the development of romantic understanding derive from the sense of an autonomous reality referred to above. One strand will be evident in the variety of ways in which thought will seek to conform with reality rather than shape it into story patterns. Not that the story-shaping will disappear, but it will find our psychological functions, while non-narra-tive structures will become increasingly important in making sense of the world and of experience. So, in this volume, attention will be given to non-narrative sense-making techniques, such as lists, formulae, recipes, tables, and so on. In particular, we will consider the formation of theories; theories represent the form of thought most committedly shaped to conform with the external world. Theory is a kind of opposite to narrative; the latter shapes the world to the mind's predisposed forms of order, whereas theory strains the mind's predisposed structures to conform with the external world. As with all such "opposites," our job is not to take sides on the greater value of one over the other, but to see how both might be used most valuably.

The scale of reality

If you stop for a few days in a North Italian town, you can follow a number of strategies in order to explore it effectively. Even if you have a map, you have first to coordinate that with the reality, if only to get some sense of its scale. We might begin by locating the major attractions, and take in a palace, the cathedral and piazza, an old monastery, and get high enough to see where the town walls are. Once the walls and the main attractions are located, you feel a sense of the scale and overall structure of the town. It would obviously be silly to look for too close an analogy here with students' developing understanding, but the early stages of exploring the autonomous real world do have some features that might be illuminated by this analogy.

To begin with, we need to be aware that the modern hotel in which we are staying, while certainly in the town, may not be a typical part of the town, and so we should not allow our familiarity with the international fixtures and the anonymous style of wall-covering and carpeting to fix our expectation that the rest of the town will be like this. Obviously we need to learn how to get around in the hotel, learn meal times and where the bars are, how to get the *Wall Street Journal* or the *Financial Times* at the earliest possible moment, and so on. But learning the conventions of the hotel, while important, should not be seen as an appropriate alternative or an equivalent to exploring the town.

This part of the analogy does not need to be explicated perhaps, but we might see it as a means of emphasizing Bertrand Russell's observation that an early educational task is to destroy the tyranny of the local over the imagination (Russell, 1926, p. 143). We all begin, and most of us remain, insufficiently aware that our local environment and its conventions are neither typical of the world at large nor privileged by nature. It is obvious that one should not assume that one's hotel room is typical of the rooms to be found in the North Italian town, nor that the functions of one's hotel are typical of those of the town at large, nor that getting to know the hotel for various utilitarian purposes is the same as exploring the town. Yet two of the more prominent curriculum and teaching principles commonly employed today tend to encourage analogous kinds of confusions. First, the "expanding horizons" form of curriculum assumes that one should begin with the material of students' everyday lives and move from these known entities gradually outward to "unknowns" by connecting them with the local things that are already familiar. The problem with this principle, as I argue at length in the previous volume, is that it tends to reduce unknowns to the known—tends to make everything conform with the norms of the hotel. Most commonly, what is known is interpreted in terms of the content of students' experience, which also limits considerably the new content that may be expanded towards. If one interprets what is known, however, in terms of abstract underlying concepts such as are evident in students' everyday discourse—good/bad, fear/hope, strong/weak, security/fear, etc.—then connections can be made directly with any content that can be articulated on those concepts. Second, a related principle that influences much teaching practice assumes that new content to be learned must be made "relevant" to students' everyday experience. This again tends to encourage students to remain intellectually tyrannized by the conventions of their immediate surroundings— they can appreciate only those parts of the Italian town which are like their hotel. If we interpret relevance not in terms of the content of students' everyday experience, but in terms of their imaginative lives, then we again have a way of connecting directly with content distant and different from their experience. I will explore these alternative principles for enhancing romantic understanding as we go along.

The close and careful exploration of our immediate hotel environment, then, does not begin an exploration of the town. And even if we begin to explore by gradually moving outward from the hotel in various directions, we will be following a rather ineffective method, one certainly that encourages the belief that the hotel is clearly the central and archetypical feature from which and in terms of which the town is to be understood. While perhaps a bit strained, this analogy with much current educational practice seems depressingly accurate. The main problem with the gradual exploration outwards in all directions from the hotel is that we do not know how typical what we first learn is of the town as a whole, nor do we have any sense of how extensive the town is. The parts begin to become proportionately meaningful only as we develop a sense of the whole. (The same slightly paradoxical point is the message of the parable of the blind men and the elephant. Each blind man concentrating on the part of the elephant he immediately feels gives a totally different and wildly inaccurate account of what the whole creature is like.)

An effective strategy in the educational exploration of the world and of experience seems to be analogous to the more sensible strategy for exploring the town, and it is a strategy which students seem predisposed to pursue in Western culture, regardless of how they are taught in schools. I have already mentioned the ready engagement by *The Guinness Book of Records* kind of information, or *Ripley's Believe It Or Not*, or the T.V. shows devoted to attempts at exotic achievements, or expositions of mysterious artefacts and unexplained phenomena, and so on. These are all straightforward descriptions or explorations of the limits and scale of reality. Once one has some sense of the scale of things, then one can get some grasp on the meaning and proportion of oneself and one's everyday world. Again, paradoxically, it is the exploration of the distant, the different, the exotic, the "other" that can tell us most about ourselves—a paradox to be explored later in this chapter.

The exploration of the scale of reality, of the limits within which one's immediate surroundings exist, sets up an intellectual context within which proportion and meaning can be better established. Without such a context, without what I am calling a romantic exploration of the scale of the world and of human experience, knowledge of the world and of one's individual experience remains somewhat adrift; meaning is indeterminate and subject to disproportionate evaluations. I am not, incidentally, suggesting that the early attraction to the extremes of reality and experience is a natural impulse. Nor am I suggesting that the logical structure of any discipline requires such a procedure. The predisposition is, like all features of romantic understanding, a cultural artefact—a theoretical point to be argued in Chapter 8—and also, an empirical observation, a sensible strategy for exploring and making sense of the world that students of middle-school age employ very commonly.

What is the attraction of knowing who was the biggest person who has ever lived and who was the smallest, and the heaviest and lightest, and so on? Such knowledge may seem trivial, but educators would be unwise not to consider what motivates students so keenly to absorb information of that kind. Clearly it is fulfilling more than casual interests. We would be wise to consider such phenomena, not so that we can fill our curricula with such knowledge, but that we might detect some principles that we could then adopt for educational purposes. That is, the kind of answer we will look for is not so much a psychological or psychoanalytic or sociological one—though any of these might be suggestive—but one which bears on the practical problems of education. My answer is only a partial one, given in the previous chapter in the discussion of Herodotus' enterprize and drawing on Whitehead's rich conception of romantic emotion, and augmented by the observations above. That is, the attraction of knowing who was the biggest and smallest person is caused by a dawning sense of an autonomous reality, the scale of which is unknown. By getting a grasp on the limits and scale of that reality, one also establishes a realistic sense of oneself and one's proper scale and one's boundaries. This is rather crudely exemplified by the concern with the biggest and smallest, but is more subtly evident in the attraction of knowledge about the extremes of human behavior— about extremes of courage and cowardice, self-sacrifice and selfishness, self-discipline and self-indulgence, and so on.

It is not the sense of reality that is new, but rather the sense of reality's autonomy, and consequently the reciprocal sense of one's distinct and autonomous "self." The new sense of an autonomous reality and the new sense of the status of knowledge about it—the self as the subjective knower of objective knowns—can lead to the kind of excitement which, following Whitehead, I am calling romantic. The excitement is typically keenest at the beginning, with the realization of the unexplored implications of one's early knowledge of the autonomous reality, and the exploration focuses most sensibly on its limits, on its most exotic and bizarre and extreme features. It is these which help to define what is normal, and help us to locate ourselves and our daily experience, and so give meaning to those within the larger scheme of things. Normal size, that is, is half way between the biggest and smallest.

An additional part of the attraction of knowing who was the biggest and who was the smallest person involves, I think, the persistence of somewhat transformed features of mythic understanding. I described the common fantasy of that layer, borrowing from Ted Hughes (Hughes, 1988), as its major factory of conceptual elaboration and meaning-making. In other words, we can see in children's fantasy not the idle mind-wandering froth so many traditional educationalists have discounted, but rather the rich realm in which the conceptual foundations for later intellectual activity are being laid down. This fantasy does not properly just die out when faced by the growing sense of autonomous reality. Rather, to echo Freud's phrase, a fragment of the earlier form of thought lives on to cope with the laws of reality. The fantasy worlds in which giants might be two miles high or little people no bigger than your thumb nail, frequently employ such binary opposites to structure stories. Those serve as a kind of template for the realistic exploration during the romantic layer of what *really* is the largest and smallest sizes than can exist. But we also see in romantic understanding a persistence of fantasy's easy transcendence over the boundaries of reality. It produces that ambivalence we noted earlier in Romanticism, represented crudely in the hero. The hero is bound by the constraints of reality but is able to transcend at least some of the constraints within which we are bound. Students in early adolescence, in particular, are bound by endless everyday constraints, and are relatively powerless to transcend them— to stop going to school, to leave home and become a film star, to drive a powerful car or motor-bike, to be *famous*. At this time of life, the ambivalence between the romantic excitement at growing knowledge about the autonomous real world and the intense desire to transcend its limits, leads readily to the association with those figures who seem most able to transcend the constraints that bind them. Commonly the association is with pop-stars, or football teams—who are transcendently wonderful or great. The educational task will involve representing physics and mathematics, history and geography, in such a way as to engage students' desire to associate with the transcendent.

I have perhaps represented the early engagement with the limits of reality too much as a purely intellectual affair. I should emphasize what is no doubt evident in the choice of the term "romance": that there is a powerful emotional or affective component to this search for the scale of things. During early adolescence this affective component is not some tame and consistent feature of intellectual inquiry, but can rise and roar and drive all inquiry into ferment and chaos. Often it takes the form which George Eliot catches well in her description of Maggie Tulliver feeling "wide, hopeless yearning for that something, whatever it was, that was greatest and best on this earth." The romantic ferment involves not a cool strategy of exploration, as of the North Italian town, but a desire to possess it, or an unnameable sense of reverence for its ancient stones, or an unassuageable yearning at the beauty of its monastery's cloisters, or a passion to understand some secret of its existence, and so on. In adolescence this romantic ferment will roar in and ebb unpredictably. When it ebbs, students can experience a desert of boredom more intense than at any other period of life. I want here only to point out that, in considering romantic engagement with knowledge, we will need to be alert to qualities of that engagement beyond the purely logical. Making sense of the world and of experience in the romantic layer involves, as at the mythic, a powerful affective component to which we need to attend.

The engagement with knowledge of the limits of reality is echoed in the common fascination of early adolescents with the extremes of human experience and the emotions associated with such experience. The kinds of events and incidents we see students most energetically interested in are, again, the most extreme and exotic: the exhilaration that follows great achievements after overcoming immense obstacles; the horrors of human cruelty and suffering; the terror of innocents caught in brutal conditions; superhuman patience and persistence against indifferent authorities; cool cleverness in the midst of great danger; the persistence of love in the face of hate; the highest heights and the deepest depths of human behavior. Again, by getting a sense of the limits of human behavior and experience we begin to grasp a proportionate sense of the range of the possible.

Details and distance

Another example of the romantic exploration of the limits and scale of reality may be seen, I think, in early adolescents' obsessive hobbies or collecting. Immense energy goes into collecting one or other of a huge variety of things—bottle tops, foreign coins or stamps, stones, pressed leaves, glass marbles, toy guns, almost anything. The energy is intensified if one can complete a *set*—the most obvious examples, because the most exploited commercially, include things like football stickers, hockey cards, outfits for dolls' houses, tiny model animals. We may occasionally see the same kind of energy go into an apparent obsession to learn about costume through the ages, or the kings and queens of England, or minerals, or astronomy, or Victorian postage stamps, or whatever.

It is, incidentally, odd that educationalists have paid relatively little attention to this common and powerful drive to learn, that is evident in very many students during early adolescence. The "problem of motivation" that properly distresses educationalists may be seen as regret that so many students so much of the time seem uninterested in learning a great deal of what we would like to teach them. Yet these same "unmotivated" students can often hardly wait to get out of the classroom to perfect their mastery of some area of knowledge. We might indeed be unenthusiastic about their drive to learn the scores made by their favorite football player in every game played or to learn to lip-sync the words of every song recorded by their pop-star idol, but if we are interested in learning it is curious that these obsessive accumulations of detailed knowledge receive so little attention. (For one of the fullest studies and discussions of the obsessive collecting of early adolescents one has to go back to the work of Caroline Frear Burk, supervised by G. Stanley Hall, in 1907.)

How can we account for this very common obsessive learning–an experience we can all surely remember ourselves? What were we doing? (No doubt there are psychoanalytic explanations which focus on aspects of this, but here I want to consider it with educational eyes.) As I suggested above, I think we can sensibly see this phenomenon as another thrust of the initial exploration of autonomous reality. While one strategy for initially exploring reality involves getting some grasp on its extreme limits, we can also get some sense of its scale by exploring some aspect of it in minute detail. This autonomous reality can be threatening, of which we cannot bear very much, and initially it may seem virtually limitless. One value of exhaustively learning something, of completing a *set,* is that it provides some security that the world is not limitless in extent, that it is intellectually graspable, that we can hope to make sense of it. Completing a set, or exhaustively exploring some area in detail, provides some further sense of the scale of things in general, and provides a degree of security in establishing that our "selves" can domesticate the fearsome unknown, can gain conceptual control over reality. In the world of our hobby we find a recourse from the uncontrolled reality, as we do in the pages of that novel just read for the sixty-third time.

This obsessive drive to master something in exhaustive detail is not a quirk to be found in just a few rare students. What is rare is to find it expressed in terms of mathematics or history or the stuff of schooling in general. But we can see it in nearly every student, though in some in a more muted form than in others. The objective of the obsession may be a film star, an athlete, a rock singer, spiders, or even torture instruments through the ages. But in students' rooms throughout the Western world we can find evidence of this passion to master *something*. We may explain for individual cases why this student should have developed a passion for earthworms, this one for motorbikes, that one for computers, that one to write endless derivative novels, or these for making replicas of Buckingham Palace or the Empire State Building or Toronto's CN Tower or the Sydney Opera House with match-sticks. It is what they have in common that is of interest here for its educational implications.

There are, at least, two distinct things of educational interest. First, is the intense drive to understand something in detail; second, is the particular things on which the intense drive is exercised. The first has some implications for teaching, the second for the curriculum; they will be explored in Chapters 9 and 10. Here we might note in passing that the focus on the details of reality noted in Romanticism finds a direct echo in this feature of students' romantic understanding today. That we might reasonably hope to find a way of engaging this drive with detailed knowledge of history, physics, or mathematics, is supported by the vast range of topics that different students do engage in this way. There seems something arbitrary about the objects students engage. Not arbitrary in the sense that there will not be a perfectly adequate explanation for each individual's particular obsession, but in the sense that the common drive seems able to achieve satisfaction with almost any content. The task for the chapters on teaching and the curriculum is to discover how to engage students romantically in the pursuit of detailed curricular knowledge.

The kind of intensity of learning we see in obsessive hobbies and collecting, as with fantasy at the earlier stage, suggests that they represent another of those little factories of meaning; underlying the particular content we can see categorization, organization, refinement of perceptual discrimination, and conceptual elaboration actively underway. So under the particular obsessive hobbies we might look for the accumulation of new sense-making capacities, new things to think with. These non-narrative forms of classification can be encouraged by various forms of "data-processing," whether using computers or cards or sheets of paper. Organization in lists, which are then sub-categorized, is a simple form of non-narrative organization of knowledge. Listing musical instruments, for example, can be followed by categorizing the instruments listed into those one scrapes, those one hits, those one plucks, those one blows, and so on. The sub-categorizing will commonly stimulate recall of additional items for the list. Similarly, construction of flow-charts, formulae, recipes, and so forth, can stimulate the use and sense of utility of non-narrative forms of classification.

We might look, too, for the development of the ability to engage in sustained intellectual work. The results of studies of attention span in children and students look very odd when we consider the lengthy and intense engagements in children's fantasy games and in students' obsessive hobbies. Fulfilling hobbies can teach us to recognize that learning can present us with difficulties but can also provide us with intense rewards that feed back, as it were, into the work of learning and make the labor itself satisfying.

What we can observe about students' engagement with particular details can be balanced by their also being engaged by overarching perspectives. I have touched on this, and will again, in terms of their easier engagement in knowledge if it is set within some more general story-context. These observations might be clearer if we think of them as a kind of intellectual analog to the attraction of the perspectives given by microscopes and telescopes. There is something quite simply romantic about looking through a microscope or telescope. We see the world in different proportions; we see afresh and differently what is commonplace. The immediate engagement on seeing a pin head or a piece of cloth or one's finger nail through a microscope is analogous to the kind of intellectual engagement one finds, on the one hand, in obsessive hobbies, and on the other hand, in day-dreaming great schemes and plans for one's life. The attraction of Gulliver in Lilliput and in Brobdingnag similarly catches the interest that comes from different perspectives.

We will want to ensure that these features of the romantic engagement with detail and distance also find a prominent place in our teaching and curricula.

The persistence of binary opposites and stories

In the following chapter I will discuss some characteristics of the kind of stories students find most engaging in adolescence and what we can infer from them about romantic understanding. Here I want to consider some aspects of the story form that seem related to the theme of reality and its limits.

Two of the sense-making techniques examined in some detail in the previous volume include the story and the use of binary opposites and mediation. Clearly these do not simply go away with the development of the techniques of romantic understanding. Students continue to use the story form and continue to use binary opposites to get an initial grasp on a topic. But neither do these techniques remain unchanged while romantic understanding develops. By observing common uses of the story form and binary opposites we can see something of the way in which capacities developed in an earlier layer can continue to perform sense-making functions in the later layer. What also seems evident, however, is that some functions of these originally mythic layer capacities become shaped by new capacities developed in the romantic layer, while other functions seem to remain unreconstructedly mythic. This is a complication undermining any attempt to represent intellectual development as a neat progression from stage to more or less discrete stage, or layer to discrete layer. It suggests that our mental lives are not neatly integrated into some overall consistent form of thought. Rather, they seem ragged, in that functions are not necessarily neatly coordinated. What is it about the persistence of binary opposites and stories that encourages such a view?

One aspect of "the primary role which storytelling plays in the household of humanity" (Benjamin, 1969, p. 101) is its power to shape experience and the world into what I called affectively meaningful patterns. Within the structure of a story the listener or reader is instructed how to feel about the events that make it up. One of the primary thrusts of romantic understanding is the development of sense-making techniques that try to grasp the world and experience as they really are. The basic tools of rationality, of literal thinking, are being refined in this layer to create a distinct kind of understanding that is in some degree hostile to story-shaping. Or so it would seem in part at least. But the techniques of romantic understanding clearly do not simply displace those of the mythic layer. What, then, happens?

Clearly students still enjoy stories during early adolescence, even if they are different in some significant regards from those prominent earlier. But does the story *form* continue to play the same crucial sense-making role identified earlier? Certainly the basic tools of rationality— consistency, coherence, literal accuracy, theory formation—are becoming prominent in romantic sense-making, and certainly story-shaping with its metaphor-based connections, seems incompatible with these. I think we can see two things happening with the story form within this layer: first, we do see competition, or at least distinct views of reality, between developing rationality and story-shaping; second, we see some coalescence and cooperation in the move of story from a central role to a context setting role in sense-making.

The competition is evident in the alternative views an adolescent might take of, say, a natural scene. One can adopt the role of the rational observer, noting the conditions which have led to the growth of these kinds of trees in this place, the incline of the land that has led the water to follow that particular course, cutting its banks in that particular fashion due to the nature of the soil and sub-soil, and so on. Alternatively, one can adopt the role of the appreciative participant, feeling caught up with the beauty of the scene, and seeing it as representing a pure natural condition threatened by the despoiling of exploiters, and so on. These are competitive in the sense that they represent alternative stances we can adopt before things, stances that determine how and what kind of sense we make of them. They are stances that are often not well coordinated within us. We can recognize that rational calculation and affective storying need not be incompatible, but we do at best observe some tension between them, and sometimes indeed they seem like strangers to each other within the same mind.

The coalescence is evident in cases where we see students attain a rational grasp of some particular area of detailed knowledge whose significance or wider meaning is determined by a story-shaped context.

Specific details of medieval building techniques can be meticulously accumulated within a context of a romantic fascination for castles and their place in the story of security against attack in earlier times. The *Cosmos* television shows and book chapters by Carl Sagan are examples of precise knowledge, rationally determined and ordered, narrated within an overall romantic story structure (Sagan, 1980).

The story-shaping of the romantic layer is more diffuse than the tighter form most common earlier, and so the term narrative is perhaps more appropriate. Typical of romantic understanding, then, is a rational grasp on particulars bound within a more general narrative context. This is exemplified in Romanticism by what Lukács and Walter Benjamin call the "arch-romantic genre"—the historical novel (Steiner, 1988, p. 168). The historical novel straddles "the open boundary" (Gearhart, 1984) between fiction and reality, between invention and record, giving us a structure of some factual details bound within a fictional narrative. Students' understanding of history, mathematics, and physics will not, of course, depend on our providing a *fictional* narrative context. The comparison with the historical novel is intended to draw attention to the typical romantic combination of a strong overall narrative and vivid detail within it. In the history writing of Romanticism, one may see similar overall story-like themes—the decline and fall of the Roman empire as "the triumph of barbarism and religion," to use Gibbon's words—exemplified with rich, vivid, and accurate particulars. The romance, as with Herodotus, encourages the selection of whatever vivid particulars can be used to give body to the overarching narrative, and so we learn, for example, that after the battle of Liegnitz in 1241 the Mongols filled nine sacks with the right ears of the slain. What students' understanding of history, mathematics, and physics does depend on, however, at least for their meaning and significance in students' lives, is our providing a more general narrative context within which the particulars make some affective sense. That is, romantic understanding is compounded of a literal grasp on the particulars of the world and experience within a context that uses some of the significant sense-making functions of the story-form. In particular these context-setting narrative forms will preserve the affective orienting role of the story. So myth, in the sense used in the previous volume, does not leave us; rather, it is domesticated to reality and provides the contexts within which particular knowledge is established and thus it governs the meaning and significance such knowledge has for us.

The persistence of binary opposites has been touched on above and may be more briefly dealt with. On the one hand we may again see this constituent technique of mythic understanding domesticated to reality.

The oppositions common in the fantasy stories of young children—good/bad, big/little, brave/cowardly, fear/security, love/hate, and so on—serve as a kind of template for early adolescents' exploration of the extremes of reality—who was the best and worst, the biggest and smallest, the bravest and most cowardly, and so on.

Such binary opposites are techniques of sense-making in that they provide the most basic orientations to whatever is expressed in terms of them. This is not to say that we will want to teach everything in terms of binary opposites. Indeed, as I argued for the previous layer, greater understanding develops through the mediation of such opposites. While the binary opposites provide access to a topic, and provide the basic coordinates of understanding, it is the mediation that makes our grasp on the topic more sophisticated and secure.

Again, the techniques of rationality that try to grasp a topic in terms derived from the nature of the thing itself will be, in some sense, incompatible with the binary opposites and mediation procedure. Rather, as with stories, we can see one form of persistence of binary opposites in their withdrawal from the particulars to the more general contextual realm. If we see the detailed story of the decline and fall of the Roman empire in terms of the triumph of barbarism and fanatical religion over the civilized and tolerant virtues represented by the empire at its best, the binary opposites need not be present in the details of our text. Instead, they persist as orienting features of the overarching narrative, focusing our attention and our affective responses to the particulars.

On the one hand, then, binary oppositions and their constant mediation are increasingly found inadequate to represent the complexity of reality, and their breakdown "leads by a dialectical process to the formation of more complex systems" (Goody, 1977, p. 102). As the opposites hot/cold and their mediation warm, and the mediation cool between cold and warm, and the mediation lukewarm between cool and warm, etc., cannot provide enough discriminations of temperature for all our disparate modern needs, so we have formed the more complex system of arbitrary temperature measurements as in the thermometer. In this system, disembedded from our daily activities, we can distinguish an infinite number of temperatures. Crucial to the adequate development of romantic understanding is the ability to master such disembedded, sometimes called abstract, conceptual techniques. But even while we become familiar with such disembedded systems, we continue to use the other conceptual system built up from opposition and mediation.

So we see within romantic understanding various kinds of accommodation, and some failures of the accommodation between mythic techniques and those new techniques for trying to represent the world and experience as they really are. It is the persistence of the techniques and capacities of mythic understanding that gives to romance its peculiar ambivalences. Particular truths have only a limited meaning by themselves; it is within the larger, epic contexts that their meaning is enhanced and can be attached to our lives. The conceptual adventures of fantasy provide templates for the early exploration of reality, but increasingly reality gives shape and definition to the arsenal of concepts elaborated in the earlier layer, but yet, the coordination of the array of mythic sense-making techniques with those of the romantic layer seems never to be fully achieved. The sense of the reciprocal importance of particular and general, and fact within narrative, will need to be borne in mind when designing curricula and planning teaching—for mathematics and the physical sciences no less than for history.

The self and autonomous reality

From so portentous a sub-heading one could no doubt launch into a book-length discussion. But fear not; I want only to emphasize a single point, already touched on above. It is a point that seems to me of great educational importance, especially during the stimulation and development of romantic understanding. It is a point, also, that seems in need of particular emphasis as a considerable number of diverse trends in educational theory and practice run exactly counter to it. It is that we discover, some would say invent, the self by exploring the autonomous world. The sense of self is a kind of side product of the sense of an autonomous world. In perceiving the world's autonomy, we come to perceive that it is from our "self" that it is autonomous.

Ong describes the cultural adumbration of this as the splitting up of the original unity of consciousness, separating the knower from the known (Ong, 1977, p. 18). The internalizing, or recreating of, literacy, and the stimulation of the forms of thought that go with it, will be changing the *bias* of students' minds during early adolescence—to draw on the metaphoric language used earlier. The "participatory" ear will become less significant in the acquisition of knowledge, and the "distancing" eye will become increasingly well trained at rapidly reading the fine discriminations of print. Whatever the terms we use, whether the language of writing and print technologies or more familiar psychological terms or even the literary language that uses archetypal images such as losing Eden, one central feature of what I am calling romantic understanding is the growth of self consciousness.

✓   The fundamental principle undergirding the development of self knowledge is that it comes through understanding that which is "other," different and autonomous from the self. As our very consciousness of ourselves is a product of the sense of an autonomous reality, so the elaboration and understanding of ourselves comes with the elaboration and understanding of the world we find ourselves in—of other people, of an historical condition, social contexts, physical forms and processes, human psychology, mathematics, and so on. This is an observation that finds different forms in the language of St. Francis of Assisi, and virtually the whole of religious teaching in the Western and many other traditions, and also in the work of the psychologist on whom this essay draws selectively but profoundly: Vygotsky concludes that "we may say that we become ourselves through others and that this rule applies not only to the personality as a whole, but also to the history of every individual function" (Vygotsky, 1966, p. 43).

There is, of course, a reciprocal relationship between the growth of knowledge about the self and about the world. (I include other people, of course, in the "world" outside the self.) We make sense of the world initially be seeing it in some degree in terms of the emotions and intentions which constitute our consciousness. We try, in Piaget's terms, to assimilate the world to these. As features of the world cannot be adequately assimilated, so we accommodate to them. The reciprocity is a complex and multi-layered one, that echoes to and fro between self and world. We do not just learn about mountains. We learn about mountains in terms of their persistence, grandeur, their rocky hardness—that is, partially in terms of affective qualities of human experience. In the process we also elaborate our sense of persistence, grandeur, and rocky hardness; their stability and endurance enhances our understanding of what stability and endurance can mean. These enlarged concepts become accessible to further understanding of human experience. Somewhat metaphorically we may say that, in learning about mountains, we increase our potential to be mountain-like. And in turn this enlarges the conceptual grasp we may have on mountains, which in turn, and so on, and so forth.

We do not seem able to learn very much about the self by dwelling intellectually on our selves and on our own experience. Indeed, perhaps oddly, the more we try to focus on ourselves the less we seem able to see. Unfortunately this knowledge is usually much plainer to others than to ourselves if we are the ones who are self-absorbed. The self-regarding stance is one that results in collapsing what is learned about the world and others to the limited categories of self concern and self interest. The educational problem with this kind of narcissism is that it undercuts the educational task, which is to extend the concerns and interests of the self by intruding them into the diversity of interests and concerns the world can make available to us.

Karen Hanson summarizes her argument about the way in which knowledge of ourself is constructed by our imaginative sympathy with others:

> There is at least one object in this world that none of us can ever behold from exactly the same real perspective as any other's. That objective is oneself. If we are to match others' perceptions of us, of ourselves, and our behavior, we must reach out imaginatively and identify with those others, try—in and through imagination—to take their perspectives. If we can do this, if we can imaginatively identify with others, we can at once achieve both a better sense of ourselves and of those others. And when we do this . . . we live with those others in truly common ground. We move from isolation to a kind of communion . . . (Hanson, 1988, p. 140).

This seems worth emphasizing because so much of current educational practice seems to take it for granted that the opposite is true. It seems to be assumed that a curriculum structure which starts with the self in kindergarten, at the beginning of school experience, begins with what the child knows best, and extends concepts constantly from children's and students' everyday experience in order to ensure that new knowledge is both logically connected with what is already known and will also be "relevant." The kind of curriculum structure that results from this assumption seems to me profoundly at odds with the perhaps paradoxical observation that it is through understanding others and the autonomous world in which we find ourselves that we can come to understand ourselves. This is not some vague mystical principle. It is a practical observation of great importance for the curriculum. The current "expanding horizons" kind of curricula constantly collapse the external world and human diversity to the limited categories children and students have available to make sense of their own limited experience. "Expanding horizons" curricula, ironically, constrain environments. Of course they introduce students to new knowledge, but they inevitably limit and restrict students' conceptual growth at precisely the times when students most need access, for educational purposes, to the different and the distant from their experience. The result so commonly is intellectual provincialism, chauvinism, narcissism, narrowness, lack of sympathy— that group of related mental stunts.

If we discard the principles that give structure to "expanding horizons" curricula, how will we make the distant and different accessible to students? How can we make the strange and exotic "relevant"? A number of answers to this will be given in the course of this book. First, we might ask what is it about the biggest person who ever lived, and the smallest, the hairiest and so on that is "relevant" in terms of the expanding horizons curricula? Second, the problem of access is resolved if we think of students' experiences as encompassing not only their everyday practical activities but also their imaginative lives. That is, we can make anything accessible that can be made "relevant" to the experience of their imaginative lives no less than to their everyday practical activities. And third, romance provides us with alternative principles, which cohere with the complexity of students' personal and social experience.

There is unquestionably a paradox at the heart of romance. Self-definition is central to romance, as it was to so much of romantic art and literature. Yet there is a profound engagement with the extremes, the exotic, and the distant from daily experience. The paradox is resolved in our discovery that it is indeed by knowledge of others and of the diversity of the world that we define ourselves. If we pause for a moment and consider what are the discoveries that have most added definition to the sense of self in Western cultural history, it is not meditations on the self, but rather it is the discoveries of Copernicus and the theories of Newton and Darwin and Einstein. Today it is the astronomer and the physicist to whom we look for further self-definition, more expectantly than to the psychologist.

The point of this is to prepare for a significantly different kind of curriculum that will follow from the principles of romance than has followed from the limited logical principles of content associations we find in current expanding horizons curricula. It will also lead to some significant differences in teaching practice, and in the framework I will articulate for planning teaching.

Conclusion

Roughly around the age of eight students begin to attend in a new way to what is increasingly perceived to be an autonomous world. Their intellectual exploration of that world commonly engages most eagerly with its limits or extremes. Students seem most readily engaged by descriptions of the extremes of the physical world or the extremes of human achievement and experience. Whatever the cause of this prominent feature of students' thinking, which echoes a prominent feature of romantic thought and expression, we may simply observe that it seems a sensible strategy for beginning to explore the reality of the world and of human experience. War, romantic love, interplanetary travel, the actions of heroes and heroines, the greatest and most amazing things done and said and suffered, most readily engage students in the romantic layer. (And if such observations seem equally applicable to many adults, this is a contribution romantic understanding leaves with us; like characteristics of the mythic layer, it is not displaced by subsequent layers, but might be qualified and changed in some ways to be explored in future volumes.)

Along with the engagement with extremes of experience and the physical world comes intense interest in the self. These two are closely related. Knowledge and understanding of the self grows along with knowledge of others and of the autonomous world, and comes most fully through imaginative sympathy with the distinctness and autonomy of others and of the world.

Romance is represented here as constituted by mythic capacities confined within reality. There results a kind of ambivalence that focuses attention on details of reality while also preserving an urge to transcend reality; an ambivalence also common in the works and lives of romantic poets and artists ("Wordsworth's love for the fantastic tales that he read both as a child and as an adult was combined with an intense love for the ordinary" [Sturrock, 1988, p. 62]). Romance involves an urge beyond our everyday lot, an urge to transcend the conventions that surround us, to remake the world closer to the heart's desire. That partner of Romanticism, the Industrial Revolution, was able to work out that urge in the real world; today's students typically lack the power to affect the real world very much, but nevertheless, what we can see on the stage of our cultural history we can see analogously on the stage of students' mental lives today. Let us then consider some characteristics of the romantic urge towards forms of transcendence.

4
Associating with the transcendent

Introduction

We saw within Romanticism an ambivalence between the imaginative attraction towards myth and fantasy on the one hand and a reverence for the particularity of the real world on the other. This ambivalence seems to be a central characteristic of romance, and a commonly evident feature of students' mental lives in the middle-school years. In Romanticism, romance, and modern students a most prominent exemplar of this ambivalence is caught in the figure of the hero. A hero is, it has no doubt been said before, a partially domesticated god. Gods absolutely transcend the constraints of humanly perceived reality; heroes are caught within the natural order but they transcend the constraints of fear, ignorance, powerlessness, or whatever, that hem in our conventional lives. By associating with their courage, wisdom, or power, we pulley ourselves along a little in their direction, or we vicariously enjoy transcending the limits that shape our humdrum daily lives. There are numerous literary, philosophical, psychoanalytic, and other theories that attempt to describe and account for the nature of such associations, their mechanisms, and functions; it is enough for us here simply to observe that such romantic associations are common among students of middle-school age, and to consider how we can use such an observation to best educational advantage.

Such associations are evident in students' devotion to football teams or pop-stars. There is an obvious common element between this phenomenon and the engagement in obsessive hobbies discussed in the previous chapter. These romantic associations are often enormously powerful, as is evident from the time and emotion expended on them, and in the degree of pleasure taken in the achievements or successes of the objective of the association or the sorrows in its losses or failures. The intensity of elation and dejection in Canada, around the time of writing this, as the sprinter Ben Johnson won the gold medal in the 100 meters race in the 1988 Olympic Games and then lost it when he tested positive for performance-enhancing drugs was prodigious—and vividly so among both boys and girls in this age range. Some part of the strength of these associations turns on what we might loosely call the imagination. The ability to feel sorrow, to feel diminished in some way, when one's favored football team loses a game requires imagination. When the actor, caught up in his role, weeps, we might with Hamlet wonder "What's Hecuba to him, or he to Hecuba,/That he should weep for her?" We may prefer that students' sorrow be moved by Hecuba's distress in flaming Troy than by their favorite football team's failure to win at the week-end, but in both cases we see an association being forged by an act of imagination. It may be that greater knowledge and imaginative power is required to feel with Hecuba, and that the human rewards are greater, but we will likely not understand how to connect our students with Hecuba if we ignore or deprecate their imaginative associations with pop-stars and football teams.

The topic for this chapter, then is to explore further the kind of romantic associations we commonly find students making during the middle-school years, and to explore some related features of their imaginative lives. In as far as we find these useful for making richer sense of the world and of experience we will want then to consider how to use them to educational advantage. They are a further constituent of romantic understanding.

Romantic associations

What is going on when students cover the walls of their rooms with pictures of a particular pop-star or football team? Why should people prefer the athletes from one—"their"—country to defeat those of other countries? They might find some of the other countries' athletes individually more admirable and likeable, and some of their country's quite despicable. Why, indeed, do some people become emotionally entangled with so indefinable a thing as "their" country? Why do some people take pride in being an employee of a particular company, enthusiastic about its power and achievements? What is going on when historians narrate their accounts of, say, medieval Christianity, ancient Greece, or the careers of Marie Curie or Isambard Kingdom Brunel in such a way that the reader is clear about their delight in their subjects' excellences, ingenuity, or power?

The objects of the pride or pleasure are imbued with heroic qualities. This does not mean that there is necessarily any *falsification* going on: the team may be excellent to exactly the degree the fan claims; the company may be just as powerful as the employee asserts; Curie and Brunel did all the things the historians narrate. The heroic quality is evident not in any falsehood but in the way the object of the romantic association is put into sharper focus, as it were, than the surrounding world; it matters more; it stands out; some emotion is invested in it to distinguish it.

This mental highlighting, this investing with particular significance, is a central capacity of romantic understanding. It may focus on a particular hero and remain relatively stable over time. But the ability to form romantic associations can be a much more fleeting and flexible mental ability. Learning about the fight between David and Goliath, we most easily form a romantic association with David. But we can reflect a moment that Goliath was some mother's son, with his joys and sorrows, and we can flick our romantic association over to bring the giant into clearer focus. To see the fight from his perspective, or to see the battle with Beowulf from Grendel's perspective (Gardner, 1972), and to associate with the poignancy of doomed power, shows that this aspect of our capacity for romantic understanding can be used as a flexible instrument that can enliven and make more richly meaningful whatever it brings into focus. To consider Grendel in a prosaic way is to see only a monster; to focus on Grendel romantically is to see the monster imbued with qualities that can engage us in his plight, against the bleak-eyed, stone-hearted Beowulf.

Or at a more mundane level, we can go out into the vegetable garden in the spring and behold the struggle between our seedlings and the implacable, remorseless, inexorable Morning Glory (Convolvulus). We can hurl ourselves into the fray, pushing back this intrusive agent of nature's chaos, preserving the neat domesticated seed beds of civilized order. While doing so, or seeing it as so, in however undramatic terms, we can also—carefully disinterring a meter long pale root—associate with the remorseless ingenuity of our foe. Such a way of seeing the activity of weeding the garden enlivens the world by imbuing it with human motives and qualities. While projecting such attributes onto the Morning Glory, or seeing the Morning Glory in such terms, we obviously do not believe it consciously plans its forays through the peas and leeks. But to see it fleetingly so enables us to make prosaic acts into transcendent dramas, which do not confuse us—except in pathological cases—and so enrich the meanings and significance of our acts.

This, then, adds some definition to our accumulating sense of romantic understanding. Romantic understanding entails this capacity for making rapid and either stable or fleeting associations; it is a mental capacity that we can use to vivify the world and so make it more readily engaging and meaningful. We may see it dramatically in the development during the Romantic period of a personalization of nations, and continuing during the middle-school years today in students' association with the qualities of their personalized nation.

The highlighting of whatever is brought into focus is what makes film and television such powerful and almost inescapably romantic media. Whatever is in the focus of the camera is highlighted and given significance, and the rest is suppressed by being out of vision or being background. Significance can so easily be picked out: the character is driving home, and the camera focuses for a moment on the wheel that is about to blow or the timer of the bomb in the trunk, or we move from the cowboy struggling to rein in the runaway horses to the slipping bolt that will disconnect the horses from the wagon they are pulling. The selection of one wheel or the connecting bolt by the camera signifies what is especially important, and the rest fades into the background. By extension, the romantic sense of experience being either highlighted and significant or background and more or less meaningless finds expression in such notions as Andy Warhol's, that everyone should appear on television and be seen by everyone else, so becoming famous for five or fifteen minutes, or however long he felt was required. The notion of being famous, of having one's acts recorded on film or television, is tied up with the way romantic understanding grasps at the bright bits and pieces, highlighting some things and suppressing the rest. It is also reflected in typical adolescents' swings between sensing the significance of all their acts in some cosmic eye or their meaninglessness and futility.

Romantic understanding, useful for investing events with significance and meaning, can also be abused or reach pathological extremes. One extreme is when the romantic view cannot be switched off, as it were: when one's acts are seen always as the proper focus of the cosmic eye; one's own acts in all their detail are seen as ultimately significant and the world and other people are seen merely as background. The other related and more common danger of romantic understanding is that the object of the romantic association is taken as disproportionately excellent. Falsification can easily creep in. The assessment of the skills of the admired football team or the company's power or Curie's or Brunel's behavior can all be twisted out of proportion as a result of a romantic association with them.

We need not, of course, dwell on the peculiarities of others to explore what is going on in the formation of romantic associations. We need only reflect within ourselves. We all make such associations, whether with film stars, historical characters, athletes, makes of automobile, culture heroes and heroines, institutions, ideas even. It is not just that we admire their prowess, skill, depths of compassion, ingenuity, or power; we invest them in addition with a romantic quality. We associate with the tincture of the transcendent that we either see in or project into them. The hero, as a paradigm of romance, is distinguished from someone we simply admire by the glow of transcendence. Those who take Socrates or Einstein as an intellectual hero do not simply consider him as the source of precisely the ideas he generated, who may also have had trouble with lower back pain, draughts, and dandruff. He is transformed somewhat by the romantic focus. The flow of transcendence shines from him, as in the posters one can get of Einstein, or the T-shirts with his image on the front. This is not the everyday man; this is an embodiment of the romantic image of the genius.

It is not easy to mark precisely the difference between a romantic and more prosaically realistic view, especially as romance is not a binary condition that is either on or off. There are clearly degrees of this kind of romanticizing of figures we associate with, from a slightly heightened admiration to an excessive worshipping. It is a capacity that, once developed, we can clearly apply flexibly and rapidly, as well as one that can set in place certain stable associations with particular figures or institutions or whatever. And we can apply it in various degrees, changing the volume, as it were, at will. At least, these kinds of control over our use of romantic associations are what we will expect in the later parts of this layer, after its appropriate stimulation and development.

Another observation we may make about the objects of romantic associations is that, again like the obsessive hobbies of the previous chapter, they seem almost arbitrary. It is clear that almost anything can serve as an object for romantic associations. While there will no doubt be explanations for each particular romantic association in each individual, it is important to note, given the educational use I want to make of this capacity, that the associations are not necessarily tied to any particular content or objects.

Earlier we noted some of the characteristics that make Napoleon so ready an object for romantic associations. It is easy to see in him transcendent power and energy. That is—it is important to note—the association is with the transcendent qualities which the particular object, in this case Napoleon, expresses. Students commonly associate with some things and some people whose cleverness, power, ingenuity, energy, virtue, courage, and so on, transcend the anonymity, powerlessness, and indefinite formlessness of their sense of themselves (perhaps stimulated by a drive to resolve the "identify confusion" described by Erikson, 1963). The common feature of these associations is that they are with qualities that transcend the everyday normality of students' lives, while their objects are a part of the real world. Clearly such associations are important to students who are, ambivalently, increasingly familiar with the conditions of their local environments and social *mores,* while increasingly sensing these everyday routines as constraints on their developing powers and on their imaginations' images of what is humanly possible. Their minds are exploring the limits of what is real and possible, and while this contributes to a realistic appraisal of their place, proportion, and bounds, it is a contribution that sits uncomfortably with the persisting desire to transcend those limits. In the association with the hero, students may feel a responsive recognition of their own dawning sense of autonomous power, self-consciousness, courage, sexual attractiveness, or whatever.

The above paragraphs are useful, I think, in putting the struggle to transcend in its starkest and simplest terms. I should qualify this, of course, by observing firstly that this reflects the early, medieval kinds of romance rather than its development in Romanticism, and secondly that it is a distinctively masculine form of romance. One contribution of Romanticism was to naturalize or demythologize medieval romance; rather than struggles to overcome foes, we find struggles to attain illumination. The feminine forms of romance show less interest in winning struggles and more in saving life, helping, and surviving, and using imaginative ingenuity to escape from the constraints of the conventional world. Dwelling on heroes is also perhaps a mistake, even though they do loom large in the romantic view of things. Heroes are seen today perhaps as more common in male than in female imaginations. And the ways females typically explore roles and seek to transcend the everyday constraints of their routines commonly take different forms than are presented by the hero struggling with his foe. Perhaps I might describe one female strategy that exemplifies the basic principles I have tried to characterize but in a rather different form.

The Catherine to whom this book is dedicated recently began high school. After the first few weeks of becoming oriented and learning the routines, she announced to her classmates that she was an identical twin whose sister had been sent to a different high school because they caused so much trouble together. But they had decided they would switch schools occasionally to see what each other's school was like. A few friends from elementary school supported her claim. She then announced on random days that she was Kaci, the twin. Initial skepticism began to give way bit by bit as she pretended not to know her way around the school, and in undefinable ways behaved rather differently. Clearly Kaci was a quieter, more demure young woman than Catherine. One day Catherine claimed to be angry that due to some confusion, Kaci had also come to her, Catherine's, school that day. There was a test for which Kaci had not studied, and if Kaci reached the classroom first she would flunk the test and pull down Catherine's grade. She then went into the washroom, changed clothes, combed her hair differently, and emerged as Kaci to be greeted by a number of her class-mates telling her to leave because Catherine was really cross. And on it went: from the boy who told Kaci not to tell Catherine, but he thought Kaci was the prettier of the two, to the father who agreed to fake photographs of the "twins" together, until Catherine recently confessed that there was only one of her. Some of her classmates still do not believe the correction; they remember seeing the two of them together, or have other evidence that the twins exist. Transcendence, döppelganger-impulses, and a range of romantic qualities have been evident in this adventure, even though it lacks the particular character of hero-in-struggle-with-foe that I have used as the simplest case of romantic transcendence.

The educationally important observation, I want to repeat in conclusion, is that it is not the object that is the anchor of the romantic association but the transcendent quality which the object embodies. There was a time when a typical middle-class English bureaucrat might form a romantic association with the Bank of England. It was seen, not quite proportionately, as a rock of stability, a foundation of civilization, and so on. Or a Catholic journalist might form a romantic association with Medievalism, seeing in the Middle Ages an ideal of harmonious and civilized life. Or a middle-American, middle-executive might form a romantic association with the IBM Corporation, seeing it as a beacon of the free world, spreading peace through trade. It is not the particularity of the Bank of England, or Medieval life and its institutions, or IBM that forms the anchor of the association, but it is the transcendent qualities of stability, harmony, or power that these embody that make them suitable targets for particular individuals' romance.

The sense of awe and wonder

Another aspect of romantic transcendence is the capacity to perceive the world with awe and wonder. There are psycho-sexual theories that attempt to account for its common development during adolescence;

here I am concerned largely with the educational implications of the phenomenon and with its role as a constituent of romantic understanding.

Awe is an "overflow of powerful feelings" that results from confronting everyday features of the world and experience as simply external forms of some internal mystery. The external features of the world and experience contain many problems and puzzles that we may rationally seek to explain, such things as the structure of the physical world, the origins of life and the universe, why the bread always falls butter side down, and so on. But beyond these there is the mystery of why there is existence rather than non-existence, or, as Leibnitz put it, why there is something rather than nothing. When we face the underlying mystery rather than the superficial puzzles, we have no applicable methodologies of inquiry and our only available response, as the reality of the mystery becomes meaningful, is awe. Most commonly people have directed their sense of awe to religion, and one may say indeed that awe is the religious emotion. And while God in various forms has commonly been the object of this sense, awe also finds many other kinds of expression. Whether it is the pantheism that some claim to observe in Romanticism, or Wordworth's overflowing emotion on seeing daffodils or mountain streams, or the farmer on a summer evening filled with unnameable emotion as he watches the sun set on his ripening wheat, or a mother watching her sleeping baby, or any of us feeling some sense of ecstatic awe in times of fullest meaning, we recognize a quality of human experience that enriches our lives. It is a quality connected with love, and it is when our experience is infused with this emotion that we most understand what it means to have a love of life. It is what stimulates us sometimes to dance rather than to walk, to sing rather than to talk.

One November morning, I sat in an unheated convocation room with my fellow Franciscan novices waiting for our first lesson on the Psalms. Father Adrian, old and very thin, came in and sat at the small table in front of us. He waited for silence and began in his clear, quick, clipped voice: "If you look at any religion in operation, you will find a morality; when you look at it reflecting on life and itself, you will find a theology; but, my dear brothers in St. Francis, when you get to the heart of a religion, you will find a song." At the heart of Judaism and Christianity, he said, were the Psalms. Whatever one makes of this, it suggests the relationship between the sense of awe that is at the heart of a religion and the enriching of experience. The sense of awe, however, reflects a mental capacity to be developed by the atheist no less than by the religious. It begins to appear early in adolescence, commonly in a passionate delight in the more spectacular natural phenomena—the mountain views, the gold and scarlet sunsets, and so on.

To be without this sense of awe at the mystery of things is to lack an important constituent of an educated understanding. To be without it is necessarily to lack an understanding of what has generated huge parts of western and eastern cultures. To be without it means that while one may be able to learn about outward features of those cultures' achievements and products, one will be unable to understand and appreciate them except in the most superficial way; they will not, that is to say, engage one's sense of awe. To be without it is to lack a capacity that can transfigure mundane experience into something rich and strange.

Now I recognize that this discussion of awe is somewhat removed from the common experience of classrooms today. Planning lessons and units, getting resources, arranging for audio-visual media, designing evaluation instruments, and so on, tends not to leave much time for considering how to stimulate students' sense of awe. My point is that it is an important constituent of romantic understanding whose stimulation and development is of educational importance. So my planning framework and curriculum content will need to take account of it.

This constituent of romantic understanding also has nothing much to do with equality of opportunity for social and economic advancement. Even so it is an important human capacity that any educational—as distinct from, say, socializing—institution should be committed to develop in students. As I will make clear later, it is not something to be touched on perhaps in literature or art classes only. Rather, as a constituent of romantic understanding, it will need to be stimulated and developed across the whole curriculum. Science and mathematics no less than poetry can stimulate our sense of awe, and can be better understood if they do so.

There is probably little point trying to distinguish wonder from awe, as they are so commonly used as synonyms. I would like to note a difference, however, between the sense of awe at the mystery underlying the most commonplace features of our existence on the one hand and wonder at the most amazing and exotic features of reality on the other. Awe is the preservation of the sense of magic that is consistent with rationality; wonder is a related response to what is comprehensible but amazing or unique in some way. Wonder is concerned with the rationally graspable, awe with the mysteries of existence that are the ultimate and inaccessible backdrop against which the rationally graspable is played out. This is not a distinction that will probably count for much in practical terms. I will later be concerned with evoking, stimulating, and developing the sense of wonder in teaching mathematics, science, history and so on, but I want to keep somewhat distinct from this wondering engagement with knowledge a deeper sense of awe that we need also to stimulate.

Wonder seems to need much less elaboration than awe. This is not to suggest that it is any less important nor any less a constituent of romantic understanding, but only to acknowledge that much more has been said and written about it. And while it is not exactly a common topic in educational textbooks, it is something that most teachers readily recognize and acknowledge as educationally significant.

Romantic stories

To see the Morning Glory or Goliath or Grendel—or the gardener, David, or Beowulf—as embodiments of some transcendent qualities, and thus in some degree wonderful, requires an act of imagination. To see them so is indeed an exercise of imagination. What we do by projecting such transcendent qualities onto them and then romantically associating with those qualities is to see the objects no longer as something we may simply learn about or observe but as something we also feel about. And we feel about them because, however fleetingly, we fit them into narratives with aims, intentions, causes, conflicts, ends, and human emotions. We put them, that is to say, into stories. The Morning Glory is no longer a particular weed to be uprooted, but a protagonist in a drama. The garden becomes an arena, the world a stage.

This "storyfication" of the world shows both the power and the weakness of romance. Its power is to vivify whatever it touches; its weakness is that it leaves largely meaningless what it does not or cannot touch. This volume is about its power; its weakness is that it cannot provide the kinds of understanding to be explored in subsequent volumes.

In the previous volume I considered at some length the importance of the story form whenever we want to communicate meaning and feeling together—what I have called affective meaning. At the earlier stage, I argued, meaning and feeling are often closely tied. This tie persists, in a gradually loosening way, into this romantic layer. While the use of romantic associations does not create elaborated stories with beginnings, middles, and ends, such associations *plot* their objects into some story scheme. The image of the inexorable Morning Glory does not involve an articulated story, but it *suggests* a story, in this case, the common one in which there is a conflict between two forces bent on conquering or repelling attack. One of the persisting capacities developed in the mythic layer is the flexible and rapid deployment of a wide range of story plots; the meaning of the romantic association with gardener or

Morning Glory, or with both in succession, is enhanced by its being fitted, if only momentarily, into an available story form or plot.

The simplest form of overt romantic stories (as distinct from the more covert kind of romantic plotting that may go on all the time) has a hero or heroine who struggles against unattractive opponents and prevails. The events unfold in such a way that we can associate with the hero's or heroine's transcendent qualities—of ingenuity, goodness, energy, toughness, or whatever—and share the glory of their success. Given the way television series have routinized the stimulation of admiration for the central character(s), of distress as they are threatened, and of that curious pleasure when they prevail, we may find our responses may have become casual to the point of being subconscious. Such stories encourage an easy association with a character who embodies transcendent qualities. The appeal, to males in particular, of cowboy stories or science fiction stories commonly involves the romantic association with self-reliant loners, isolated from the securities of life, facing a generally hostile environment that neither knows nor cares about them. The Sergio Leone films, with Clint Eastwood as the largely silent hero vengefully overcoming his foes, take this stock romantic character to what must be some kind of limit, or make a stereotype of it. They clearly attract the immature romantic association to self-reliance and toughness, while at the same time allowing a kind of "high camp" pleasure to more mature audiences.

This kind of figure has been common in romantic literature from the beginning. The archetypal romantic hero is the knight on a noble quest, meeting mysterious dangers, performing wonderfully valorous deeds, and prevailing in the end. In later Gothic romantic fiction "the crucial figure is that of the anachronistic hero, representative of an older and nobler world who survives into a world that has lost integrity and honour and who serves as a reminder of other possibilities and other values" (Morse, 1982, p. 4). Anne Radcliffe wrote hugely popular Gothic romances of this kind, which prominently included also that other romantic role of the noble but beleaguered heroine.

We do, of course, have romantic stories in which the hero loses in his struggle and we may deliciously associate with the defeat, while knowing that in some better world the transcendent quality will prevail. Such stories are quite different from tragedies; the supports of our sanity are not at stake, but are, rather, reinforced. Perhaps a judicious re-editing might bring us a better *Star Wars* sequence as the Faustian romantic saga of Darth Vader.

Fantasy stories, we noted, are usually built on simple binary opposites and the protagonists tend to be made up of just a name and a couple of characteristics (ugly but good; handsome and brave; wrinkled and greedy; small and noble; and so on). The characters in romantic stories tend to be more sophisticated but still rather less than (or perhaps more than) life-like, especially in that their common transcendent self-reliance obliterates the kind of fears, insecurities, and ambivalences that contribute to most human personalities.

Another aspect of this association with transcendent self-reliance is evident in the common early adolescent interest in spying and keeping secret diaries, and preserving secrets and communicating them in codes. This aspect seems more common in girls in Western culture so far (see, e.g., Bowen, 1964). For whatever reasons, boys' engagements with this realm tend to focus on code-making and communicating in code and also quite commonly in magic—conjuring and card-tricks. A related area where boys' and girls' interests seem often to come together is that of piracy. At least this seems common in middle-class students who have access to the Arthur Ransome books, with their sea-going boys and girls and exotic female pirate chiefs like Missee Lee. Domesticated piracy, spying, diary-keeping, codes, and secrets all bolster the sense of self as secure, powerful, and knowledgeable against an everyday world which so frequently seems to embody those characteristics against the insecure, powerless, and generally unknowledgeable early adolescent self. The girl's secret diary with elaborate locks and hidden key transforms the daily events of her family and school into scarlet dramas, with the knowing writer at the center of the web. By turning others' actions into one's own words, in which one can ascribe motive, one gets a measure of control over the otherwise alien and mysterious interiority of others. Girls particularly, for whatever reasons, often weave worlds in their imaginative play. The roots of the tree around which they sit are woven into magic countries and elaborate romantic adventures. When the imagination has had less literary material to draw on, it may be boys or pop-stars who are woven into imaginative and romantic narratives. In more literary backgrounds it can generate worlds of an intense vividness such that reality becomes the shadow world. This is especially the case when female lives are confined and their imaginations are allowed no adequate range of action in the world. Anne and Emily Brontë, for example, invented the imaginary world of Gondal, which became the setting for many of their dramatic poems. Branwell and Charlotte Brontë collaborated to create the imaginary world of Angria about whose history and characters Charlotte wrote many stories which foreshadowed many of the themes of her mature novels.

A couple of the teachers who read a draft of this book suggested I should mention *Dungeons and Dragons* here, as an example of the engaging power of some of the characteristics of romantic stories. Boys particularly can become totally involved in a *Dungeons and Dragons* adventure, which typically involves searching for hidden secrets in exotic locales, with masses of realistic (plausibly impossible) detail, associating with transcendent qualities, chance encounters with dangers of various kinds, and so on.

We can find some clear differences between the narrative forms most eagerly read, or acted out, or followed in imaginative constructions by boys and girls or by middle and lower class students. But it is not fanciful, I think, to see beneath these differences some common features. What I have tried to describe here are those common features, even though the particular illustrations I have chosen may be more evident among some groups of students than others.

Conclusion

"Real life was only a squalid interruption to an imaginary paradise" (Shaw, 1988, p.191) is how Bernard Shaw described childhood and adolescence. It is a fair characterization of life in the romantic layer for those who are fortunate enough to have, as Shaw did, access to the kinds of cultural materials that feed the romantic imagination. But one sees it also in adolescents who are full of life and energy when caught up with their romantic associations and who become like a dull rag, overwhelmed with boredom, when having to engage the routine matters of everyday schooling. Romantic understanding grasps well the kinds of features that I have described in this chapter, but it is poor at grasping the everyday routines; they remain relatively meaningless. The girl dragged from her imaginative world-construction with a friend to rake leaves or the boy dragged from being a Dungeon-master to lay the table typically show that these conceptual capacities are tied powerfully in with emotional engagements. What is brought into focus by romantic understanding is bright, larger and bolder, and more noble and better than daily life, but what romantic understanding does not bring into focus is diminished, suppressed, darkened. The main conceptual problem for romantic under-standing is proportion.

Despite its constant tendency to distort, romantic understanding does not necessarily falsify whatever it brings into focus. I put it this way to introduce what has become a contentious matter in some areas of educational discourse. The problem is the hero. "I don't like heroes; they make too much noise," Voltaire said. Typical nine-year-old boys do like heroes; indeed, they want to be heroes and make noise. A number of traditionalist or neo-conservative voices in education have bewailed the absence of heroes for today's young people, and have argued for their importance as ideals exemplifying particular values, or as role models. More progressivist or radical voices have argued that the very idea of the hero gives a false view of the world and experience to the young, and tends to imply an élitist conception of society. Heroes are typically leaders with powerful personalities who cause events by their strength of will, ingenuity, or whatever. History, seen as the arena of successive heroes, is a process driven by particular strong wills in which the masses are mere fodder and economic and social forces are largely discounted. The British used to have a strong line in military heroes, whom the lower classes were to admire and to recognize as their social superiors. Moreover, of course, heroes are generally males. Girls, it is sometimes claimed, do not respond to heroines—indeed do not have heroines available to respond to—as boys are taught to respond to heroes. Is my analysis of romantic understanding, with its prominent place for heroes, simply reinforcing dysfunctional class and sex-role stereotypes? If this is a cultural recapitulation theory, perhaps heroes represent a crux in our culture's class and sex-role history that we would do well not to recapitulate?

The first point to be made is that those who are wary of heroes and heroines in the curriculum have some good reasons to be so. While supporting the importance of heroes, I do not want to support their use for reinforcing either forms of submissive class consciousness or sex-role stereotyping. Providing role models of black women, for example, as doctors or managers of corporations is no doubt socially useful today, but is only a subsidiary part of my concern with the educational importance of the hero in stimulating romantic understanding. The question I need to answer is this: if one wants to avoid using the hero to condition students to certain social and sexual roles, is there any legitimate educational use for heroes?

The second point is a reflection of one of the arguments made in the previous volume about the potential stereotyping involved in the use of binary opposites. That is: binary opposites and heroes represent techniques that can be used in sense-making but can also be abused. The abuses are contingent, in that one can use these techniques perfectly well without falling into the abuses. Vivifying one's struggle with the Morning Glory uses this technique but does not necessary further undesirable social conditions nor lead to sexist, or even animalist, views. It is a kind of momentary fiction, in which the gardener or the Morning Glory figures as a hero in an imaginary drama. The momentary fiction vivifies and makes however slightly and briefly, one's mental representations more richly meaningful. One does need to learn to distinguish such momentary fictions from reality, and this is learned much more effectively through their constant and flexible use than by trying to ignore and suppress them. It is inexperience with fiction that leaves one most vulnerable to confusing one's fictions with reality.

Stereotyping, we need to remember, is one of the undesirable products of our commonest sense-making technique. We form mental categories in order to deal with the ungraspable diversity of things; we simplify. We do not have distinct concepts for each individual chair; we lump together a massive diversity of things that take a rough general form and fulfill a particular purpose for us and call them all "chair." This lumping of things into general categories to suit our purposes is a condition of effective thought. But it can be abused and can be dysfunctional when applied inappropriately. Stereotyping involves lumping into the same category things that should be distinguished. We will not cure stereotyping by restricting the use of categorizing—that is, by restricting thinking. Restricting the use of heroes as a cure for certain socially damaging forms of class consciousness or sex-role stereotyping will not be very effective. In both cases the more effective answer is to increase the sophistication of the sense-making techniques and to sensitize students to their potential abuses.

A third point is that it is a contingent matter what is selected for highlighting by this romantic capacity for "heroizing" individuals, institutions, ideas, weeds, or whatever. While it may indeed have undesirable social and personal consequences to feed students a diet of glorified male military heroes, one need not feed their predisposition to respond to heroes in this layer with such a diet. One might instead make heroes of a wide variety of women and men, and children, and ideas, institutions, weeds, mathematical procedures, physics concepts, and so on. That is, anything in the universe is amenable to romantic highlighting. The kinds of people who were typically represented as heroes in the past were selected according to the values of past societies. We can reflect quite different values by our choice of quite different people, ideas, institutions, or whatever, for treatment by this highlighting technique. What we cannot do, and also hope to educate, is represent no values. That is, this romantic heroizing of phenomena is indeed value-laden, but, first, this cannot be avoided, and, second, its use does not commit us to any particular values. Its use does not, in particular, commit us to submissive class consciousness nor sex-role stereotyping.

A fourth point derives from my general cultural recapitulation argument, to be elaborated in chapter 8. This is, that the heroizing technique of romantic understanding is one of the conditions of making the world and experience meaningful to students in the middle-school years. Indeed, this technique tends to distort knowledge, or distorts the relationship between what is highlighted and the suppressed backdrop. If it could be argued that this romantic technique in some way prevented movement in the direction of more sophisticated understanding, then this would be a powerful objection. Not only does this seem untrue generally, but also the vivifying power of this technique seems more commonly to stimulate the pursuit of further knowledge and deeper understanding. That this heroizing is a condition of making the world and experience meaningful to middle-school students is a point that will be addressed later in my argument for the overall scheme.

What I have tried to describe in this chapter, then, are some further capacities that are constituents of romantic understanding. Central among them is the capacity to form associations with people, things, institutions, or rather with the transcendent human qualities that can be embodied in, or projected into, such people, things, institutions, or whatever. We can use this capacity to "heroize," to highlight and vivify, aspects of the world and of experience, by associating with the qualities we find in them that most transcend the routines of the everyday world or that most resist its constraints and limits. In the romantic vision, certain selected things stand out bright and clear and somewhat larger than life against a dull and diminished backdrop. The students' view of themselves, their group or gang, and their "associates"—whether people, events, ideas, games, institutions, weeds—takes on, if only momentarily, a special importance and significance, and the rest of the world, including adult *mores* and concerns, are proportionately considered insignificant or meaningless.

It may seem odd that in discussing these capacities I am attending very little to their development *within* the romantic layer. The sense of awe, for example, can be significantly different in its objects, intensity, and psychological uses at nine years and at fourteen years. To try to describe in detail a process of development of these capacities within the romantic years would no doubt be possible and desirable, but it would require a considerable book. I will touch on the most general changes in Chapter 6 but my aim here, as for each of these books, is mainly to make a preliminary attempt to sketch this dimension of educational development that is generally little dealt with.

The romantic urge to associate with the transcendent is well captured in the writings of G. Stanley Hall who, as I shall discuss later, is commonly credited with first extensively defining the character of adolescence:

Youth seeks to be, know, get, feel all that is highest, greatest,
and best in man's estate, circumnutating in widening sweeps
before it finds the right object upon which to climb. . . . It is
the glorious dawn of imagination, which supplements
individual limitations and expands the soul toward the
dimensions of the race (G.S. Hall, 1904, Vol. II, p. 302).

This is a romantic way of putting it, of course, but it catches at, as well
as exemplifies, one distinctive characteristic of romantic understanding—one to which our teaching and curriculum will have to be responsive. I should perhaps note that Hall's "romantic way of putting it"
seems not entirely devoid of racialist overtones (Karier, 1986).

5
Human and inhuman knowledge

Introduction

A feature of Romanticism and romance that I have touched on a few times is the vivifying of knowledge and experience. One aspect of this is evident in the way knowledge is made engaging when "romanticized." The journalistic principle of searching out a "human interest" angle to make a news item more engaging is very much an exemplification of a romantic approach. But romantic understanding is also supported by learning the basic tools of rationality, by absorption in details, in "inhuman" systematic categorizing and theorizing. How do these two kinds of developments come together?

In this chapter I will explore some further characteristics of romantic understanding, focusing first on the "humanizing" of knowledge, and later on the relationship to this of the rational systematic forms of knowledge that seek to reflect only what is the case about the world. That relationship, very generally put, is an elaboration of the process seen above in the survival of the story form as the narrative context which makes more generally and affectively meaningful the particulars organized within it. I will try to show that students' access to understanding "inhuman" knowledge comes most readily be seeing it within contexts made up of the human courage, ingenuity, and energy that were involved in the invention or discovery of the knowledge in the first place. That is, our access to rationality comes through seeing its products as extensions of common human intentions, hopes, and fears. But this is not the only route of access to the early tools of rationality. Sometimes the contexts can be quite distant and other principles come into play, principles that will allow us to encourage the development of disembedded, "abstract" thought by recapitulating the forms of their appearance in our cultural history.

Knowledge, learning and some metaphors

"Today," I sometimes begin one of my classes, "is the anniversary of the birth of the inventor of the past tense. Last Friday was the anniversary of the inventor of the subjunctive." Bowing the head: "Let us remember them with gratitude for a few silent moments." There usually follow a few silent moments, but these are succeeded by comments which suggest the moments were not spent in grateful remembrance.

I suppose this is an overly cute way of introducing a topic, but it tends to lead to a lively argument, focusing first on whether it makes sense to suggest that someone *invented* the past tense. Usually some students will argue that it *developed* as a by-product of the evolution of the brain. In response I suggest that the theory of relativity, then, should be similarly considered a by-product of this evolutionary process and should not be credited to Einstein. That, I am assured, is different.

What seems to propel such a discussion is a difference in the metaphors used in thinking about knowledge. The storage of knowledge in symbols—the great achievement of literacy—and their housing in encyclopaedias and text-books encourage some people to think of these symbols as the natural habitat of knowledge. Knowledge can thus be seen as leading a life independent of minds. From such a view we can come easily to see knowledge as evolving by itself, unfolding according to its own inherent rules and logic, parasitic on minds perhaps, but having, as it were, a life of its own. In this view we may yet discover, bring into "the bright circle of our recognition," in Auden's phrase, the perfect complete system of, say, mathematics. Our job is to discover it, not invent it. The form knowledge takes is seen as a function of the nature of the world, affected by our purposes only contingently. The typical text-book introduction to any area of knowledge tends to reinforce this view (Luke, de Castell, & Luke, 1983; de Castell, in press). Such textbooks often organize their knowledge historically, presenting its growth as an evolutionary process. Thomas S. Kuhn, whatever one makes of his more general claims, has shown convincingly how the history of science is seriously misrepresented by such presentation (Kuhn, 1962).

This metaphor of evolving knowledge has its uses, of course. It helps us to make sense of some important aspects of the way knowledge has been accumulated in Western culture. But, as with any metaphor once its metaphorical character is underestimated or forgotten, it can also tend to cover up other aspects of how we accumulate knowledge. It tends to cover up the fact that minds are the only sources and repositories of knowledge. They are not, as it were, simply hosts for the independently living knowledge to parasitically grow in and evolve according to its own internal dynamic life.

The metaphor of evolving knowledge becomes an educational problem when its easy acceptance as a literal truth leads to seeing the educational task as getting into the students' minds the knowledge that exists in the textbooks. It is only this metaphor that encourages us to see the stuff in textbooks *as* knowledge. Books do not contain knowledge; they contain symbols. Knowledge is a characteristic of minds. Knowledge requires a knower. The educational task is to convert or, as we are being sensitive to our metaphors, transmute the symbols into human knowledge within students' minds, or, alternatively again, reconstitute the dead symbols into living knowledge.

These metaphors are most hidden in educational discourse. They are usually hidden inside the word "learn." What is hidden is that people mean different things by "learn." During this century the word has gathered a significantly new meaning due to the considerable influence psychology has had in educational discourse. "Learn" has come to mean increasingly what psychologists have used the term for in their research. This has most commonly been students' internalizing of symbolic forms and their later reproduction of them. The topic of the experiments may be prose passages, random numbers, lists of unrelated terms, or whatever. "Learning" thus comes to mean something closer to "memorizing" than its traditional meaning, which was tied up with coming to understand one's culture's "lore." The influence of psychology has been largely to strip "learning" of its associations with understanding. This is no one's intention, of course. It is simply a product of the term's use in psychology, whose methods are effective in dealing with relatively clear matters of memorization but much less effective in dealing with relatively vague or complex matters of understanding. And, because psychology has had such a powerful influence on educational discourse of late, the common use of "learn" has tended to gather its psychological meaning at the expense of its traditional meaning. The psychological meaning is much more hospitable to metaphors suggesting that knowledge is made up of symbols which may exist in books or in minds equally well.

Educational discourse might benefit by our becoming more sensitive to the influence of the evolutionary metaphor applied to knowledge and the related restriction in the common meaning of "learn." We might note more carefully the work the metaphor does and, perhaps more importantly, its limitations in helping us to think about knowledge and learning. We might usefully seek further metaphors that will help us to focus on the distinction between the symbolic coding of knowledge and knowledge living in minds. Such metaphors might proliferate through educational discourse, indicating more clearly what students have to do when they "transmute" the symbols into knowledge, or "reconstitute" knowledge from the symbols. Had such metaphors been more prominent, we would not at this time be fighting back the restricted and simplistic conceptions of learning that have been able to gain so much ground during this century. It would simply not have been taken for granted that learning involved the reproduction in children's minds of the symbols in books, with all the associated assumptions of more or less passive minds having "knowledge" impressed into them, nor that "learning" might be evaluated from the students' ability to reproduce the symbolic codes. It would not now seem so novel to have more appropriate metaphors spun out of "learning": as when, say, Wolfgang Iser notes that "the reader receives [textual material] by composing it" (cited in Bruner, 1986, p. 24). Once the metaphor of "composition" is embedded in our conception of learning, we make much more complex and realistic what happens between symbol and knowledge. The composing mental activity that finds a polished outlet in poetry comes to be seen as a constituent of all learning. We do not "internalize" knowledge, nor are we "initiated" into it; both *these* metaphors have their uses within "learning," but both carry with them the sense of symbols being knowledge indistinguishable from its form in minds. But we are also active *makers* while we learn.

"Composing," "poetry," and "making" all highlight a constituent of learning that has tended to be rather suppressed as a result of psychology's influence, and the difficulty the dominant methods of psychological research have had in getting much hold on this constituent of learning. These alternative metaphors point to an element of learning which became prominently recognized, in somewhat different ways, in the Enlightenment and in the Romantic movement; i.e. the imagination. David Hume was driven, despite his radical empiricism, to conclude that the senses and their impressions could not account for our perception of a continuous, stable, external world—because that is certainly not what we perceive. In the most simple forms of learning—interpreting objects in the world from perceptions—Hume argues for a necessary imaginative act. Kant took this further, arguing that there must exist in us an active faculty for the synthesis of manifold perceptions, which faculty he identified with the imagination. The enormous elaboration of the roles conceived for the imagination in the Romantic period do not need to be revisited here. But the inheritance of both these traditions today is found in such claims as: "Imagination . . . is involved in all perception of the world, in that it is the element in perception which makes what we see and hear meaningful to us" (Warnock, 1977, p. 152), and whose exercise and education "will certainly lead to [children] inhabiting a world more interesting, better loved and understood, less boring that if [they] had not been so educated" (Warnock, 1977, p. 153).

My point is the radically different ways of conceiving of such things as learning that follow from the hidden metaphors we employ. If we recognize that a more adequate conception of learning necessarily involves imagination, then we will find much of the current research that supposedly yields implications for learning largely irrelevant to what we mean by learning in education.

The transmutation of inert symbols into living knowledge should, then, be at the heart of any metaphors we use about learning in education, and the imagination plays a crucial role in this. Our metaphors are not simply tools we think with; they tend to do our thinking for us, especially if we are insensitive to them. The metaphors that represent knowledge as evolving and living in symbols are enormously influential in educational thinking at present. Without them, and with more appropriate metaphors, we would not likely be involved with such educational peculiarities as multiple-choice tests, "thinking skills," the panoply of assessment devices that threaten to choke education and teaching, distinctions between "process" and "content," and so on through the desiccated wasteland of current fads, jargon, and so much "research."

Reasserting metaphors that highlight the imaginative reconstitution involved in making living knowledge from inert symbols tends to have a number of influences on educational discourse. First, it emphasizes that coming to understand something can never be simply a matter of replicating in minds what exists in books. That is to see learning crudely as accumulating symbols in minds in the same inert form as they are preserved in books. The common result is to make the inert form the paradigmatic form and then impel all learning to conform to it. By emphasizing the complex and little understood imaginative reconstitution of living knowledge from inert symbols, we keep clear in our minds that only evidence of knowledge living in students' minds will count as educational success.

If educational evaluation is to have educationally beneficial uses, it needs to be able to measure the degrees or qualities of life students attain with particular knowledge. We do this intuitively while teaching. There is no point evaluating other things that can be measured more easily and offering these instead. They will be at best educationally irrelevant, and at worst educationally damaging because they encourage teaching towards the achievement of what can be measured. All sensible evaluators of course recognize that there are important educational aims that cannot be measured. They try to isolate indices of these aims. or constituents, and measure these, recognizing that they are not the aims themselves. But, unfortunately, education is not a process in which such procedures make much headway. Unfortunately, the enormous technical complexity disguises for so many the gross conceptual confusions underneath. Such disguise, indeed, sometimes seems part of the purpose of the technical complexity.

That the process whereby we imaginatively reconstitute knowledge from inert symbols is largely mysterious is largely irrelevant to our daily tasks in education. As we do not need to know the chemical structure of chalk in order to be able to write on the chalk-board, so knowing the psychological processes involved in learning are not necessary to teach well. In both cases the relevant skills and knowledge concern quite different levels of the phenomena.

Second, these reconstitutive metaphors help to bring into focus the realization that knowledge is all human knowledge. That is, people, like us, made it, invented it, discovered and formulated it, for human purposes, with human motives. For it to be reconstituted in our minds some sense of the role and place it has had in other lives is important, as is some sense of the human motives that stimulated its invention or discovery.

"Cats and dogs seem not to have a use for the subjunctive but long ago Ug-Nor felt a purpose for it, and with enormous creative genius just invented the damn thing. Clearly some of the greatest geniuses lived long ago and left us their amazing invention of language," I sometimes continue my class. The idea that language comes from individuals inventing it bit by bit clearly strikes most of my students as bizarre. They argue for an evolutionary view by noting the cats' and dogs' apparent lack of use of the subjunctive is tied up with the evolutionary condition of their brains. Conceding this, I ask again whether the evolutionary condition of human brains is to account for eighteenth century people not knowing the theory of relativity. That, I am told, is different: a matter of prerequisite knowledge not yet having been discovered. But surely, I reply, the brain capacity for the subjunctive probably existed for ages before Ug-Nor. If "evolution" is to be credited for her invention why should Einstein's not similarly be credited to evolution? A distinction between biological and cultural evolution might then be raised, and so the discussion would go on.

Well, this is a kind of joke introduction. It is intended to bring to the fore the fact that when we use the idea of evolution with regard to cultural things we are employing a metaphor, and that it is a powerful and pervasive metaphor. If we are not sensitive to its metaphoric nature, we let it do a lot of our thinking for us, leading us to conclusions that would be reasonable only if the metaphor was a literal truth. Only in a metaphoric sense can we talk of cultures evolving. Cultures do not evolve; we make them. We make them bit by bit in response to human needs, hopes, fears, intentions, and pleasures. This is not to deny we can discover logical sequences in cultural history, just that any account of cultural development that does not prominently bear in mind human psychology, and our needs and purposes, is unlikely to get much grasp on the phenomenon.

Third, the reconstitutive metaphor brings into focus an aspect of the role of the teacher that tends to get suppressed in the evolutionary metaphor. If the problem is seen as initiating the child into the knowledge held in our data sources, or of getting the child to internalize the knowledge contained in the text-books, then the teacher may be seen either in traditional didactic terms or as a "resource person" or "facilitator" who helps the communication between external knowledge and the child's mind. The reconstitutive metaphor focuses us on the teacher as a kind of magus who is to help transmute the inert codes into living knowledge. The hint of magic here is, I think, entirely appropriate. Learning, in its traditional educational sense, remains a mysterious process. I emphasize this not to encourage mumbo-jumbo, but rather to properly recognize just how little we understand about it. All our available models of learning from Plato's *Meno* to the current cognitive science crop, are hopelessly inadequate to account for this most commonplace phenomenon. We will not make much progress in understanding learning—in its educational sense—unless we clearly see the gulf between our simplistic models and the complex reality.

While this might seem comforting to teachers and should indeed be an index of the specialness of their professional role, it carries a burden. That is, in order that the symbolic codes be transmuted into genuine living knowledge in students, the knowledge must be seen to be of value in the life of the teacher. This is perhaps a seemingly obscure and roundabout way of stating the cliché that teachers, to properly fulfil their role, must be exemplars of what they teach. I hope it is not so much obscure and roundabout as clarifying and rounding out a dimension of what the cliché means. At a professional level, it means that in order to educate, teachers must be in some significant sense scholars; teaching is properly a learned profession. I'm not sure this is adequately recognized in the time and opportunities provided for teachers at present to consistently pursue their own educational and imaginative development. But more of this in Chapter 10.

I have perhaps labored my point here, but I have done so because, while it seems a simple truism—that human knowledge is dissimilar from our forms of encoding it—we use a bunch of metaphors that sometimes disguise and confuse this. We talk of books containing knowledge—as I have and shall in the rest of this book—which leads so easily to assuming that educational success can be achieved by getting what is in the text into the student's brain and that that success can be measured relatively unambiguously by getting the student to reproduce the text codes on a sheet of paper. This, however, is best achieved by simply retaining the codes in memory as codes, and so preventing them from becoming genuine knowledge. I think this common student activity, which, it perhaps needs emphasizing, is what very many students genuinely learn that schools and learning are all about, exemplifies the fact that students often "learn to cope with school tasks by means of strategies that actually have the effect of subverting learning" (Bereiter and Scardamalia, 1989, p. 367). Bereiter and Scardamalia emphasize that "*The skills a student will acquire in an instructional interaction are those requested by the student's role in the joint cognitive process*" (Bereiter and Scardamalia, 1989, p. 383). Until it is made clear that the students' role is imaginatively to reconstitute knowledge from symbolic codes, they will continue to try to retain the symbolic codes in memory. Now, obviously these are not water-tight compartments in minds. Some human meaning will be derived from codes once in minds but, if we want genuine long-term understanding, then it is the imaginative reconstitution that we must require of students as their part in the joint cognitive process of education.

And this seeming excursion is here because romantic understanding cannot grow from inert knowledge. The middle-school period is that period during which we try to convey nearly all the knowledge we think is fundamental to being a responsible citizen today. It is also the period during which students experience the most intense excitements and the most awful boredom. As Christopher Nolan puts it after what is generally a most favorable view of his school, all the students welcomed a trip away because "after all anything was better than school" (Nolan, 1987, p. 133). The danger is that our focus on the important knowledge the students must learn can very easily lead to our focusing away from how the learning can vivify or revivify the knowledge. And that can lead to the common boredom that results from struggling to internalize codes whose meaning is wrapped up in themselves and does not extend to the student's life. Romance is the perception of the human meaning of knowledge.

Rehumanizing knowledge

"There are men, and there are gods, and also there are creatures like Pythagoras," said the golden-thighed Pythagoras. Why was Pythagoras considered a magus, even by himself apparently? The secrecy in which his sect held the knowledge he had discovered about harmonies and regularities in sounds, shapes, and materials suggested their sense of the magic of discovering such hidden and mysterious knowledge. Their religious sense of the mystery and magic of mathematics is something entirely purged from its typical teaching today. Maynard Keynes acutely described Isaac Newton not, as he is conventionally thought of, as the first and greatest of modern scientists, but rather as the last of the great magi in the tradition of Pythagoras. Newton was the last great inquirer who saw the universe as a vast puzzle made by God but solvable by human beings from the clues God had scattered throughout his creation. Such a view brings together and makes sense in a single whole of Newton's scriptural exegesis, his alchemical work, and his scientific research. When his elegant and apparently bloodless *Principia* is seen as a part of this great and passionate attempt to solve God's puzzles, the theorems take on a somewhat different light (Fauvel et al., 1989).

Mathematics in particular seems an educational victim of dissociation from its human source. Science teaching, too, perhaps because science's "objectivity" is so greatly valued, fails to interest large numbers of students who seem unable to engage knowledge so dissociated from human motives, purposes, hopes, and fears. One oddity of the dissociated form in which mathematics and science are commonly taught is that it presupposes precisely the capacities it is best able to teach.

One simple way of reversing the dehumanizing of scientific knowledge is to introduce it as the product of, and in the context of, its inventors' or discovers' transcendent qualities. The biographical or historical approach to science teaching is hardly new, of course. Let me describe a dramatic example of its use before coming back to the basic principle.

Richard Eakin taught his college introductory course on zoology by lecturing in a somewhat atypical style. He would come to class wearing an early seventeenth century wig, hat, and frock-coat. His lecture began: "Gracious Ladies and worthy Gentlemen, before presenting a discourse on the heart and the circulation of the blood, listen I pray you to some personal history. I was born on All Fools' Day, 1578 . . ." In his book, *Great scientists speak again* (1976), Eakin describes his methods and his repertoire, which included among others Darwin, Pasteur, and Mendel. Students' access to the relevant scientific knowledge, and their understanding of it, seems to have increased entirely disproportionately to the simple shift of lecture format.

What Eakin has done in rehumanize the knowledge he is teaching, and help his students imaginatively to reconstitute the knowledge by putting it back into the human context out of which it came. He reconstitutes the knowledge as a product of individuals' energy, ingenuity, persistence, and so on, not as something inhumanly "evolving." He places the knowledge particularly in the context of the time of its invention or discovery. This is important because it makes clearer the questions and concerns its invention or discovery was a response to, the alternative hypotheses, and the personal qualities and interests, hopes, fears, and ambitions that directed the individuals' search, experiments, and discoveries in that particular direction. What one can teach by such a method is not only the scientific knowledge in a meaningful and engaging context, but also something about the qualities which are required to produce it. The students see science as an engaging, even passionate, human activity, not simply, and falsely, as an ordered and objective set of products.

The methods of science seem so obvious to some people years after they learned them that they forget, or cannot understand, why it took many centuries of rational activity by many great geniuses before anything recognizable as empirical science emerged or was invented. We must not expect it, then, to become immediately obvious to students quite early in their education. Rather, we need to be careful not to assume that students have the capacities that science can stimulate and develop, and we need to remember that science is a peculiar human activity engaged in for particular human purposes.

Approaching science through the transcendent human qualities that produced it, then, is not to be seen as merely a motivational ploy. We can, of course, distinguish between the romantic context-setting which can help to make science accessible to students and the hard scientific knowledge itself with its logic. We certainly want to be clear that our purpose is not teaching history marginally related to certain scientific discoveries nor teaching about the biographies of some scientists, but is to ensure through them an understanding of science. But we should qualify what may seem an easily drawn sharp distinction between context on the one hand and science on the other. During this romantic layer, which recapitulates an understanding of science preliminary to the sophisticated conceptions articulated in the Royal Society and in modern times, the distinction between human purposes and the scientific knowledge they led to is not to be etched so sharply. That distinction does indeed become much sharper later, for reasons I will discuss in the next volume, but the tie between context and science is not one that we should feel overly concerned about during this romantic layer.

If we teach mathematics, beyond the basic steps, through its history, through the motives, hopes, and passions of the people who invented it bit by bit and elaborated its implications, then we might expect many more students to have access to higher mathematics, and this passionate subject might become more meaningful to nearly all students. Of course it is not always easy to achieve such a manner of presentation. It is especially difficult in mathematics, even more than in the sciences, because we commonly dissociate the products of mathematical invention or discovery from the inventors or discoverers and their human qualities. Mathematical knowledge can be seen to stand alone, and pride has been taken in disembedding it from its human context and viewing it as an independent structure of abstract relationships. Whatever our philosophical conclusions about the nature of mathematical knowledge, our educational conclusions about how to make it accessible to students, following this principle, will move us in the direction of reconnecting the knowledge with the transcendent qualities of the individuals who produced it.

What, in the beginning, were the ancients counting and why, and then, how? And after the utilitarian beginnings and the discovery of unsuspected relationships among numbers and between numbers and things in the world, can we understand better the sense of magic and mystery in mathematics, and the sense of power it might give to creatures like Pythagoras? And why did the monks need to measure time so precisely, and what discoveries in mathematics and engineering did this lead to? What were the motives that led the medievals to make their small but crucial steps in logic and algebra? Why did Ramon Lull think he could build logic machines that could discover the truth about the world? What did his machines look like, how did they work, and what did he do with them? (Peers, 1929; Gardner, 1982). Mathematics, so often abstracted and inhumanly structured, contains within its cool webs endless human dreams and passions. The way into those webs, to make sense of them, is by means of the motives and purposes of the passionate dreamers who have spun them.

So this sense of it all being human knowledge yields us a straightforward pedagogical principle. To the fore in our planning of lessons and units we should place the relevant transcendent human qualities that can give access to whatever knowledge we wish students to understand. Individuals' motives and purposes are the context that can help to make knowledge romantically understandable. We will then ensure that they do not merely internalize codes, but will bring them to life in their minds by seeing what makes them humanly meaningful and humanly worthwhile.

Surely I am not recommending this principle for *all* teaching in *all* subjects for *all* the middle-school years? Yes and no. Yes, in the sense that to engage students with an area of knowledge, this way of providing "romantic" access to it is necessary to make it humanly meaningful. No, in the sense that once the romantic context and access is provided, the related knowledge may be taught any way at all. No, also, in the sense that this biographical/historical approach is only one of a large number of ways this principle may be implemented. But more of this in Chapter 10.

Literal thinking in narrative contexts

Romantic understanding, as we have seen, is not hostile to or in any way incompatible with rationality; indeed this kind of understanding is generated as a result of the early development of rational capacities. If an early intellectual engagement of children is, to echo Richard Coe, to establish their inventories, a task that follows on is the organization, classification, categorization of those inventories. In the previous volume I suggested that children's initial forms of organization and classification may be intellectually no less sophisticated than those used later; they will not seem so, of course, if our focus is only on logical forms of classification and we ignore or cannot measure those tied into emotional, affective categories. I think we may read the available data as indicating that children's early forms of organization are idiosyncratic and tied in with personal purposes and feelings about the elements of their inventories; as they become literate and attend schools, we see increasingly forms of organization that conform with their inventories' overt characteristics and logical properties (Donaldson, 1978; Piaget, 1952, 1954).

I have tended so far to emphasize the contextual and narrative features of romantic understanding and have not dwelt on the kernel of rational forms growing within. This is due largely to the fact that the early appearance and growth of these rational capacities provide the focus of so much of the research and writing on this period of educational development. I have indicated why I think that this focus on the rational capacities by themselves cannot provide an adequate conception of students' understanding, and hence of their learning, motivation, development, and so on. Here, however, I will consider the way in which narrative contexts and, within them, rational kernels grow together. By emphasizing the contextual features of romantic understanding I have perhaps tended to suggest to some that I think that no important learning can take place during this "layer" unless it is explicitly tied into some general narrative context. I do not think this is the case; rather, one can clearly teach rational skills successfully while making no contact with any evident narrative context. I do think, however, that basic rational skills can be taught more successfully if the teacher is aware of how they contribute to the stimulation and development of romantic understanding. They are, that is to say, one constituent of romantic understanding and one can sensibly focus on developing this constituent by itself, though one does need to remember what it is a constituent of. Perhaps I can make my point clearer by dealing with two examples, one the development of a basic rational skill that makes no reference to any more general context, the second of a rational skill embedded in a powerful narrative context. Let me make a few more theoretical points, and then the examples.

"We all know by now that many scientific and mathematical hypotheses start their lives as little stories or metaphors, but they reach their scientific maturity by a process of conversion into verifiability, formal and empirical, and their power at maturity does not rest upon their dramatic origins" (Bruner, 1986, p. 12). This distinction between stories and theories, what Bruner settles for calling "narrative" and "paradigmatic" forms of thought, is common in observing the mature differentiated forms they have achieved in our cultural history and can achieve in individuals' educational development. A couple of points relevant to my theme are worth making, however.

The first is that during the middle-school years we are not dealing with a form of understanding in which this differentiation has reached "maturity." We are, rather, at the beginning of that differentiating process. We need, then, to be sensitive to what the early stages of that differentiation of story and theory, of the narrative and the paradigmatic, are like. And, again, I think we can find useful clues to this by considering the relevant stages of our cultural history, augmented by empirical observations of students' typical ways of proceeding to recapitulate this differentiation.

The second important point to emphasize is that the sharp dichotomy between these two forms of thought is not as sharp as it has sometimes seemed. Rational forms of thought do indeed strive to mirror reality and its processes, but they can only hope to do this according to the forms whereby we make sense of reality (Rorty, 1979), which can never be entirely independent of our storying capacity. We do not simply copy the world in thought but rather recreate our experience of the world as well as we can in the alien stuff of thought.

Rationality is made up of the set of techniques we have invented for reflecting the literal truth about the world and experience, regardless of their personal meaning to the knower, and for predicting things that are testably true on the basis of unambiguous evidence. But, of course, all these terms do not etch an absolute distinction between rationality and other forms of thought that people have used in "pre-rational" oral cultures. And Dan Sperber properly qualifies Bruner's attempted distinction, pointing out (echoing Vernant, 1982) that "the very notion of evidence and testability comes not from science but from the law, hence from the 'narrative' rather than the 'paradigmatic' mode" (Sperber, 1986, p. 1308).

Well, these disputed philosophical issues are hardly up for resolution here. I mention them only to suggest that the mixing of narrative context and rational kernel that I see as a central component of romantic understanding is not something epistemologically weird, even if rather unusual in educational discourse. What are commonly taken as mutually repelling forms of thought, I am arguing, are precisely what, in first coming together, generate romantic understanding.

It will be obvious, then, that I am not looking for ways to characterize how students develop *from* stories and narrative, contextual thinking *to* theory, and rational, paradigmatic thinking. Rather, I am looking for way to characterize how rational forms of thought grow within and into narrative forms. The trouble with our cultural intellectual development is that it seems *sui genesis;* it seems impossible to come up with any adequate analogy or metaphor for it. Most of the models of intellectual development we have, seem to be built on rather simple, usually hidden, largely unavoidable, analogies and metaphors—like development, growth, evolution, progress, and so on. I have used the term "kernel" of rational capacities, suggesting that these grow, elaborate, and differentiate within as it were, corn husks of narrative contexts. The inadequacy of this metaphor is that the husks and corn grow somewhat independently and when the corn is ripe the husks are cast away. But in our cultural and intellectual development we properly use the developing rational capacities *also* to develop our narrative capacities. "My metaphor," writes Frank Smith, "pictures the brain as an artist, a creator of experience for itself and for others, rather than as a dealer in information" (Smith, 1985, p. 197). And while this is an important metaphor to emphasize in the face of an educational establishment that has, perhaps reluctantly, accepted the metaphor of students' minds as dealers in information, it must be noted that a better metaphor would encompass both.

What are the early forms of rational thinking like, then? How can we characterize the beginning developments of what I chose in the previous volume to call "literal thinking" because of its connections with the inventions that led to the alphabet and relatively easy literacy. I will take a specific example here to try to indicate a general principle of that early development, and I will then elaborate it in the later chapter on the curriculum. The example deals with the early developments of rationality in cultural historical terms, but it is one whose appeal we can also see today in students of middle-school age, if only because of its commercial exploitation.

Jack Goody, having argued for the transforming influence of writing on ancient Near Eastern cultures, focused on a few very particular examples of new literate techniques to exemplify his case. I will borrow one of his examples for my rather different but related argument. He pointed out that one of the earliest uses of writing that proliferated rapidly was the keeping of lists: lists of produce, lists of priests and kings, lists of events, lists of merchandise, and so on. The list is very distinctly a device that belongs "to early literacy rather than yet earlier orality" (Goody, 1977, p. 102). Once a list was written, its terms were, firstly, released from the tight mnemonic networks that held them in preliteracy and, secondly, they became available for visual inspection. Once lists are available for visual inspection, they are open to, and often invite, manipulation, categorization, classification (and one need not fear that their manipulation will mean their loss to memory). There begins what Goody has described as "the dialectical effect of writing upon classification" (Goody, 1977, p. 102), which sets in train the succession of changes that gradually over time influence forms of thought by means of the new categories made available.

> The lists is transformed by writing and in turn transforms the series and the class. I mean by 'transforming the series' simply that the perception of pattern is primarily (though not exclusively) a visual phenomenon. . . . In saying that the list transforms (or at least embodies) the class, I mean that it establishes the necessity of a boundary, the necessity of a beginning and an end. In oral usage, there are few if any occasions when one is required to list vegetables or trees or fruit (Goody, 1977, p. 105).

To revert to the example mentioned earlier, it is this boundary setting, or category generating, that raises first and trivially such questions as whether a tomato is a fruit or a vegetable and later leads us into epistemology. Or if our list is about gods and their qualities and characteristics, it leads us first into trying to regularize varying accounts and later into theology. That is, the use and manipulation of written lists (among other things, of course) stimulates thought about thought, and thought about the categories it has been and is using. It is this meta-level of inquiry, this self-consciousness about our thinking, this explicitness of what had been implicit, whose stimulation and development is central to romantic understanding. "Lists are seen to be characteristic of the early uses of writing, being promoted partly by the demands of complex economic and state organization, partly by the nature of scribal training, and partly by a 'play' element, which attempts to explore the potentialities of this new medium" (Goody, 1977, p. 108). I think the last two uses are of particular interest for the educational recapitulation of this intellectual tool but the utilitarian functions of the first are also significant and will need attending to.

There is nothing "natural" about making lists, despite its evident appeal to students in the early middle-school years. Prosaic listing is an extension of a common human activity made possible by writing: "It seems to me," observes Goody, "an example of the kind of decontextualization that writing promotes, and one that gives the mind a special kind of lever on 'reality.' I mean by this that it is not simply a matter of an added 'skill', as is assumed to be the case with mnemonics, but of a change in 'capacity' " (Goody, 1977, p. 109). Now 'skill' and 'capacity' are not entirely pellucid concepts, so neither is the distinction to be drawn between them, and this crucial claim of Goody's is much disputed, perhaps because its meaning is not entirely clear. If "capacity" is understood just in terms of what effects the first tools of rationality have on some people's forms of thought and expression, then the claim seems in general unobjectionable (One might want to haggle about exactly what forms of thought and expression are due to what particular tools while accepting the overall claim.) What seems more objectionable is interpreting "capacity" in a way that asserts some general superiority to "literate" minds. Hand in hand with such an interpretation goes a notion of "reality," which rationality gives a special lever on, and which suggests that the thought evident in oral cultures deals with something else. (Nothing in Goody seems to me to imply these more questionable interpretations of his claim.) But it seems clear that rational, decontextualized thinking comprises intellectual tools for dealing with "reality" in a rather peculiar way. It is a way that, paradoxically, finds its "special kind of lever" a grip-hold by abstracting or disembedding thought from the concrete particulars of reality and while not—to switch metaphors—looking away from the concrete particulars, it somehow looks at them through the ways we look at them; we *reflect* on them; we focus in part on the categories we are using to make sense of them. This kind of meta-level of intellectual activity gives us two objects of thought that we blend together in rationality, partially analogous (but only partially) to binocular vision enlarging our visual "capacity."

So it is the development and coordination of this kind of meta-level, decontextualized, disembedded, rational, paradigmatic, and so on, and so forth,[1] intellectual activity that we need to recapitulate in order to stimulate and develop romantic understanding. I will here consider just list-making and consider what use we could make of it in the early middle-school years to stimulate the kind of meta-level thinking that Goody characterizes in early literate cultures. I will try to suggest much more varied and subtle ways of achieving this in Chapter 10, but it might be of some value here to deal quite starkly and simply with list-making in order to show up the kind of connection I am seeking to draw between cultural historical developments and individuals' cognitive developments today.

From Goody's account we may infer that central to our teaching activity concerning lists is the visual inspection and organization, categorization, classification of terms representing concrete particulars. At the simplest level, we could ask students to compile a folder of lists: list of rivers, list of places I have been, list of sports, list of films, list of stars, list of buildings, list of furniture, list of countries, list of fruits, and so on. Next we might consider a variety of ways in which the students might begin to organize their lists: the list of fruits might be categorized into those whose skins we eat, those whose insides are in segments, those with pits in the middle, those we grow in our country, those that grow on bushes, those that grow in clusters; the list of countries might be categorized into those that do not touch the sea, those that have more than one official language, those with fewer than thirty million inhabitants, those that do touch the sea, those whose capital is not the biggest city, those that are completely surrounded by the sea; the list of sports might be categorized into those in which a ball is kicked, those in which a ball is hit with something, those in which the goal is off the ground, those played indoors, those in which more than two teams compete, those that can be played with only two people; the list of buildings might be categorized into those people usually live in, those we have to pay to enter, those that are usually noisy, those in which books are important, those in which we eat, those in which money is important. And so on. No doubt, dialectically, in the categorization process, additional items will be brought to mind and can be added to the lists.

From simple listing we can move on to other forms of making features of reality visually accessible: diagrams, flowcharts, tables, data bases, sociograms, recipes, and so forth. In many of these, events and processes can routinely be made available to a different kind of thought than is

---

[1] The proliferation of terms with their different shades of meaning and associations hints at the looseness of our grasp on our meta-meta-level thinking!

usually brought to bear on them. Flowcharts might be composed of the events and decisions involved in the student's morning routines. These can then be restructured experimentally and analysed for efficiency, and compared with others. Planning behaviour in an uncoordinated society should, incidentally, be helped by such exercises. Computers with flexible data-base programs could also be helpful in stimulating this form of thought about the categories we use. We might tie in this activity with the "collecting instinct" discussed earlier. Listing one's collections and ordering the lots in various ways can also stimulate thought about the ordering as well as the contents of the collection.

Teachers who have not engaged students in list-making activities might be surprised by how eagerly many students will get involved in them. Of course, list-making can be made into an educationally useless activity if its educational purpose is ignored. The purpose is not simply to make lots of lists and divide them up in various ways. The purpose is to engage students' intellects with the categorizing level of the activity. One will need to avoid excessive rigidity in setting the task, and encouragement should be given to odd and quirky ways of organizing lists. The teacher might even arrange competitions in which each student, or a set of students, takes a list and categorizes it according to some principle that is not announced. The class or other sets then have to discern the principle underlying the categories into which the list is broken. I guess the winner would be the student or the group who had a clear principle that was least easily detected.

If my general claims are anywhere near true, this kind of activity is likely to be engaging not because we are "naturally" attracted to such things but because there are subtle but pervasive cultural pressures that encourage such activities as literacy becomes "internalized." Caroline Frear Burk's comment on the collecting "instinct," which she studied to such interesting effect earlier in the century, was that the powerfully engaging quality of such activities "is no accidental affair, no merely acquired trait" (Burk, 1907, p. 237). She meant, of course, following her mentor, G. Stanley Hall, that it was a feature of the recapitulation of human psychological development. I think the first part of her observation is true, but the latter is false. It is an acquired trait, but not accidentally acquired; it is acquired in the forms in which we see it as a product of students becoming educated in Western culture. But I will come to the theoretical argument in Chapter 8.

A transition from story to theory, from narrative to logico-mathematical forms of thought is not, I have suggested throughout, an adequate way to account for what goes on in middle-school education. We will not ideally leave story behind, but rather will develop theory within story contexts which are in turn affected and modified by the developing theory within. In what may be considered a kind of transition year, usually about age 8 or 9, one can help the development of literal thinking, of non-story forms of thought, by placing them firmly within stories. I have discussed and exemplified some features of this in *Primary Understanding,* but again, a rather stark example of the basic principle may help here to clarify what I mean. I will use an unoriginal example, as it has been developed by a local teacher. Let me simply quote Scott Sayer's version, with thanks to him. He illustrates this story of the old, old Western frontier with a felt-board and cut-out figures:

The Ghastly Deed
(fractions as part of whole; renaming)

Once, long ago, when numbers still walked the earth, there was a little town in the hills. The town was a quiet place, with little crime, because the numbers who lived there could always be counted upon to do the right thing. Besides, the sheriff knew immediately who the culprits were if something were stolen. You see, FOUR always stole four objects; no more, no less. If SEVEN turned to crime, he would always steal seven things, and so on. Ninety-nine was the sheriff, because he could never find 99 things to steal.

One day, as 99 was having his morning cup of tea, he was startled to hear cries for help. (Help! Help!) He immediately put his cup aside and went outside to see what the trouble was. It was the baker, 13.

"Sheriff! There has been a terrible crime!" exclaimed 13. "Some of a cake has been stolen!"

"No problem," said 99, "I'll go and arrest 1 immediately."

"But you don't understand," continued 13, "I didn't say one cake had been stolen. It's much worse than that! The cake has been (gulp) CUT and (horrors) PART of it has been taken!"

By this time a small crowd had gathered and the onlookers expressed their horror at this ghastly deed. (Gasp, shriek, etc.)

"But this is impossible," said 99. "One would take one thing, two would only steal two cakes. What kind of number would steal part of a cake?"

However, impossible as it seemed, there could be no doubt about it. Part of a cake had indeed vanished. The thief had even left the weapon behind with which he had done the horrible deed (Hold up a large knife).

That night the sheriff was on watch when he saw a dark, cloaked form leaving a shop. He chased after it and grabbed the cloak. The cloak pulled away, and inside was something horrible! It wasn't a normal number at all, but a monster. It had a two on the top and a three on the bottom. The sheriff fainted dead away (He later claimed that he must have struck is head on something).

The following day, a posse was organized, and, armed with all the squirt guns they could muster, they set out to track the criminal to his hide out. Far up in the back hills, they came upon an old cabin and they saw a weird shape through the window. "Come out with your hands up," demanded 99, and he fired off a warning squirt to be sure the point was made. The door creaked open and Two-thirds sidled out. An initial gasp from the posse quickly gave way to dead silence. Everyone shrank back. Two-thirds was carrying an odd-shaped box.

"Is that some kind of weapon?" asked Two nervously.

"Not at all," laughed Two-thirds. "It's a pizza." And he took out a pizza cutter and showed the numbers how he would cut the pizza into three pieces and eat two of them. The other numbers began to get used to Two-third's rather strange looks. He was so easy going that someone asked if it would be possible to have a number with a four on the bottom and a four on the top. "Certainly," replied Two-thirds. "He's right over there." The posse turned apprehensively to see the new creature, but they saw only 1.

"Me?" asked 1.

"Certainly," said Two-thirds. "Let me explain. If I cut this pizza into four parts, how many would you take?"

"Why all four of them of course!" replied 1.

"Well, think deeply about four. Engage your active imagination on the topic of fourness."

One concentrated very hard and soon a tiny four over four appeared shimmering within his very being. A second later, he had transcended himself and had become Four-fourths.

The crowd broke into applause to show their appreciation of this wonderful feat.

"Can I do that?" asked Four.

"Certainly," said Two-thirds. "What number would you like for your bottom?"

"I'd like to be like my old friend Two," said Four.

"Well then, if I cut these four pizzas into two pieces each, how many of them would you take?"

"Why, all eight of them, of course!"

"Then think deeply about two and highly of eight," instructed Two-thirds.

Four soon managed to transform himself into Eight-halves.

(At this point it may be possible to get some input from the students about what other changes the numbers could make, starting with possibilities for One and then for others. I would have a felt board with felt "pizzas" ready.)

When the numbers had calmed themselves and had all changed back into their usual forms, the sheriff looked around for Two-thirds. "This is all very interesting, but I've still got to arrest him for the theft of that piece of cake!" But no one could find Two-thirds.

Just then, Four-sixths ambled up to the Sheriff. He was chewing thoughtfully on a piece of hay. "I reckon Two-thirds must of went that-a-way," he said.

As time goes by the story context may gradually recede into the background. But it is important, it seems to me, always to remember that it will never recede completely, even at the most austere edge of the most logico-mathematical disciplines. And certainly during the middle-school years it will not recede very far at all. I should add quickly that the above kind of overt fictionalizing around the content is not at all the only way to acknowledge narrative contexts for lessons. And I should quickly repeat that placing the content explicitly in narrative contexts all the time is not necessary either. But more of this in Chapter 10.

Conclusion

The educational dimension in communicating knowledge to students, then, lies in revivifying it in the process, enabling them to reconstitute from the codes used some living meaning. We should be sensitive also to the fact that once knowledge is brought to life in another mind it is always something new and different; however slightly or significantly, it is never the same; there is no "internalizing" of identical concepts: "It is quite certain that, however great the convergence among a community on definitions of concepts and concept prototypes . . . there is variation from individual to individual in the content and structure of the vast majority of concepts, scripts, and categories" (Nelson, 1977, p. 223). Knowledge, in the sense distinguished from its coded forms above, is living material that takes distinct shapes, associations, and affective coloring in each individual mind.

Literacy can provide the capacity to transform lived experience and living knowledge into codes for purposes of communication and preservation. Whatever may be disputed about the causal role of literacy in transforming our material lives and our consciousness, its very great importance in human cultural history cannot be doubted. It is generally recognized as absolutely essential and central to education—a kind of prerequisite to nearly all the rest of the educational program. I think it is important to recognize, however, that it is also the cause of perhaps the greatest and most persistent problem faced by educationalists, and addressed most energetically by the greatest educational thinkers. This problem is not, perhaps surprisingly, ignorance or illiteracy. Something much more educationally dangerous exercised the ingenuity of Plato and Rousseau. The greatest educational enemy for them was clearly what we might call conventional thought, or the informed, conventional mind. That is, in the terms used above, the mind that has successfully "internalized" literacy and whatever codes are given it to learn, but who has failed to convert those codes into distinct and unique living knowledge is the paradigm of *educational* failure. Such a person may be well socialized, happy, capable of doing a useful job, etc., but represents precisely what *education* is supposed to transcend. Plato put it powerfully in his story of Thoth and the invention of writing. Plato put into the mouth of the god Thamus, who was the god of the whole of Egypt to whom Thoth was hawking his various inventions, severe doubts about the values of writing which Thoth's sales *spiel* advertised. Thamus, with great prescience, counselled Thoth that his invention of writing will simply persuade people "to trust to the external characters" and will give its users "Not truth, but only the semblance of truth; they will be the hearers of many things and will have learned nothing; they will appear to be omniscient and will generally know nothing; they will be tiresome company, having the show of wisdom without the reality" (*Phaedrus,* 275: cited in Jowett, 1937, p. 278). This last point is echoed in Whitehead's despairing comment, which I'll echo again, on the conventional, informed person as the greatest bore on God's earth.

Plato elaborated an extensive curriculum and methods of inquiry that were designed to propel the mind out of the level of *doxa,* out of conventional thinking. Rousseau concluded, with a kind of desperation, that only if children could be kept away from everything that seemed to induce this unimaginative, unoriginal, conventional thought was there any educational hope. Thus Émile was to be carefully preserved from reading and writing and all deliberate instruction until on the threshold of his teens, and then his access to information was to be very carefully restricted. Ignorance is no great problem to the great educational theorists; either people persist perfectly contentedly in it, or they can be educated. The real danger was and remains pseudo-education, the learning of the techniques of literacy and learning the codes in which knowledge is stored and preserving them as codes in the mind, where no original idea sees the light of day, no play of metaphor invades and enlivens the codes and brings the imaginations to life to convert them to living meaningful knowledge.

In our current distress at how small a proportion of even coded information many students seem to retain, many educational administrators are attracted to proposals that seem to promise an improved retention of conventional information and improved literacy skills. That is, most prominent and most energetically promoted are—and have been in mass educational systems virtually from their beginnings—precisely the kinds of pseudo-educational programs designed to socialize and produce conventionally literate minds. The reason such programs tend to fail rather spectacularly, even in their own terms, is, I think, involved with their lack of a sense of how to convert or transmute codes into living knowl-edge. The truth is that human beings are generally not well equipped to store coded information, so programs that aim at this are inevitably in trouble from the start, and can generally display "success" with only a very small percentage of their subjects. Ironically, human beings are superbly equipped to deal with living knowledge. The educationalists' job is to focus on how we can stimulate its development. My answer, in part, turns on the importance during the middle-school years of introducing new skills and information into the little factory of meaning which I am calling romantic understanding.

6
Rebellion, ideals, and boredom

Introduction

The period between about ages eight and fifteen is rarely dealt with in "developmental" theories as a unit. Most observers note a radical division at around puberty, when physical and psychological changes are typically more evident and rapid than at any other period of life apart from the earliest years. I think the main characteristics of romantic understanding do span this whole period, but they are somewhat affected by puberty. In this chapter, then, I want briefly to explore some of these effects. I do not want to dwell on adolescence and the changes that constitute it—about which there are many books and theories—but rather I want to see how romantic understanding changes between its earlier and later phases. Even so, some characterizations of adolescence clearly overlap with those characteristics I have been noting as constituents of romantic understanding.

"Adolescence" is the term we have come to accept as denoting the period of change, common to all cultures, from being a social outsider without any of the rights, privileges, and powers that go with being a social participant and agent, to becoming an insider, an initiate, an adult. Childhood dependence begins to give way to adolescents' developing power to accept or reject or modify the image of the world and of themselves represented to them by adults. The particular characteristics wherein we tend to see adolescence as a distinct stage of life have been most influentially described by G. Stanley Hall. He saw adolescence as prominently a period of inner absorption, of an efflorescence of imagination, of a tendency to self-criticism and oversensitive conscience, of "overassertion of individuality" (G. S. Hall, 1904, Vol. I, p. 315), of heavy reliance on imitation, of a dramatic stance towards life, of indulgence in "folly," of a new consciousness of speech indicated either by lavish flow or reticence[1], of "the dominance of sentiment over thought" (G. S. Hall, Vol. I, p. 318), undirected bouts of energy, of an exaggerated sense of the significance of what one does or suffers, and so—now rather familiarly—on.

Hall had a very, perhaps over, vivid sense of adolescence as a distinctive period of bursting, energetic life, of something unique to that period of our experience, which he felt was underestimated and undervalued by contemporary adult society. He helped make adolescence into a distinctively perceived period by the vividness with which he contrasted its generative vigor with the enervation of conventional adulthood: "The life of feeding has its prime in youth, and we are prematurely old and too often senile in heart. . . . What we have felt is second-hand, bookish, shopworn, and the heart is parched and bankrupt" (G. S. Hall, 1904, Vol. II, p. 59). While perhaps exaggerated, this does catch a note that is crucial to my argument in this essay: about the losses that seem commonly to accompany educational gains and the need for sensitivity to what is potentially being lost if we hope to preserve it or to minimize the loss. Let me again quote what seems to me an important insight of Hall's:

Gifted people seem to conserve their youth and to be all the more children, and perhaps especially all the more intensely adolescents, because of their gifts, and it is certainly one of the marks of genius that the plasticity and spontaneity of adolescence persists into maturity. Sometimes even its passions, reveries, and hoydenish freaks continue (G. S. Hall, Vol. I, p. 547). [This is a theme he echoes in the observation that genius "consists in keeping alive and duly domesticating by culture the exuberant psychic faculties, of which this is the nascent period" (G. S. Hall, Vol. I, p. 309)].

While I would hardly use Hall's terms, and while I crucially differ from him on the "natural" bases of these developments, I think he helps

---

[1]As I have turned so often to Wordsworth for illustrations, one might recall his rough agreement here with Hall:

Thirteen years
Or haply less, I might have been, when first
My ears began to open to the charm
Of words in tuneful order, found them sweet
For their own sakes, a passion and a power
(*The Prelude*, V, 1805 version)

(Later, for the 1850 edition, the thirteen is revised down to twice five years.)

acutely to identify a central educational task: how to keep alive the energy and vivifying power of what I am calling romantic understanding, with its "exuberant psychic faculties," as we get older. Coleridge, focusing on poets rather than on gifted people in general, had earlier stated a similar conclusion: "The poet is one who carries the simplicity of childhood into the powers of manhood; who, with a soul unsubdued by habit, unshackled by custom, contemplates all things with the freshness and the wonder of a child" (Coleridge, 1960, p. 112). Keeping the soul unshackled by custom follows on the task addressed in the previous volume of how to preserve the capacities that were developed within mythic understanding. We have seen how one may contribute to that by introducing the new kind of understanding in a manner that builds on and extends the former kind rather than replaces it. Mythic story-forms have led us into romantic narrative contexts, for example, and in the next chapter I will address, as a preliminary to the next volume, how both of these are maintained into philosophic understanding, and how the rational kernel of romantic understanding can be further elaborated and developed in the subsequent layer.

I will, then, focus on just a few characteristics of adolescence, those that seem most obviously to affect the forms of romantic understanding. They are all characteristics that have been touched on in one way or another above, particularly in the long discussion of Romanticism. I will not labor the connections between these characteristics and Romanticism, as they seem fairly self-evident. A study of "teenage culture in contemporary society" from a few years back, whose main conclusions seem still valid, observed of the various forms of teenage culture that all "seem to be to varying degrees manifestations of a similar rejection of the established way of life, the self-conscious assertion of youth as a self-justifying age-group and a strange mixture of reactive narcissism and nineteenth century romanticism" (Mays, 1965, p. 27). In looking at these particular characteristics, we will hear echoes of that ambivalence we have encountered throughout romance, in these cases seeing them as expressions of adolescents' efforts "alternately to resist the adult world and to find a place in it" (Spacks, 1981, p. 15).

Revolt and the idealized self

"It has always seemed to me that every child is by nature a delinquent, that the only difference between us as children was the extent of our delinquency, whether we were found out or not and how we were punished for it" (Joyce Carey, cited in Coe, 1984, p. 169). No doubt this particular child perception is largely a product of social conditions, even though of rather widespread conditions in Western culture and its history. It does catch also at something about the relationship between generations, in which the powerless young are the inevitable inheritors and displacers of the currently powerful adults. The adult consciousness of this can lead to an ungenerous resentment and hostility towards youth, or an unreflecting sense of one's responsibility and right to civilize their actual or potential wildness, or more generously to try to help them prepare for the adult world while giving them some breathing space in the process. In any case, to the adolescent, adults seem fairly constantly to be pushing and prodding and constraining and frustrating and trying to shape them. The adult world just won't leave the young alone.

During adolescence the growing sense of power of the young, and the growing sense of their powers that adults recognize, leads to accommodations and conflicts. The powerless outsiders are, sometimes gracefully, sometimes clumsily, rarely without some pain and distress on both sides, gradually introduced to some of the powers and freedoms that are a part of adult status—however constrained those powers and freedoms may be by other social and political circumstances. In this century, when freedoms have been expanding for many, the normal envy of youthful vigor by those in whom it is perceptibly waning, has been augmented; they sense that today's adolescents will inherit greater freedoms from the religious or sexual or whatever constraints that knotted up their own lives, fondly imagining "everyone young going down the long slide / To happiness endlessly" (Philip Larkin, 1988, p. 165, "High Windows").

Most visible and intrusive of adolescents' attempted readjustments of their status is revolt against adult norms, conventions, or constraints. While such overt revolt is often taken as the most characteristic symptom of adolescence, it is worth bearing in mind that most adolescents, even in the heyday of adolescent rebellion during the 1960s, identified with the values and ideals of their parents rather than with those of their outspoken "revolutionary" peers (Springhall, 1986). For most students, the change towards adult status is a piecemeal process of adjustments over a period of years, rather than a vivid climacteric of acute generational conflict. To say this, however, is not to deny the pain that can accompany these adjustments: put for males by W. B. Yeats as "The toil of growing up;/The ignominy of boyhood; the distress / Of boyhood changing into man;/The unfinished man and his pain / Brought face to face with his own clumsiness" ("A dialogue of self and soul").

In autobiographies—not, of course, the most reliable source for views of the typical adolescent—most commonly the years between about twelve and fifteen are represented as a kind of gap between the comprehensible remembered child the author was and the comprehensible adult the author became. In that gap appears some rather awful, sulky, foulmouthed, sneering, adult-hating, violent, subversive, and sneaky stranger; at best the stranger has a kind of reckless boldness, crusading against adults (Coe, 1984, pp. 174ff). A common self-image of the adolescent is as an excluded "outsider," treated shabbily by an adult world that is, for motives that never seem entirely clear, by turns indifferent and hostile. Nearly all adolescents can recognize Pip's feelings, despite his *Great Expectations:* "I cried a little . . . and felt vaguely convinced that I was very much ill-used by somebody or by everybody; I can't say which." Dickens as usual catches with precision the complex imprecision of the basis for the adolescent's agonistic stance against the adult world. That stance quite commonly involves a hostile and distasteful resistance to the dreary conventions that adolescents are expected soon to become a part of: "The criminal adolescent supplies a forceful image of the young as ferocious critics of the world they are expected to enter" (Spacks, 1981, p. 274).

Apart from the effects of such psychological conditions on kinds of understanding, these features of adolescence are also relevant to our theme because of the intervention of the school in this generational shuffling of the school. If the school's role were simply to socialize or domesticate the young, our problems might be simpler. But it also seeks to educate them, and a significant feature of education is to encourage a critical consciousness towards the dominant conventions of the time. The school, then, is in a rather peculiar position. On the one hand, it represents and justifies its coercive powers by reference to adult authority and, on the other, it is supposed to encourage critical reflection on the legitimacy of that and other authorities. A hard act to get right. A problem with schools, from authority's point of view, is the massive inequity in the size of the troops on either side. This is redressed, of course, by authority's control of vastly more coercive power. So a *modus vivendi* exists, a kind of balance of terror within which—so we are encouraged to believe by geopolitical authorities—we can live out our everyday lives in calm and peace. So the adolescents who could wreck the school, or at least leave it deserted, and the administrators and teachers who could call in the police, carry on daily in a kind of harmony, maintained by an implicit balance of terror. This may appear a startlingly inappropriate way of representing state-controlled compulsory schooling in a quiet suburb, but the front line troops on either side are aware of the psychic stakes and balances, and even in the quietest places eruptions of violence or defiance testify to the underlying realities of power, while in the least quiet places the weapons of coercion are visible in the corridors.

Like all authorities, however benign, schools tend to be not very good at encouraging those who are subservient to them to examine the bases of their authority critically. This is a particular problem for schools because a proper education in history, for example, would encourage a sense of the arbitrariness of most institutional claims to authority. It is no wonder, then, that the kind of social studies curriculum served up in schools tends to be largely vacuous (Ravitch, 1987) and focuses on uncritically supporting rather than critically evaluating the prevailing institutions and authorities of the state, and so also any sense of "change, conflict, and men and women as creators as well as receivers of values and institutions are systematically neglected" (Apple, 1979, p. 102). That is, the school's role as an agent of the adult state tends to undermine its educational role, and this tendency is one that has been perceptibly increasing throughout this century.[2] The current curriculum and the technologies of assessment, grading, and sorting students seem designed to conventionalize them to prevailing adult norms, with very little encouragement given to the common adolescent criticism of prevailing norms and conventions.

However subservient and acquiescent adolescents are in the face of adult authority and the institutions through which it impacts on them, and however benignly it is expressed, it seems very rare that a sense of injustice is not felt. Injustice stimulates resentment, and resentment stimulates revolt. The revolt may not be expressed outwardly, or may go no further than sulking reluctance in conforming with adults' will. Within groups of adolescents it may find oblique expression through styles of clothes, hair, music, etc. But along with this comes too a sporadic sense of hope, of possibilities, of growing power. In revolutions generally, according to Crane Brinton, there is inevitably a "honeymoon" period of expansive hope and the sense of new possibilities and of one's

---

[2]Einstein records how his bouts of reading in his early teens convinced him that many of the stories in the Bible could not be true: "The consequence was a positive fanatic orgy of free-thinking coupled with the impression that youth is intentionally being deceived by the state through lies; it was a crushing impression. Suspicion against every kind of authority grew out of this experience, a skeptical attitude towards the convictions which were alive in any specific social environment—an attitude which has never again left me" (Einstein, cited in Sampson, 1985, p. 33). Educational institutions cannot with an entirely easy conscience hold Einstein up as a kind of educational hero and disregard this message on behalf of a kind of skepticism which they do so little to encourage. It is indeed positively discouraged when we seek to inculcate only what we can clearly evaluate. I know of no instruments for measuring students' skepticism.

will becoming effective in the world, also a period of "thermidor," of a new harmony with the repressive authorities as one's growing power is recognized and accepted (Brinton, 1965).

Adjustment to the adult world is one side of the adolescent's task; the other side is adjusting to a changing self. I have already touched on this above, and referred to a range of writings that deal with it extensively. Dealing with the adjustments between self and world can easily lead to absorption with this fascinating self that comes so prominently to consciousness during this time. This reflects, in Romanticism, the conscious self-cultivation, the *Bildung,* that can so easily become, or seem to others, excessive and narcissistic.

Uncertainty about one's developing self and what its powers and qualities are commonly leads to "trying on" different personae, seeing how well they seem to fit or are accepted by peers and adults. The set Peckham identified as originating in Romanticism (Peckham, 1970, pp. 41–47) are not unfamiliar as models still used in perhaps updated forms today—the Byronic hero, the artist, the bohemian, the virtuoso, the dandy, and so on. In adolescent females we see the same person "trying on" such roles as the serene lady, the tease, the hoyden, the fashion plate, the rebel, to name a few.

The uncertainty about one's "self" leads, relatedly, to what is often called adolescent fantasizing. The trying on or playing out of roles is the external reflection of a kind of fantasy life in which one imagines oneself as an adult. This is often not altogether based on realistic assessments of one's possibilities because it is precisely such realistic assessments that adolescents are unable to make. One common product of this kind of activity is a sense of oneself embodying unrealistic perfections—of power, beauty, influence, wealth, nobility, or whatever. And while this "daydreaming" or fantasy can become somewhat morbid or dysfunctional, it seems also to be connected with students' development of various ideals. One part is an image, or images, of one's ideal self, another, obviously connected, consists of ideal images of the world, of politics, of family life, of human relationships, and so on. Such fantasy-generated ideals seem an extension of the kind of fantasy life of children considered in the previous volume, but beginning to accommodate to reality.

Romantic understanding, then, is colored in the latter part of its development by adolescents' adjustments and resistances to the roles and responsibilities of adult society. Along with uncertainty about the capacities one actually has or will develop goes a tendency to successively over- and under-estimate one's potential. From this we revolt, feel injustice, form high ideals, and exhibit all those other common features of adolescence.

Stumbling on authenticity

This subtitle paraphrases a central aim of Dorothy Heathcote's educational uses of drama (Heathcote, cited in Robinson, 1980, p. 11). By encouraging students to inhabit roles and helping to free-up their imaginations and undo their inhibitions, she enables students to feel their way into situations, emotions, characters. She does this in ways that enable students to resonate, one might say, with the role, to discover bits that fit themselves while also extending their sense of what their self can be. Drama, especially in Heathcote's hands, can perform an especially important role in this romantic layer; it can help students' imaginative extension into other lives and experiences. It can also provide a kind of *recognition,* as they play roles, of elements of their "true self," and help extend their emotional range to make contact with elements of their "buried life"—to revert to Matthew Arnold's lyric. If drama is made to live, then indeed "From the soul's subterranean depth upborne / As from an infinitely distant land,/ Come airs and floating echoes" (Arnold, "The Buried Life," cited in Allott and Super, 1986).

These lyric lines are not, I recognize, the usual language of instructional methodology and curriculum discourse, but I think they are truer to what we are supposed to be about in education. The "soul's subterranean depths" are indeed not open to much in the way of multiple-choice assessment, but they are a central concern to romantic understanding. This is a period of very significant adjustments at the most fundamental levels. It is worth bearing in mind when discussing the mass of students of middle-school age that, to use again the words of their most dedicated observer: "Not a single young person with whom I have had free and open conversation has been free from serious thoughts of suicide" (G. S. Hall, 1921, p. 144). Hall also found that, once over thirty, all of them suppressed and denied that they had ever had such thoughts.

Heathcote's educational work also overlaps with the psychotherapeutic concerns of Erik Erikson, as I suppose educational development must constantly be doing. This latter part of the romantic layer is also characterized by Erikson's "identity crisis":

I have called the major crisis of adolescence the *identity crisis;* it occurs in that period of the life cycle when each youth must forge for himself some central perspective and direction, some working unity, out of the effective remnants of his childhood and the hope of his anticipated adulthood, he must detect some meaningful resemblance between what he has come to see in

> himself and what his sharpened awareness tells him others
> judge and expect him to be (Erikson, 1962, p. 14).

To this I would like to attach the earlier qualification about the degree
of intensity suggested by "crisis," and perhaps wonder, along with
others, about how far the use of the generic "he" may focus more
precisely on typical male experience somewhat to the neglect of that of
females. If taken generally, though, the description seems relevant to
both—something I'll touch on in the conclusion of this chapter. Springhall adopts as a kind of irreducible definition of adolescence that it is
the period during which people learn who they are and what they really
feel (Springhall, 1986). This, however, is the outcome; during adolescence they are caught up in that great adventure, trying on and casting
off bits of selves, bits of behavior, styles of being. We can often say of
those we grew up with that we knew them when their characteristics
were affectations.

Developing with this self is a place to view the world from—a sense
of "I" that is behind one's eye. The source of this sense of one's self as
a viewpoint, as a separate, private, and unique vantage point, is another
feature of romantic understanding. I discussed earlier the arguments for
seeing this as a product of alphabetic literacy, or at least some of the
distinctive sense of private identity located behind the eyes is tied in
with the development of literacy, and with the visual access to records
and one's own and others' written thoughts.[3]

> Compound nouns beginning with *self* almost all apply readily
> to adolescents, immersed in a life stage of heightened
> narcissistic energy. The young person's absorption with his or
> her own growth, discovery, and pain are reason enough for
> proclaiming ours the century of the adolescent (Spacks, 1981,
> p. 9).

I think this is valid, but, I would also want to add that, since the
period of Romanticism, the capacities that constitute what I am calling
romantic understanding have been evident in public forms of expression.
That is, it is not so much adolescence that has become evident in a new

---

[3]The most dramatic claims on this are, as discussed earlier, Marshall McLuhan's (1962
and *passim*). He sees this sense of identity as an historical phenomenon whose period of
tenure is now coming to an end under the force of electronic media—the electronic
extension of our senses through the global village. Who knows? As Tom Wolfe noted
(1968) "What if he is right?"

way but it is romantic understanding that has become a part of most adults' consciousness. If this notion of layers of understanding is at all accurate, once the capacities of romantic understanding are learnt they do not "go away" as succeeding layers are learnt. Rather they coalesce with them, change their forms in some ways, but remain as a part of our developing consciousness. Also, I think many people do not get extensive mastery over the capacities of succeeding layers, and consequently a relatively unmediated romantic understanding characterizes their dominant ways of making sense of the world and of experience. The "yuppie syndrome" may be an instance of this, as may the fact that nearly all public media aim to engage this romantic kind of understanding. So ours is not so much the century of the adolescent, I think, as the century in which romantic understanding has dominated public media and discourse. This romantic impulse is, in itself, neither good nor bad, of course. It has given us the moon landing, *Dallas,* and Fascism—to isolate three rather purely romantic phenomena of our century.

The features of adolescence considered in this section are largely familiar from our earlier consideration of Romanticism. They color romantic understanding during the latter portion of this "layer," adding or heightening some characteristics to which we will have to attend in planning the curriculum and appropriate methods of teaching. In large part, all these features are connected with the development during puberty of what has been called our sixth sense—the growing consciousness of sex and love.

Boredom

It is useful to remember that this period of irregular bursts of energy, of growth, discovery, and pain, is also the period during which we seem most susceptible to boredom, and during which boredom tends to *hurt* more than at other periods of life. Boredom comes when the defences of our romantic associations with the transcendent are down, that is, when we have to do things or live through things on which our imaginations either cannot or do not get any hold. It is no secret that very many students identify this sense of arid boredom most readily with school: "After all, anything was better than school." The dulling effect of routine activities or of learning that lacks imaginative engagement generates what Wordsworth has described as "a universe of death" (Wordsworth, *The Prelude,* XIV, 1.160). I don't think this is a bad metaphor for boredom; it is a kind of intellectual death, it presages the death of something in us. We can handle some boredom, but too much can kill elements of our mental life. We see this too often in schools, where matters of the most intense fascination are unconnected with students' imaginative lives and so become merely dead ground for the students. During this layer I think we have to take particular care to ensure that boredom in students occurs as rarely as possible.

Conclusion

I have described romantic understanding as a cultural artifact. It seems to me to structure our consciousness by our interaction with the cultural world we grow into, which is prominently pervaded by forms of expression and communication that are consequences of literacy and print. The effects of electronic media may well have transforming effects on our consciousness, as McLuhan and others argue. But, as I noted above, these media seem, at least at the level of their "messages," to be intent on conforming with, and thus possibly confirming rather than undermining, current general kinds of understanding. No doubt the undermining and transforming may be going on and in future years will be evident to all. At present, however, it seems to me that the characteristics of romantic understanding remain clearly evident in most middle-school-aged students in Western countries.

The impact of puberty, which marks a decisive stage for most developmental theories, seems to play a significant but not major layer-shifting role in this scheme. Or, at least, while it plays a significant role, it seems to me that many important and distinctive characteristics span puberty. I suppose I could recognize the significance of the influence of puberty by inserting perhaps a mini-layer. I prefer just to distinguish the single major layer distinctions at about eight and fifteen, acknowledging puberty as I have done briefly above.

Another major source of differentiation to which I have paid only occasional attention is sexual. Here again, while I recognize clear differences in the ways our cultural environment impacts differently on male and female lives, I think the rather general cultural influences I am trying to chart affect males and females quite similarly. That is, males and females both seem to me subject to taking on the characteristics of romantic understanding in the process of becoming educated.

"Because in adolescence men and women alike typically confirm their sexual roles, writings about the young often convey with particular sharpness the dichotomies and inequalities between male and female experience" (Spacks, 1981, p. 18). Those sharply etched dichotomies with which we are all so familiar do not seem so vivid in terms of this scheme, though I recognize that some of the characteristics I have sketched are more common to males than to females and vice versa, and that the illustrative examples I have chosen are often less appropriate for males or for females. Given my own experience and imaginative life, I realize that my examples are probably more commonly and characteristically male. I don't think this implies that there is something about these layers that reflects male experience rather than female, but merely that I am less good at exemplifying female imaginative experience.

For example, it seems that social pressures through most of our culture's history have encouraged middle-class male imaginations to locate a sense of self that anticipated power and multiple opportunities. Such pressures persist, and our literature and institutions tend to support them. The social pressures on females growing into adolescence and searching for a definition of self have been much less encouraging. It was quite common (Spacks, 1981, Ch. 2), and no doubt this influence persists too, for girls to adopt a partial-play convention of being "Nobody." This is perhaps most vividly and articulately expressed and examined in Fanny Burney's diary, as in her angry reflection "Why must a *female* be made Nobody?" (Ellis, 1889, Vol. I, p. 5).

I am suggesting, then, that from an educational point of view some differences that loom large in our experience are not so important as some other changes, that often don't seem to loom much at all. It would be foolhardy to say that sex isn't very interesting from an educational point of view, so I'll be careful not to say it.

7
The romantic imagination and philosophic understanding

Introduction

This brief chapter is divided into three sections. In the first I will consider some of the distinctive forms of imaginative activity during the romantic layer and, as a preliminary to the later chapter on teaching, describe some implications for how we might go about engaging the romantic imagination when teaching. This will serve as a summary of a number of the features of romance considered in previous chapters. I don't intend it to be exhaustive so much as indicative of how the more general discussion of Romanticism and romance can lead fairly directly to principles for teaching. In the two following sections I want to begin pointing towards the next distinctive layer of understanding, which I am calling philosophic. First I will look at some of the limitations and problems with romantic understanding as a way of grasping and representing the world and experience, and some of the losses of mythic-layer capacities that its acquisition seems to entail. Then I will briefly sketch the main distinguishing characteristic of philosophic understanding. This will be of use for this book in that it will suggest a sense of direction for teaching and the curriculum during the last year or so of this layer. Year 9 will be designated a "transition" year in which a somewhat distinct curriculum will be designed in order to evoke and stimulate the capacities of philosophic understanding. I will describe that curriculum in the next volume, as I will describe the transitional year 4 curriculum to romantic understanding in this one.

The romantic imagination

I have emphasized a number of times that romantic understanding and its distinctive use of imagination is intimately tied in with the developing

164

capacities of rationality. Indeed, this book might be read in part as an attempted explication of Wordsworth's insight that imagination is "Reason in her most exalted mood" (Wordsworth, *The Prelude*, XIV, 1.192). There have obviously been fanciful, weak, and whimsical strains to Romanticism, but at its core, especially evident in the work of the great English poets, Blake, Coleridge, Wordsworth, Keats, Shelley and Byron, is the belief that "the imagination stands in some essential relation to truth and reality, and they were at pains to make their poetry pay attention to them" (Bowra, 1961, p. 5).

Among their contributions to our culture and potentially to each student's educational experience is a sense and use of the imagination that can enlarge our perception of the everyday world around us and enrich our experience within it. We can get some better inkling of their contribution to the imagination's powers if we recall the sense of it, and the range of activity assumed appropriate for the imagination, before their time. Bacon's *Advancement of Learning* or Addison's essays on Imagination in the *Spectator* represent it largely as a faculty that can throw an ornamental gloss over objects in the world, and so provide us with an additional, if relatively superficial, pleasure in them. Addison, for example, concludes that "The pleasures of the imagination, taken in their full extent, are not so gross as those of sense, nor so refined as those of the understanding" (*Spectator*, Monday, June 23rd, 1712). Understanding, after all, requires "labour of the brain," whereas imagination easily delights and "bestows charms," offering "a kind of refreshment" (*ibid.*).

How different is such a view from that expressed by Coleridge: "The primary IMAGINATION I hold to be the living Power and prime Agent of all human Perception, and as a repetition in the finite mind of the eternal act of creation in the infinite I AM" (Coleridge, 1907, Vol. I, p. 202). In the Romantics' view, the imagination was the source and center of all creative power in human beings, and it was a power of particular value in exposing a world of greater meaning than was accessible to the senses locked in with conventional thinking. As Bowra puts it:

> So far from thinking the imagination deals with the non-
> existent, they insist that it reveals an important kind of truth.
> They believe that when it is at work it sees things to which the
> ordinary intelligence is blind and that it is intimately connected
> with a special insight or perception or intuition. Indeed,
> imagination and insight are in fact inseparable and form for all
> practical purposes a single faculty. Insight both awakens the

imagination to work and is in turn sharpened by it when it is at work (Bowra, 1961, p. 7).

Coleridge saw the strength of Wordsworth's imagination as due to "the union of deep feeling with profound thought" (Coleridge, 1907, Vol. I, p. 59), and it is this combination, this union, that gives the characteristic quality to the romantic imagination at its best. So it is the union of feeling and (rational) thought that we have to stimulate in order to enable students to develop romantic understanding. Let me pick up here, then, some of the features, qualities or orientations that can stimulate the romantic imagination and contribute to the development of Romantic understanding. The reason for so emphasizing the imagination is given in the previous chapter where I argue that all learning that is to be of *educational* value seems necessarily to involve an imaginative—finite creative—component. The imagination is the making, composing, vivifying power that is required if the student is to reconstitute codes into living knowledge.

Teaching that aims, then, to engage and stimulate imagination in this layer might wisely include some of the following characteristics:

Affective orientation

Students' imaginations tend to be more readily engaged by materials that are organized and presented so that they not only convey information but also involve students affectively or emotionally. The most common and powerful technique that enables us to achieve this is to organize the information on a story framework. This does not necessarily mean telling a fictional story; rather, the teacher needs to structure the information using some of the principles that make stories so engaging. I have earlier discussed some of the ways in which this might be done, and have described components of a story framework with various examples in the previous volume. Romance entails. a perspective that is colored by affective responses to what we are dealing with. Even the most purely logical tasks, such as list manipulation or flowcharting, can be made affectively engaging by being situated in a wider context that is itself romantic. We can, for example, approach the austerity and practical utility of mathematical manipulations from the romantic perspective, as on the human story of the development of this mysteriously extending web of mathematical knowledge. This context, once decisively generated in students' understanding, can then become quite unobtrusive, called forward only occasionally, reinforced as it were, to keep alive students' affective orientation to mathematics.

Obviously teachers can best stimulate imagination by first identifying what they themselves find affectively engaging about the topic at hand. Indeed, this seems to me a first essential. If teachers cannot locate in themselves an affective response to the material, then they have little hope of being able to engage students in it.

The Heroic

This does not mean teaching about male heroes performing superhuman deeds. But the quality of heroism is an effective catcher of our imaginations, and particularly in the middle-school years. We create a sense of the heroic when we emphasize those qualities that overcome the everyday constraints that hem us in. Heroic qualities can be found in anything; they need not be located only in people acting or suffering. An institution can embody heroic qualities. Even a plant can be seen as heroic, as when we focus on, say, a particular weed's tenacity in maintaining itself in hostile conditions. A rock formation can be "heroized" by focusing on its stability, its stubbornness, or its towering strength and sheer persistence. This "heroizing" of whatever we wish to engage students' imaginations in does not necessarily involve falsification; rather it is a matter of emphasizing those qualities of the chosen topic that transcend the everyday and conventional sense we might unthinkingly hold about them. If one brings such transcendent qualities to the fore, one is more likely to engage students' imaginations.

Detail and distance

Shifting perspectives provides another potential stimulant to imaginative engagement in a topic. Teachers might take an opportunity in a lesson or unit to pursue some element in minute detail and also to stand back and see the whole distantly in a wider context. Remember how common it is for people to enjoy looking through microscopes and telescopes when they get a chance. Remember, too, that we tend not to want to keep looking through them for very long periods, but just enough to get a different and romantic perspective on the material.

The exotic, wonder, and awe

One of the more accessible and imaginatively stimulating books—if only in a relatively trivial way—is *The Guinness Book of Records*. One reason I have given for its success in this regard is that it deals with the extremes of reality: the biggest, the smallest, the fastest, the slowest, and, with regard to a huge range of human achievements, human experience, and the natural world, the most exotic, bizarre, and strange. Teachers are commonly told to begin with what students find most familiar. If we want to engage their imaginations, beginning with what is most exotic and unfamiliar seems at least as good a principle, and— I have argued—generally a principle much better in keeping with the mental lives of students of middle-school age. As all sorts of things can be heroic, so everything is potentially strange and exotic if one can only see it in the right light. Even the most commonplace features of our environment can be seen as the products of amazing ingenuity, struggles, natural forces, and persisting energy. This is not to suggest that our lessons should induce incessant neuron-popping excitement, but that teachers might be attentive to some exotic features in the materials in which they hope to engage students' imaginations.

Relatedly, students' imaginations are stimulated and engaged by the wonderful. And, again, everything we look upon is wonderful, in one light or another. The artistry of teaching is expressed in being able to make evident to students some sense of what is wonderful about whatever material is being dealt with (Rubin, 1985). Wonder is a kind of surprise mingled with admiration or curiosity or bewilderment (suggests the Oxford English Dictionary). A significant feature of wonder is the combination of exclusive attention to the object of wonder and the desire to know more about it, either because there is something rare and puzzling about it or because it is intrinsically fascinating. Here, too, the teacher will sensibly not seek to stimulate incessant wonder in students, creating wonder-addicts who can then not bear to deal with more routine learning. Rather, pointing up some features of a topic that can stimulate students' sense of wonder is occasionally useful in keeping their imaginations engaged while learning.

Similarly teachers might be attentive to stimulating a sense of awe about some aspect of the subject matter to be learned. Awe is the emotion resulting from the perception of something mysterious underlying the everydayness of things. It is an important ingredient in the stimulation and development of the romantic imagination, and it can be evoked at any point when one can show a glimpse of some mystery underlying what might normally be taken for granted. Attached to awe is a hint of fear: basically, I think, a fear that our routine ways of making sense of the world and experience are ultimately inadequate, and that our claims to secure knowledge are either groundless or wildly mistaken. The stimulation of a sense of awe seems to me of considerable educational importance; it can provide a source of proper humility about the intellectual grasp we gain on reality and about our claims to knowledge. This sense of awe, I will in a later volume argue, is one of the roots of irony—the dissolver of certainties. Awe is often associated with religious experience—the sudden sense of something mysterious and quite other than the routines of church going or religious services. It comes to some people as a kind of conversion experience. Though it is perhaps most commonly referred to in a religious context, awe seems to me to be equally appropriately a quite secular emotion, and appropriately stimulated in educational contexts. And again, one would not want lessons that constantly induce awe-struck numbness, but occasional hints of it will stimulate imaginative engagements with subject matter.

I have prudently omitted from this sub-heading another colleague of the exotic, wonder, and awe, and I might be more prudent simply to ignore it here. But, as you can see, I am being imprudent enough to discuss a related stimulant of students' imaginations in the relatively peaceful, routine, socially-quite-well-disciplined democracies of the West. That is, horror. Horror, like awe, is an emotion induced by the threatened breakdown of the sustaining intellectual frameworks of our lives. Those frameworks seem so secure to typical early adolescents that our psychic preparation for the emergencies of their breakdown finds an attraction to horror. My concern about imprudence here is that some careless reader may think that my mentioning this commonplace of students' mental lives means that I am recommending lessons and units that induce crawling horror and screaming terror for the average classroom. Careful readers will, I trust, note that I do not do this. Rather I want to draw attention to the fact of the immense attraction horror has to typical students in this age period. It is (I clearly believe) no coincidence that Mary Shelley, wife of the romantic poet, wrote *Frankenstein,* or that horror is a significant element of romantic literature. The only conclusion I would draw from this observation is that the protective sanitizing of everything permitted to enter the classroom is far more likely to be psychologically damaging than recognizing, particularly in placid and peaceful times and places, the therapeutic role of horror. Perhaps this might mean no more than being more tolerant of literature that includes horrific elements, and recognizing that horror, too, is a stimulant of the imagination. And, of course, one must be cautious about the potential effects of any of the above on students who may be unstable in one way or another. That caution is misguided, however, it seems to me, if it goes to the extreme of ignoring the potential of the exotic, wonder, awe, and horror in stimulating the imagination.

Literal thinking

Graphic display and organization of aspects of the world and of experience can be imaginatively engaging as they build some of the basic skills of rationality. Converting one's routines into flowcharts for inspection, then manipulating them in this symbolic form, or making and manipulating lists, or reflecting on and trying to sort out seemingly contradictory proverbs, and so on, can all stimulate imaginative activity. This is a topic on which educational discourse is rich and sophisticated, so I need add little here. Perhaps the one item worth inferring from the earlier chapters is that these kinds of intellectual activities can often be imaginatively enhanced for students if they are embedded in wider narrative contexts.

Humanizing knowledge

The imagination helps to grasp and reconstitute knowledge more readily if it is embedded in contexts of human emotion, human struggles, hopes, and fears. Whatever material is being taught has a place in human lives and human purposes. By seeing knowledge as meaningful in others' lives, students can get a better imaginative sense of its potential meaning for them. I have written at length about this above, but I might mention a concomitant here in preparation for the chapter on teaching: that is, that the knowledge will be meaningful to students and engage their imaginations more fully if it is clear that the teachers find it meaningful in their own lives and are imaginatively engaged by it. This is not, of course, an iron law. But is does suggest strongly that a part of planning teaching needs to be teachers' location of the imaginative meaning of the topic in their own lives. If nothing like this can be located, it seems more likely than not that the lesson or unit will mean nothing much to the students, nor will it stimulate their imaginations. So "humanizing knowledge" might be read in two senses; one, concerning the context of human lives in which the content is embedded and, two, concerning its place in the imaginative life of the teacher.

Some limitations of romantic understanding

Central to Romanticism, romance, and romantic understanding is the development of a particular use of the imagination, some characteristics of which I have tried to describe in previous chapters. In Wordsworth, this romantic conception of the imagination was tied to everyday reality, and enabled him to see how it could indeed be reason working in its most exalted mood. Imagination and reason consequently could be conceived as jointly developing together. And it is this insight, this achievement of Wordsworth's and of other Romantics that seems to me one of the greatest intellectual contributions Romanticism has made to the cultural life of the West, and one which it seems to me is both possible and desirable for students to recapitulate in their education.

Commonly, no doubt because many of the Romantics saw themselves as reacting against what they considered the excessive and desiccated rationality of the neo-classical Enlightenment, they understood imagination as the faculty that could liberate people from dull reason, and enable them to transcend its earthy bounds. They assumed the imagination was able to create its own reality and make its own reasons. We can identify a tendency in Romanticism and romance to undervalue rationality and logic—what the Romantics often called "Philosophy." So Blake refers to "Lame Philosophy," and Keats to "cold philosophy" and Wordsworth's characterization of mental life after the "visionary gleam" of imagination-rich youth is past is "the years that bring the philosophic mind." We can see the tendency in even some of the most exalted romantic poetry:

> Weave a circle round him thrice
> And close your eyes with holy dread
> For he on honey-dew hath fed
> And drunk the milk of paradise.
>
> (ll.51–54)

So Coleridge's "Kubla Khan" catches with immense imaginative verve the mystery and magic that is an important constituent of romance. It is, of course, splendid; wonderful to recite and to listen to. But it really doesn't bear very much *thinking* about. Honey-dew, one suspects, *sounds* a great deal better than it tastes—as others have observed before me.

The problem with unfettering the imagination becomes clear when we attend to what it is being unfettered from. Too often it is from reality, and from the intellectual tools forged within rationality for attempting to grasp reality. The abstract languages of science, mathematics, logic, and philosophy were taken by too many Romantics as a kind of enemy. Consequently another of the legacies of Romanticism to modern Western culture is a sense or suspicion that reason and imagination are somehow necessarily at odds; that we inhabit a world of two cultures not one (Snow, 1963). It is useful to remember that this sense of opposition, between imagination and reason, between arts and sciences, is not common in the Renaissance or in the greatest figures of the Enlightenment and Romanticism—perhaps most obviously they were harmoniously integrated in Goethe. Certainly Plato helped to prepare for such a dichotomy, but the sense of romance that we have inherited from Romanticism has underscored it, in ways that have been neither educationally nor socially beneficial. One purpose of this book is to emphasize as clearly as I can Bowra's point that: "there is no external or necessary quarrel between abstractions and imaginative vision" (Bowra, 1961, p. 289). Indeed, I would go further and suggest that an education that stimulates and develops either one at the expense of the other is necessarily defective. Abstraction and imaginative vision together constitute the first major step in becoming educated in a literate culture.

Similarly, the romantic stimulation of awe and of the sense of the mysterious, while at their best they enrich everyday experience and perception, can also be trivialized and become a technique or affectation, encouraging vacuous wonder. The sense of the numinous, of the mystery of things, can be a source of imaginative energy and even religious experience, but it is also prone to ineffectual vagueness. It is particularly evident in the displacement of thought and articulate expression by a language of impenetrable, mysterious, and ineffably vague claims. With such a language we can easily fool ourselves and often others too that we are expressing profundities that mere words can only haltingly approach. The best exploitation of this weakness of romance, as Bowra wickedly points out, is Edward Lear's nonsense poetry. But Bowra was perhaps not familiar with the outpourings of the "mystical poetry" and myth-entranced experiences that sold in millions of copies of during the sixties in the United States. Today we see this weakness of romance turned into a major industry—television religiosity, mysteries of the universe, astrology, tabloid sensations, and so on. Romantic understanding, then, when inadequately stimulated and developed, is particularly prone to whimsy, sentimentality, weak mysticism, and high-sounding vacuousness taking the proper place of reason.

Another kind of failure to which an inadequately developed romantic understanding seems particularly prone is cynicism. Cynicism, it seems to me, is inherently romantic, but it is decaying romance—too-literal romance undermined by experience. No doubt there are endless causes of cynicism, but one that is relevant here seems to result from making romantic associations with a person, institution, or object rather than with the transcendent qualities that these are seen to embody. That is, to take a simple example, instead of associating with the transcendent qualities of courage and integrity—which students recognize in a particular person and identify as burgeoning within themselves—they form the association directly with the particular person and with everything about him or her. They value the person, whether pop-star or politician or religious leader or whatever, as human perfection, rather than as an exemplar of certain qualities which the students also share, in however embryonic a form. The person, not the transcendent quality, forms the romantic object of association. The later realization that the person is not all perfection, that perhaps the romantic object has clay feet, or a clay head, can lead to a kind of disillusionment that undermines faith in any kind of romantic association. What is left is cynicism—the belief that there are no transcendent objects worthy of association. If, more properly, the romantic association was made with the transcendent human quality, the realization that a particular person did not adequately represent it does not undermine faith that such qualities can exist in some people, and, most importantly, it does not undermine faith that such qualities can exist in oneself. The mark of the cynic is less the lack of respect for, or faith in, others' transcendent qualities than the belief that such things do not exist and, therefore of course, cannot exist in themselves.

Among the various capacities I have tried to sketch as constituting romantic understanding I have described the ability to generate "momentary fictions" that highlight certain features of the world and ascribe to them motives and emotions. This highlighting I have described as an important technique for vivifying knowledge and experience and for helping to make them more engaging and meaningful. The potential limitation of this vivifying capacity is the suppression of whatever is not vivified. A romantic view of history, for example, tends to highlight great figures and dramatic events. It is indeed the kind of historical sense that most Western adults carry with them after their schooling, when they have forgotten most of the details that initially generated it. It begins with the ancient civilizations of Mesopotamia, takes in the pyramids and pauses for the birth of democracy amidst the glory that was Greece. Then there was Alexander and his conquests. There are then a few blank centuries until Julius Caesar came along and the Roman legions carved out a huge empire and built roads and towns, and had a few colorful early emperors, but then an anonymous decline, leaving even more blank centuries until the building of the cathedrals and then the Renaissance, and so on. This is a slightly silly way of putting it, of course, but it describes the ways in which history becomes a story with particular highlights and large *lacunae*. (The *lacunae* tend to include pretty much everything that happened everywhere in the world apart from Europe and its colonies.) One part of the potential limitation of this romantic vivification of history lies in the *lacunae*. Another part lies in the lack of any systematic grasp of history beyond that represented by the generally progressive story line. A systematic conception of history would not leave such *lacunae* because all of history would be required to make up, or be accounted for, in whatever system was being constructed.

One person's *lacuna,* of course, is another person's highlight. I don't want to suggest that this characteristic of romantic understanding necessarily prevents people from attending romantically to what used, romantically, to be called the Dark Ages. The tendency, however, is to skip over such centuries, seeing them just as barbarians milling about, doing nothing of particular interest. But one *could* focus romantically on precisely such topics, highlighting the dramatic movements of peoples, the details of excavations and what we have learned about their daily lives and arts and crafts. It could become like one of those obsessive hobbies, and one can easily imagine some twelve-year-old with huge maps on a wall marking burial sites and excavated settlements, or photographs of objects of daily use or arts, and so on. To such a person perhaps the Renaissance or High Middle Ages are a bore.

Romantic understanding, then, is often just a bit too susceptible to glitter and sparkle of the kind that the imagination can be trained to generate. While praising Wordsworth, Coleridge seems always to go that little way beyond the toughness and restraint that one finds in Wordsworth and in the direction of "the depth and height of the ideal world . . . of which, for the common view, custom had bedimmed all the lustre, had dried up the sparkle and the dew drops" (Coleridge, 1907, Vol. I, p. 59). Coleridge is clear and forceful on this value of the romantic imagination as the faculty that can remove the dulling effects of custom on our perception and thinking, but too much lustre and sparkle can also dazzle us, and blind us to what is not easily made lustrous. These potential weaknesses of romance hint at some of the losses of mythic layer capacities that the development of romantic understanding may bring about. The sense of reality that intrudes into child-hood fantasy and that I have associated with the onset of romantic understanding has often been taken as reflected in the loss of Eden. The intellectual security of childhood is undone with the realization of an autonomous world. We might rapidly build defences, without transcendent associations and so on, but some fundamental shift takes place in that period of transition that separates us from the garden of Eden. The immediacy of the natural world is threatened too. We can build defenses and try to recapture that immediacy in romantic wonder, but there is ultimately no going home again; we know, where'er we go "That there hath passed away a glory from the earth"—as Wordsworth so perfectly puts it.

The development of the sense-making techniques of rationality has traditionally been seen in some imprecise way as in conflict with the imaginative life of the mythic-layer child. Because of the practical utility of rationality it has been calculated as expedient to sacrifice to its better development some imaginative potential. This sense of conflict between rationality and imagination has a long history in the West, and the necessity of sacrificing the latter to the former has been a traditional theme. One of Descartes's disciples, Nicholas Malebranche (1638–1715) articulated this opposition very clearly in his *The Search for Truth*. This is "a treatise which discusses the senses, the imagination, and the passions as obstacles to the attainment of the truth" (Burke, 1985, p. 16). Malebranche offers us, instead of these, a "rational" system based on mathematics for making proper sense of the world and of experience. This opposition between reason and imagination, I have been busy arguing, is a false one, but it has played a powerful part in Western education.

Perhaps the grosser claim that education into rationality requires the curbing of imagination and emotions is less prominent today. That particular division of human beings into such distinct warring parts, the baser of which constantly threatens to cloud the pure seeing mind, is an image of human functioning that no longer carries so much authority. But Descartes' dichotomizing has left its ramified residue throughout educational discourse. Social utility, we are commonly told, for example, demands that more time be given to practical, vocationally useful subjects, even if this comes at the expense of "the arts."

Overcoming the dichotomy does not require that we fight for more time for "the arts" against more socially useful subjects. Rather, seeing the falseness of the dichotomy enables us to see that the task at hand is to teach the "practical subjects" so that they stimulate and develop the imagination, and are themselves made "arts" by having imagination injected into them. It is this coalescing of rational techniques and imagination that is at the heart of romantic understanding.

When middle-school education is seen in a modern Malebranche-fashion as the development of rational capacities distinct from romance the losses of mythic-layer capacities can be fairly catastrophic. We are too familiar with the dulling that so commonly accompanies students into their fourth and fifth years of schooling. I suspect that even with the greatest sensitivity, there will be some loss of mythic-layer capacities. The development of romantic wonder, for example, seems a replacement for, or a shadow of, the lost sense of magic. Rationality is compatible with wonder—indeed, I have argued, requires it for fullest development—but the vivid edge of magic that we had access to as young children is dulled.

The tightening of our literal grasp over the world and experience seems inevitably to entail some weakening of our metaphoric grasp. The ease with which young children slide across metaphoric connections is not entirely compatible with training in the building of systematic logical connections. They are obviously not incompatible, and ideally they can continue to feed each other's further development, but that Ariel-like fluidity of the child's thinking—which is not practically or materially productive—seems inevitably somewhat constrained by the development of the techniques of literal thought.

One task of education in this scheme, then, is not just to maximize educational gains but also to minimize educational losses. Too often we ignore the potential losses because we focus exclusively on the gains involved in learning, and particularly on those gains that lead to practical control over the world. Important to this scheme is the need to be sensitive to the losses that contingently or possibly necessarily accompany the major educational gains. We can hope to minimize the losses that are common during the acquisition of romantic understanding only if we are sensitive to them.

Towards philosophic understanding

Coalescing the values and the capacities of romantic understanding with techniques that provide protection against its potential weaknesses leads us into the next layer, which I am calling philosophic understanding.

One of the main realizations that heralds the development of philosophic understanding is the sense that all the lustrous and sparkling knowledge we have of the world and of experience is connected. In the romantic layer, of course, the student is aware that all the bright bits and pieces of knowledge are in some ultimate sense about the one world we inhabit, but the connections among the parts are not matters of much urgency. Students tend to connect themselves with particular areas of engagement directly, by means of romantic associations. Two closely related processes seem to occur: students realize that the world is a complex interconnected unit of some kind and that they are a part of it; they are no longer transcendent players but are agents in complex processes.

Let me try to clarify this distinction by turning again to the example of history. I have characterized the romantic understanding of history as a kind of story with vivid incidents and characters and with *lacunae* whose relevance to the overall story is at best uncertain. The philosophic understanding of history is of a single complex process of causal chains and networks. Instead of retaining a romantic transcendence over history, associating with the great and the good, the noble and heroic, "philosophic" students realize that they are a part of the single historical process, caught in it, and, in some significant ways, determined by it.

Similarly students begin to realize that their very "selves" are determined not as a result of their romantic predilections, choices, and associations, but by the laws of history, of human psychology, of the natural world, of social organization, and of all the general schemes that are evident working in our lives and in the world we inhabit. One result of this realization is that we reorient intellectual attention somewhat, and direct it energetically to these general, or "philosophic," schemes. We can see an index of this reorientation, this engagement with a somewhat distinct layer of understanding, in the relatively sudden appearance in students' vocabularies, and in their intellectual engagements, of such very general concepts as "society," "culture," "evolution," "human nature," and so on. Politics, economics, anthropology, psychology, at least in terms of their most general questions, become areas of quickened interest.

Now perhaps I should emphasize, again, that I am not trying to articulate a developmental theory. I am not claiming that at about age fifteen or sixteen this process occurs as a result of some inner psychological imperatives. For very many people in Western culture it does not happen at all, or only in the most marginal fashion. What I am trying to characterize are some of the constraints that affect the process of becoming educated in Western culture. (I will elaborate on this in the next chapter.) Many people do not become extensively educated. Many studies have shown that average performances in a range of schooled subjects, like math, general science, historical knowledge, indicate that the general adult population scores at about a grade eight level. Most adults in Western societies do not know how to subtract fractions, and division of fractions, which nearly every student studies at school, is a truly arcane accomplishment among Western adults. Analogously, the kinds of intellectual engagements and capacities of most adults in Western societies can, I think uncontentiously, be characterized as what I am calling romantic. Literacy seems to encourage this range of intellectual engagements and affective responses to the world and to experience. The first two layers I have tried to characterize are relatively uncomplicated, in that the cultural techniques that are learned are so pervasive that they fairly routinely carry the schooled child from mythic to romantic understanding. This is less true for philosophic understanding; its techniques are pervasive only in certain areas of Western cultural life and do not provide the same stimulation to all segments of society. This is a topic which must wait for the chapter on theory in the next volume, but it seems important to mention it here lest readers think that their not observing these "philosophic" characteristics clicking into place in all fifteen or sixteen year olds counts against the validity of this scheme. (It may be invalid for any number of reasons, but that particular observation is irrelevant to its claims.)

The fading of one's romantic "self," and romanticized identity is again no doubt an aspect of the identity crisis Erikson discusses. One of the intellectual, psychological, and emotional challenges students face is to establish conceptions of themselves as parts of general natural, social, historical, and other, processes. The drive to establish a secure sense of identity leads to a desire to understand how these general processes work. A major defining characteristic of philosophic understanding, then, is the search for *the* truth about human psychology, for *the* laws of historical change and development, for *the* truth about how societies function, and so on. That is, in the philosophic layer, students' focus is on the *general laws* whereby the world works.

What we see in this significant transition in kinds of understanding is not a further expansion "outwards" in any meaningful sense. Rather, if romantic understanding has established a sense of the limits of reality, a sense of the scope and scale of the world and of experience, and their more dramatic features, then philosophic understanding turns inward, as it were, and conducts a general and systematic survey of what romantic understanding has outlined. Students in the philosophic layer work rather like intellectual cartographers, trying to develop accurate maps of whatever phenomena make up their world and experience. The most evident of these maps are ideologies and metaphysical schemes, which philosophic-layer students begin to adopt and adapt. These schemes provide fixed coordinates by means of which all the particular knowledge is located and given meaning.

To revert to history again to clarify this point: the many particulars that students learned during the romantic layer, and which were made meaningful by romantic associations, now threaten to be merely chaotic bits and pieces littering the mental landscape. The philosophic impulse is to seek some general scheme that can organize them all and make sense of them as a part of some process. Thus a student in this layer might be attracted to an ideology such as is available in an unsophisticated Marxism, for example. It provides the student with an enormously general scheme that can not only organize all the particular historical knowledge the student has, but can reduce its diversity into a clear and relatively simple process. Once such an ideology is in place, once one knows the laws of history, the details can all be swept up, slotted into the general scheme, and so made newly meaningful. All that knowledge about knights and about crop rotation and about castles, popes, and Renaissance artists is suddenly endowed with a new meaning as the decay of feudalism and the rise of the bourgeoisie. That is, the *meaning* of particular knowledge during this layer is most commonly derived *primarily* from its place within some general scheme. A side-effect of this pursuit of meaning via the general is most commonly the final falling away from the obsessive hobbies and collecting activities that are common in the romantic layer.

While I have tried here to sketch the main characteristic of philosophic understanding by contrasting it with forms of romantic understanding, I will be concerned to show in the next volume that the capacities of romantic understanding are not "left behind," but can be, and properly are, coalesced into philosophic understanding as it develops. They remain a part of us, accessible for use, but gradually coalescing with a new layer of capacities. As with each earlier layer, I will argue that this is not all a process of gains. There are losses too, and the educational task is to attend carefully to minimizing mythic- and romantic-layer losses while evoking, stimulating, and developing the capacities of philosophic understanding.

Conclusion

The task now is to consider what kind of curriculum and teaching practices can best help to evoke, stimulate, and develop abstraction and imaginative vision together, to generate romantic understanding. Before turning to this task, however, because this scheme is somewhat atypical in current educational discourse, we might usefully take a break here and consider the nature of this scheme and the support there might be for it. What is a "cultural recapitulation" scheme, after all?

8
Cultural recapitulation: some comments on theory

Introduction

In this chapter I will try both to make clear in what sense this scheme is recapitulationary and to justify such a scheme. I will try to show *what* is being recapitulated, on what the scheme rests, and how it respects logical and psychological constraints. I need to show in addition, or as a part of achieving the above, how a recapitulation scheme can coalesce the Platonic end-focused and Rousseauian present-ripening insights. So this chapter will, as it were, withdraw a little from the particular concerns of students' thinking and consider some aspects of the scheme in general. Much of this chapter will echo Volume One in which I discuss the overall scheme. There are, however, a number of changes and additions. The main addition is a section on A. N. Whitehead's conception of romance as a stage in educational development. I will consider how this is like and unlike the conception of romantic understanding I have been articulating above.

The Platonic and Rousseauian insights have also implied distinctive ideas about what one needs to do in order to study education effectively. The Platonic tradition in the main has assumed that conceptual clarity about the aims and meaning of education, the nature of knowledge, and the language of pedagogical discourse will take us a considerable way. The Rousseauian emphasis on the student and on nature as our guide has supported the assumption that the more we can discover about the nature of the student, about how students learn, are motivated and develop, and so on, the better able we will be to educate more effectively. That is, the two major educational ideas have each encouraged somewhat distinct approaches to dealing with educational problems. These ideas are realized in the structure of typical departments of education in colleges and universities across the world. That education is full of conceptual and empirical problems seems self-evident. By and large the former have tended to be the domain of philosophers of education and the latter the domain of psychologists of education. The research of these two groups should complement each other, of course, the former providing the conceptual clarity that permits the latter to conduct more precise empirical investigations. But the products of these two branches of research have had as much difficulty in coming easily together as have the two great educational insights from which they have sprung.

I mention current research because this scheme runs somewhat aslant of prevailing assumptions about how one can support an educational program. The distinction between conceptual and empirical questions is a very easy one to hold theoretically, and it is also much exercised as a kind of demarcation line between philosophers' and psychologists' areas of expertise. The trouble with education as an area of study is that empirical and conceptual issues are knotted up in ways that make it very difficult to get anywhere by addressing one or the other separately and, for reasons I will discuss below, they have difficulty coming together. This scheme involves an attempt to bring together the Platonic and Rousseauian insights in some coherent way, and so will involve bringing together, in at least one important sense, conceptual and empirical considerations.

Consider, for example, how A. V. Kelly, in one of the clearer general curriculum textbooks, discusses how aspects of the Platonic and Rousseauian insights are to interact:

> While it is true that understanding cannot be developed in isolation from bodies of knowledge, it does not follow that decisions about the knowledge content of the curriculum should or must be made first. On the contrary, it suggests rather that they are secondary considerations. We need first to be aware of the kinds of intellectual capacity we are concerned to promote in pupils and, only then, to make decisions about the kinds of content they must be initiated into in order to develop these capacities (Kelly, 1982, p. 58)[1]

The problem with Kelly's formulation, I think, is that it presupposes that there are educationally meaningful ways of characterizing intellectual capacities apart from the kinds of contents that can evoke and realize

---

[1] I use this quotation in part because I used to think it expresses precisely how we should go about determining content. But increasingly I see it as still carrying an echo of the educationally unfruitful dichotomizing of mind and knowledge.

them. The scheme I am elaborating in this essay attempts to overcome the dichotomy, and to bring together intellectual capacities and knowledge by focusing on the sense-making capacities available in our culture.

Some radical distinction between mind and knowledge is presupposed if one is doing psychological or philosophical research, as it is if one is considering education from a predominantly Rousseauian or Platonic perspective. Or rather, one might say, because education is so pervasively thought about in terms of those perspectives, that distinction is taken for granted in the way educational problems, and research on them, are conceptualized. If one wants to bring those perspectives together, an instrument and effect will be to suppress the importance of the distinction between minds and knowledge, and to focus instead on cultural capacities. So I am not, on the one hand, trying to characterize some "natural psychological reality, in terms of which we must understand the development of knowledge" (Piaget, 1964, p. 9) as the most Rousseauian of psychologists puts it. Nor am I, on the other hand, trying to describe how knowledge is structured and accumulates in logical sequences. Rather, I am concerned with how the sense-making capacities of a particular culture can be stimulated and developed in the individual within the constraints of what is logically and psychologically possible. Another, hardly innocent, way of putting it is to say that my focus is on the Vygotskian "interlacement" of knowledge, psychological development, and cultural history.[2]

The apparent oddity of trying to coalesce considerations of mind and knowledge might be mitigated a little by reflecting on how difficult that distinction is to sustain in practice anyway. We might recall the problems involved in the various attempts to characterize minds and knowledge separately. We know minds almost entirely by what they do with knowledge—the mind is like a transparent organism whose structures only become visible when it ingests the dye of knowledge, but then it has proven immensely difficult to establish whether whatever structures we can make out are a function or property of the mind or of the knowledge. Similarly, we need to remember that we store data or codes, not knowl-

---

[2]This way of putting it raises the ghost of Vygotsky but acknowledges it only in passing. His insistence on considering cultural history and its present social effects on the child as a necessary element for understanding individual development is clearly in tune with this scheme, though his hostility to recapitulation equally clearly is not. I will leave these issues for a later volume, when there will be more material available to address them. This is hardly innocent also because of the undeveloped undercurrent of skepticism about programs of research that pursue psychological questions independently of epistemology, and vice versa; this explicitly educational scheme attempts a fruitful combination of a kind perhaps more widely interesting than its present educational concerns might suggest.

edge, in books and computers—the only proper home of knowledge is a human mind and its forms in there are tied up with emotions, imagination, intentions, and all kinds of things that make it much less accessible to precise analysis than are external data. So my attempt to bring considerations of mind and knowledge, empirical and conceptual concerns, together is not necessarily an exotic straining to overcome some invariably fruitful distinction. It is enormously complicated to distinguish between them in practice. This is not to argue that such a distinction cannot be usefully made, just that from an educational perspective it is not so important a distinction as the polarizing of the Platonic and Rousseauian insights have encouraged us to accept. What I am trying to show is that one can get a better grasp on education by coalescing considerations of mind and knowledge in terms of sense-making capacities than one can by approaching education as involving more or less distinct sets of empirical and conceptual questions.

A neat metaphor used by some cognitive psychologists is that the brain is a computer and the mind is the program it is running. It might clarify one part of my point—though, as is the common case with metaphors, run the risk of confusing others—to suggest that the brain is a computer and our culture is the program it is running.

Recapitulating recapitulationism

The superficial attraction of recapitulation theories for educationalists is fairly obvious. We can readily characterize the history of our cultural development and individual educational development in similar terms. Becoming educated is in significant part a matter of accumulating the most valuable capacities whose initial creation is our cultural history. Also, a causal sequence is evident, or interpretable, in our cultural history. Certain things are discovered, invented, or made possible as a result of prior things having been discovered, invented, or made possible.[3] We can see a semblance at least of logical progression from a Ptolemaic to an Einsteinian universe, from crude ethnocentric self-glorifying stories about one's ancestors to sophisticated modern historiography, and so on. These developmental sequences seem logical in

---

[3]For examples of such an argument see James Burke's popular television series and associated book *Connections* (Burke, 1978). See also *Art and Illusion* (Gombrich, 1960) and *Mimesis* (Auerbach, 1955).

perhaps a loose sense, but it is a sense that has constantly suggested some imprecise guidance to the curriculum designer.

Alternatively, or perhaps additionally, one can see in these sequences of discovery and invention the product of certain psychological predispositions. Given the nature of human cognition, we have of necessity had to construct human culture in these general sequences. It is psychologically necessary that we begin writing history from an ego-centric view, progress to an ethno-centric view, and then, maturing historiographically, try to describe things as they were. (This kind of argument, using Piaget's theory as its basis, has been made by Hallpike in *The Foundations of Primitive Thought,* 1979).

That is, whenever we describe our cultural history as some kind of causal sequence, which one can hardly avoid, we are asserting a logical and/or psychological underpinning to the scheme. If there are logical entailments or psychological predispositions or both underlying the process of our cultural development, then a curriculum sequence recapitulating cultural history will be based on that logical sequence or those psychological predispositions or both. And as logic and/or nature are attractive bases for a curriculum, so recapitulation schemes have an obvious attraction.

Some of the problems with this generally plausible principle become quickly apparent when we try to work out detailed curricula from it. Also, despite its general plausibility, recapitulation ideas tend to be little regarded today because of the particular and, so it seems at this remove, obtuse interpretations of them that were implemented towards the end of the last century and early in this one. Most commonly a marriage of Rousseauian and Darwinian ideas led to the belief that evolutionary theory provided nature's guidance for the curriculum. G. Stanley Hall claimed that the study of evolution for education "when explored and utilized to its full extent will reveal pedagogic possibilities now undreamed of" (G. S. Hall, 1904, Vol. 2, p. 221). The development of civilization was seen, analogously to the evolution of species, as a natural growth whose shape should thus, naturally, dictate the shape of the individual's development, and so the curriculum. "If there be an order in which the human race has mastered its various kinds of knowledge, there will arise in every child an aptitude to acquire these kinds of knowledge in the same order. . . . Education should be a repetition of civilization in little" (Spencer, 1861, p. 76).

The most highly developed recapitulationist curricula were implemented in Germany. All of them made rather literal translations from cultural history to curricula, producing a variety of "culture-epoch" proposals. These curricula seem now oddly content-tied and epoch-tied

(DeGarmo, 1895; Seeley, 1906). In North America, apart from the best known advocacy of recapitulationist ideas in G. S. Hall (1904), John Dewey was initially attracted by the ideas. He tried

> a modified system of culture epochs in his Chicago experimental school during the early 1890s. But he could not interest children in all aspects of supposedly appropriate material for their age: they loved the Roman heroes, for example, but yawned through the study of Roman laws (Gould, 1977, p. 154).

But Dewey also did not shake off the focus on content: "There is a sort of natural recurrence in the child mind to the typical activities of primitive people; witness the hut which the boy likes to build in the yard, playing hunt, with bows, arrows, spears and so on" (cited in Gould, 1977, p. 154).

Dewey came to deride the cruder kind of culture-epoch curricula, and their disrepute lasts even to the present. Recapitulation foundered in the early decades of this century under a two-pronged attack. The less influential came as a simple extension of the attack on recapitulation ideas in biology. It was suggested that educators "who base their work upon recapitulation . . . may well ask themselves whether they are not building on shifting soil" (Bovet, 1923, p. 150).

The more influential attack came from the growing present-mindedness of progressivism. Recapitulation curricula become

> absurd when tested by common sense. Although the development of the child may parallel the development of the race in certain respects, it does not follow that the curriculum should parallel the cultural development of the race. Obviously a child living in the 20th century would pursue a 20th century curriculum. There is no justification for delaying the study of current events and our present community, state, and natural life until the child has completed his study of the preceding periods of racial development (Monroe et al., 1930, pp. 408–9).

The notion of recapitulation I am developing here is—I hope it is already apparent—significantly unlike those that enjoyed a vogue about a century ago. What is recapitulated in this scheme are sets of sense-making capacities or kinds of understanding—the constituents of the general layers I am calling mythic, romantic, philosophic, and ironic. The sense-making capacities of romance, for example, together consti-

tute what I mean by a kind of understanding. I am calling th
making capacities because they are not simply mental char
nor simply forms of knowledge; they are capacities that ar
stimulated, and developed as the student becomes initiated into the forms
of sense-making available in a particular culture.

Education in this scheme, then, is the sequential accumulation of
the sense-making capacities, and associated capacities to communicate,
available in our culture. This is a recapitulationary scheme because it
embodies an argument that the sequence in which these capacities can
be accumulated by the individual reflects the sequence in which they
were generated in our cultural history. The tie between the two—cultural
history and individual development—is located in the logical and psychological constraints that have influenced the historical generation of
these capacities and that also constrain the sequence in which the individual can accumulate them. The dynamic of the process of educational
development is not located in either of the constraints, however, but in
their complex interaction with the range of sense-making capacities
available as a result of our particular cultural history.

This scheme has been arrived at by analyzing modern educated consciousness into constituent forms of understanding, identifying the logical and psychological constraints that determine the sequence in which
those forms of understanding can be accumulated and that determine how
they coalesce layer by layer, and by empirically establishing grounds for
associating each layer with a particular age-range. The analysis of modern educated consciousness has not relied on identifying the characteristics of those conventionally considered best educated, nor on inferences
from studies of the nature and forms of knowledge or of psychological
development. Rather, it has been arrived at by identifying the major
achievements in our cultural history that have extended our capacity to
make sense of the world and of experience. I have tried to interpret these
major achievements neither in terms of changing mental structures nor
in terms of the contents of the particular achievements themselves, but
rather, again, to fuse these into a way of characterizing sense-making
capacities in a form that is equally useful in discussing cultural history
and individual development. The concepts I use to characterize students'
intellectual lives are to be seen, then, as embodying—in no doubt often
complex transformations—the history of which they are the outcome
(MacIntyre, 1981, pp. 174ff.).

I use the concept of layers to suggest that we accumulate these kinds
of understanding more or less sequentially, but this does not imply that
we preserve each layer in its distinct form somehow separate from the
others. Rather, as each new layer is accumulated, it tends to coalesce

somewhat with that or those already developed. This coalescence is a complex affair, it seems, never a simple homogenizing of the set of layers, as we retain access to some distinctive qualities of each layer. This conception is articulated by Ong when he notes: "In its evolution, consciousness does not slough off its earlier stages but incorporates them in transmuted form in its later stages" (Ong, 1977, p. 49).

One result of identifying the dynamic of the educational process in cultural recapitulation may be seen in the way the curriculum is determined. The presently dominant traditions of research remain unclear about how one can move from their results to specifying a curriculum. In psychology of education, research aims to establish facts about learning, development, motivation, teaching, and so on, and whatever implications seem relevant may be drawn from these facts. While much of this research may offer more direct implications for instructional methods and conditions, one can, for example, try to infer from Piaget's theories what kinds of concepts are likely to be comprehensible at particular ages. Analyses of the nature of knowledge may provide criteria for distinguishing forms of knowledge and lead to implications for the structure of the curriculum, as in Paul Hirst's interesting studies for example (Hirst, 1974). But each kind of study separately runs into areas of opaqueness such that no precise and comprehensive implications for the curriculum can be securely established. It might seem, again, that we need only bring the results of these two traditions of research together to be able to design a truly effective curriculum— articulating the facts about learners and their development and about conditions of learning with the analyses of knowledge and criteria of education. But, again, they have not and do not come easily together. The problem, as I have argued in the more general context of the Platonic and Rousseauian insights which these distinct traditions seek to elaborate, is that each identifies the dynamic of the educational process differently. This prevents their results coming easily together and tends instead to make them pass one another by or seem even in conflict. Nor is this some contingent matter, to be overcome by collaborative research teams or by some "give" as on a demarcation dispute. The difficulty seems to lie rather at the level of the methodological presuppositions that enable each tradition of research to go forward separately. Each presupposes that one *can* study knowledge independently of what minds do to it or that one *can* study minds, or behaviors, independently of the cultural contexts and contents which give them form and meaning. Each tends to reify knowledge or mind/behavior. Ascribing to the topic of research an independent existence leads in turn to seeing it as an appropriate source for the dynamic of education; knowledge in-forms minds or minds' changing structures require knowledge to conform to them.

This is perhaps to overstate and oversimplify matters, or perhaps to state the condition of the more extreme practitioners of each tradition, or, perhaps better yet, to state the past condition of those traditions from which both have moved. The overstatement, or historical statement, is useful, however, to emphasize in what way cultural recapitulation avoids being tied to a presupposition that the dynamic of education resides either in knowledge or in minds and so scanting to some degree either the Platonic or Rousseauian insight. It gives due attention to both by focusing on the cultural development of the individual, by finding a way of characterizing—to put it tendentiously—mind in society.

Easy for me casually to assert a "right" position on matters of intense debate, but it is worth noting that these two traditions of educational research are increasingly nudging into each other's territories, acknowledging the necessity for more comprehensive perspectives. I have earlier indicated some skepticism about the continuing fruitfulness of these traditions of research if they remained independent of each other and neglected to take into full account the influence of cultural history in shaping their phenomena of interest. Easy, too, to offer such lordly advice, but I am here not trying to engage these methodological debates so much as to indicate that cultural recapitulation is not some exotic sport. It avoids precisely the presuppositions that seem at the root of the practical problems faced by the more established research traditions in education.

Cultural history and individual development

If cultural history is going to provide guidance to the curriculum, does this mean that astrology must precede astronomy, alchemy precede chemistry, magic precede physics and medicine, and myth precede philosophy and literature? Such a conclusion might be encouraged by nineteenth-century recapitulation schemes. And perhaps my constant references to oral cultures and the Greek beginnings of our rational inquiries suggests that mythic and romantic understanding require pre-rational, irrational, or non-rational forms of thinking. Also there is my insistence on searching for transcendent associations and on putting knowledge into story-shapes. The point about our rational forms of inquiry is that their first great achievement was to escape from stories and the transcendent. Theories and logic do not transcend reality and are determinedly not story-shaped, but they are precisely the tools that have enabled us to make sense of the world and of experience in ways that have given us greater control over them.

Will this scheme, then, for example, require that astrology, or something like it, be introduced to children before knowledge of astronomy? No. The particular knowledge content of our cultural history is not what is to be recapitulated. What we see in the move from astrology is indeed an accumulation of knowledge and, crucially, theory replacing story. If, however, we consider astrology in the kind of terms I have been using in the previous chapters, we will focus on the sense-making capacities at work. We will focus on the cultural achievements embedded in astrology and their contribution to enhancing our sense-making grasp over the world. We tend to dismiss astrology as nonsense, as the irrational predecessor whose displacement made astronomy possible. But, again, the move from astrology to astronomy cannot be understood if seen simply as a displacement; astronomy grew out of astrology. Our focus is on what survived in that transition. The cultural achievement of astrology was, to put it generally, the imaginative search for meaning in the stars, the consequent observation of order and pattern in complex phenomena, and the attempt to report that order in a memorable and personally meaningful form. It is this that we will try to recapitulate in providing an engaging and meaningful access to astronomy. Identifying the cultural achievement that preceded and gave early shape to astronomy enables us to formulate a principle for the construction of an early curriculum in astronomy. Evoking, stimulating, and developing the imaginative search for meaning in the stars does not require us to begin with astrological stories from Greek, Norse, African, or other mythologies—though we would be a bit obtuse to overlook their possible educational uses in encouraging an initial engagement with astronomy. But we might equally well begin with the most recent findings about the Big Bang, quasars, pulsars, black holes, and so on—if presented in the appropriate form. Similarly our language arts curriculum need not be composed of the writings of the major Romantics—though, again, we would be a bit obtuse if we ignore their potential help. We could as well focus on modern writers or ancient writers—and on the students as writers—to develop a romantic understanding of literature.

What this scheme provides for determining the curriculum, then, is not historically sequenced bodies of knowledge but rather historically sequenced layers of sense-making capacities. The historical sequence is determining not simply because of its historicity but because it embodies and reflects the logical and psychological constraints on the development of sense-making capacities. From the definition of these capacities we can identify appropriate curriculum content and methods of teaching that can best evoke, stimulate, and develop them. Astrology shows us sense-making capacities that are historically foundational to astronomy; astrology embodies, we may say, the cultural foundations of astronomy. It embodies in complex ways, to be discussed below, the logical and psychological foundations of astronomy. However sophisticated might become an individual's understanding of astronomy, the foundational capacities evident in astrology will ideally remain as constituents of that understanding. The imaginative search for meaning, that is to say, is as much a proper part of the most advanced astronomical research as it is of the foundational access to the subject. Its absence or repression might indeed permit the accumulation of knowledge and refinement of theory, but the resulting research would likely be characterized by an inability to find imaginative engagement in the work and an absence of the energetic imagination that can break through and refashion theory. (For an examination of the role of imagination in scientific research and in major theoretical break-throughs see Shepard, 1978; 1988).

But astrological stories were replaced by astronomical theories, and if we are to recapitulate this cultural enhancement of our sense-making capacities, then stories must surely give way to theories? And as one seems incompatible with the other surely this involves straightforward displacement? If our initial exploration of the stars is to be dominated by our storying capacities, and these are somehow to persist throughout our rational romantic layer education in astronomy, then surely the development of theory will be prevented? Stories cannot "coalesce" into theories. Is this not a fundamental objection to a scheme of recapitulating an historical sequence of sense-making capacities? I think not. In the discussion of stories earlier I stressed the separation between fictional stories and the characteristics of the story-form. The story-form can be used to make a particular kind of sense of any phenomena. It is a foundational form of meaning-making. The development of theory involves attempts at a more precise, literal, objective grasp on phenomena. The kind of meaning or sense, that theories try to make, takes place, as it were, within contexts shaped by our storying capacities. An imaginative search for meaning in the cosmos need not interfere with our development of increasingly sophisticated theories about black holes. Indeed, we constantly coordinate the two kinds of sense-making, and coordinate them with the further layers of understanding to be discussed in later volumes of this essay. Our storying capacities do not go away with the development of theories; as argued earlier, they provide the contexts of meaning in which theories make more precise sense of their limited phenomena of interest; they provide the ties between theoretically informed knowledge and our lives; they enable the absorption of accumulating knowledge to our imaginations and ever-active memories.

I should perhaps mention that I have used this astrology/astronomy example to make a couple of points about the recapitulation scheme, not to make a particular curriculum proposal. How we might move from historically derived sense-making capacities to curriculum principles and thence to a particular curriculum to the topic of the next chapter.

This scheme, then, identifies the dynamic of education in the recapitulation of the cultural capacities that enhance our power to make sense of the world of our experience. There are logical and psychological constraints, complexly intermingled, on the historical and on the individual's development of those capacities, but the dynamic of the process does not lie in its constraints. Romantic understanding is not achieved by mastery of any particular body of knowledge—as would be the case if the dynamic of the educational process were to be located in knowledge. Nor is it a product of psychological development; it is not a necessary stage we pass through in reaching maturity. Indeed, there are evident in human cultures forms of maturity which do not use romantic understanding. Romantic understanding is a cultural artifact, brought about by teaching particular kinds of things in particular ways during particular periods of life.

"Interlacing" psychological and logical constraints with cultural history makes it difficult to identify the dynamic of education precisely as distinct from the kinds of psychological or epistemological theories that have long held sway. My argument is that identifying the dynamic in cultural recapitulation does not make it *distinct* from psychological and logical considerations; their constraining forces are felt in different ways both in cultural history and in individual development. Cultural history is made up of the invention and discovery of an array of techniques for making sense of the world and of experience. The sequence of those inventions and discoveries was constrained by logic—certain inventions required other knowledge to be in place to make them possible, and by human psychology—certain directions are followed rather than others because of the nature of our hopes, fears, intentions, and so on. But to describe these shaping constraints in the fullest detail is still not to catch the dynamic of the process of cultural development. There is in it a creative, playful, imaginative element, something that slides sideways along metaphors rather than climbs methodically and literally. We can try to impose a causal order on the history of cultural achievements in retrospect, and that causal order depends on some logical or psychological scheme. The order, that is, can characterize something of the constraints on the process. What we cannot do adequately, or have not done adequately, is characterize the creative dynamic of the process. One can try to describe the changes as they occur—in this case from layer to layer and within layers—but the causes of the changes are difficult to isolate and characterize. If I might borrow an observation from John Bossy, who borrowed it from Clifford Geertz, who borrowed it from Gilbert Ryle: "Where explanation is implied . . . it should be taken . . . more as a contribution to the thickness of the description than as the key to open a door upon the mysteries of change" (Bossy, 1985, p. viii).

As our cultural history and our understanding of it are constrained by logical entailments and psychological predispositions, so is individual educational development constrained. Cultural history is an expression of the creative dynamic of the human spirit working within the constraints of logical entailments and psychological predispositions. The term "constraints" perhaps suggests some sluggish logic and psychology chaining down some wonderful free dynamic human spirit. This would be to miss the meaning of their interlacement. The joint constraints on cultural development are also its conditions. So, understanding cultural development requires our attending to the logical and psychological conditions/constraints of the process, but also requires our attending to the less easily grasped way in which their interlacement with the conditions of human societies in particular environments leads to new ways of making sense of the world and of experience. Similarly, understanding education requires our attending to the logical and psychological conditions/constraints on the process, but also requires our attending to the particular cultural conditions which the individual is to recapitulate. The logical and psychological constraints, and the range of sense-making capacities available in any culture, are given a graspable form in the history of the culture's development of those capacities. The logical and psychological constraints also operate on each individual but, by themselves, are inadequate to characterize the process of education. The process of education can, however, be characterized in a graspable way by seeing it as the recapitulation of the culture's historical development of those sense-making capacities.

Even if it is possible to characterize education adequately this way, and to identify its dynamic in a way that overcomes the dichotomy that has presented an *impasse* for educational theory and practice for so long, some problems remain. We need to know whether such a scheme is possible and desirable, whether it is better than other schemes presently in place, why the set of capacities characterized earlier should provide the basis for middle-school education; we need to know in short how to go about evaluating such a scheme. We have well developed methods for evaluating empirical and conceptual claims in education, but how are these to be deployed to deal with a scheme that has tied empirical and conceptual questions in a complicated way with to history?

Possibility, desirability and evaluation

Because this scheme is not like the kind of psychological theory one commonly sees in educational literature nor like the product of epistemological research, it might be worth pausing to consider ways in which it seems not amenable to the normal array of evaluation procedures. This is not so much a defensive move as an attempt towards clearer definition.

If we were to consider the empirical supports for the scheme, we might find it difficult to locate straightforward empirical claims that are contentious. That it is possible to evoke, stimulate, and develop the constituents of romantic understanding in students is an empirical claim, but hardly a contentious one that merits careful testing. This scheme is not a psychological theory to be tested against empirical observations; it is composed in significant part from empirical observations—of historical phenomena and of common student behaviors. It is a product, not of some novel empirical findings, but of exploring implications of some empirically uncontentious observations, of putting what was already known together in a new way. What is open to evaluation, of course, is the adequacy and accuracy of the observations. This scheme is not an attempt to make claims that are cross-culturally valid nor developmentally invariant, nor even necessarily the case; it is a characterization of a cultural process that *can* be brought about. That it *can* be brought about, that students can be taught the sense-making capacities of romantic understanding, seems quite uncontentious.

The empirical connection of this layer and its constituents with students of middle-school age also seems to be not particularly contentious. The characterization of romantic understanding is built in part from systematic observation and analysis of students' oral and written behavior, of their stories and games, of their grasp of the exotic and extreme features of reality, and so on. This connection, however, begins to impinge on a more general apparently empirical claim made by this scheme: that children are predisposed, in the process of becoming educated in our culture, to proceed through these layers in the sequence I am describing. For this second layer, this means that we are predisposed to acquire the characteristics of romantic understanding after those of mythic and before those of philosophic understanding. This scheme, that is to say, is not an arbitrary prescription. It reflects a predisposition. The task is to locate the source and dynamic of the predisposition in order that the scheme be appropriately evaluated.

This is not, again, a psychological claim that mythic understanding is a necessary first stage in cognitive development and romantic understanding a distinct second stage. A crucial difference is that these kinds of understanding are cultural artifacts, not reflections of some supposed underlying psychological reality. It is a layer of an educational process that need not go forward, of a particular initiation that need not take place. It is necessary, however, if one is to become educated in our culture. The problem with this claim, at least from the point of view of our traditional methods for testing empirical claims, is that it has already slid over into the murky realm where the empirical and conceptual are conjoined. The predisposition, that is to say, is not based only on the nature of human psychology—which would yield straightforward empirically testable claims. Nor again is it based only on logical entailments.

We know, for example, that children cannot understand some things that adults or adolescents can understand. In some cases we can adequately explain such failures as due to prerequisite knowledge not yet having been mastered. That is, we look to logic for the explanation. The alternative explanation for children's failure to learn certain things is psychological. It is claimed, say, that the development of certain mental structures must take place before certain things can be understood. There is a problem distinguishing these two kinds of explanations, reflecting the difficulty described earlier in distinguishing mind and knowledge. One may see an aspect of their confusion in arguments about whether Piaget's general stages are psychological structures empirically supported or whether they are guaranteed by logic (Hamlyn, 1978) and of course in the name "genetic epistemology" which Piaget gave to his complex inquiries. In the case of this scheme, the problem is compounded by locating the dynamic of the predisposition in cultural recapitulation. This does not obviate the logical and psychological influences, as I argued in the previous section. These together have constrained and shaped the sequence whereby the sets of capacities have been invented or discovered in our culture and they shape and constrain the ways in which any individual can acquire them. But we cannot neatly separate out the logical from the psychological constraints as they operate on sense-making capacities, nor can we feel confident that doing so would exhaust what we have to deal with in accounting for either cultural history or individual development within a culture. There remains that imaginative element we glimpse sliding around on mercurial metaphor, which may indeed be simply a feature of the conjointness of logic and psychology operating within cultural stuff, but we would be unwise, I think, to make any firm conclusion about this. It is not that there isn't a genetic component, but rather that it never acts or is accessible independently of the cultural stuff with which it is coalesced. Consequently, we can only hope to characterize it in terms of that cultural stuff.

This ambivalence has the effect that it is possible to amass logical and psychological supports for this scheme but that they remain somewhat circumstantial to the central claim about developing mythic and romantic understanding. For example, with regard to mythic sense-making capacities described in the previous volume, it is possible to locate considerable psychological support for the priority of metaphoric over literal or logico-mathematical forms of thought. Not a little can be found in those studies designed to locate the beginnings of particular logical procedures, wherein we see easy grasp of metaphors—though these are not commonly the focus of researchers' attention—before the ability to grasp even the simplest logical technique such as the syllogism (see Piaget, 1951, and Luria, 1979). One can see this primacy most vividly in children's own narratives (Paley, 1981). On the other hand one can make a logical case for the necessary primacy of metaphor, as the conceptual grounding which logical procedures need in order to be able to work. The most dramatic assertion of this view as plain common-sense is Nietszche's, whose views are presented along with a series of much more systematic arguments in *Metaphor* (Cooper, 1986). (See especially the section on "The Primacy of Metaphor," pp. 257–79).

Similarly with, for example, the ready engagement by the extremes of reality. It would be easy to show empirically that interest in the exotic and extreme is a common feature of early adolescents' engagement with the world. On the other hand it would be possible to make a logical case that the meaning of any particular knowledge requires a context within which it can be grasped. I have tried to provide both cases above.

When I say these kinds of support are circumstantial, I mean that they provide plausibility for the scheme but do not directly support it. That is, my arguments for the importance of metaphor in early education or for the greater imaginative engagement of the exotic in the middle-school years are based on their role in cultural development. Their role and sequence in cultural development are constrained by logical and psychological forces acting together in terms of the cultural content. What psychological and logical supports for such claims provide is some definition of the constraints that shape cultural development and individual development in that culture. These are not universal constraints, nor universal principles of cultural development, but simply principles that operate in the development of the particular set of cultural capacities that have been evoked, stimulated, and developed in our culture. Because the range of human capacities for sense-making is indeterminate, it does not make sense to assert for the set we are familiar with any more generality than our culture allows. Partly this is sensible because past guesses about "the nature" of human capacities have always been ethnocentric in one way or another, and partly because the occasional bizarre achievements of some individuals suggest we have sense-making potentials as yet largely un-evoked, un-stimulated, and un-developed.

It would be possible to take each of the characteristics of romantic understanding and try to provide the kind of empirical and/or conceptual support considered appropriate for traditional educational claims. The first odd feature of pursuing such a strategy is that, in the case of each characteristic, it becomes clear that we can turn either way for support, building a logical or a psychological case. If I am hastily passing over these kinds of arguments, it is not because I do not think they are important, or worthy of research. Nor is it because I think the psychological or the logical cases are obviously true, or not in need of much more elaborate support. It is because I do not think either kind of argument is convincing by itself nor can it be conclusive.

This set of considerations has grown from my wanting to support the claim that we have in our individual educational development a predisposition to acquire the capacities of mythic understanding first and then those of romantic understanding, and then those of subsequent layers. This is not, I am suggesting, a conceptual truth—something we can show to be the case by logical analysis. Nor is it a matter of empirical necessity—something we can show to be the case by amassing appropriate empirical support. The major empirical claim—which I take to be uncontentious, though potentially falsifiable—is that one *can* acquire the capacities of mythic understanding before those of romantic understanding, and those of romantic understanding before subsequent layers. The potentially more contentious claim, that we are predisposed to do so, *if we are to become educated,* is complicated by the emphasized conditional clause. (Nor is this simply circular: I am not defining education simply as whatever this scheme characterizes in the sequence in which it is characterized. I have committed it to satisfying the requirements of the general conceptions of education held both in the Platonic tradition and the Rousseauian progressivist tradition.) The source of the predisposition operating in the educational process lies in the interactive force of psychology and logic working within particular cultural environments, possibly along with an imaginative element (which seems necessary to account for the contingent nature of our cultural development and the play of students' imaginations). If I could characterize this in detail, obviously, I would. What I am doing, in the hope of being able to be more explicit as this essay proceeds, is pointing to the set of interactive elements from which the dynamic of the educational process is composed, and partially exposing it by charting its effects and how it works itself out in education—and so trying to contribute to the thickness of the description. Its effects are being charted by finding a level of the phenomena of education that reflects the set of interactive elements that conjointly constitute the dynamic of education—that level I am characterizing as culturally constrained sense-making capacities.

The predisposition seems to work something like this. I am identifying as crucially important, and in large part definitive of cultures, the set of sense-making techniques they have developed for making sense of the world and of their experience. This encompasses in our case our technology, arts, and sciences. To borrow some useful jargon, the set of techniques, or sense-making capacities, exist in the present in our culture in a complex synchronicity. They were generated diachronically. Education is the process whereby the individual acquires these techniques, these capacities, diachronically. As they are acquired, they coalesce into a synchronicity analogous to their existence in the culture. The dynamic that has determined the diachronic sequence of their invention and discovery in our culture is constrained by the interaction of logic and human psychology. The sequence in which knowledge can be elaborated in human minds is constrained by the logic of the various forms of knowledge acting together with the predispositions of human psychology. These same forces whose action we see in human cultural development shape and constrain the individual's acquisition of the sense-making capacities available in the culture. In becoming educated, then, we are constrained to recapitulate the sequence whereby in our cultural history these sense-making capacities were invented and discovered. Now, we do not need to recapitulate this sequence if we are not to acquire the fullest range of these capacities—if we are not going to become educated. But if we are to become educated, if we want to maximize our acquisition of the range of sense-making capacities available to us—which *is* our culture—then we need to recapitulate the sequence of their historical development. To fail to recapitulate some of the foundational capacities, for example, is to fail to acquire prerequisites for later capacities. To fail to develop metaphoric fluency or imaginative capacities, undercuts the degree to which later capacities can be developed. The predisposition derives from, or resides in, the shaping given to the dynamic of both cultural development and the individual's acquisition of the culture by logic and human psychology.

In general, I am arguing that human beings are predisposed to become educated in distinct ways in particular cultures. Each culture may be seen as a conditioning context which evokes, stimulates, and develops particular human potentials in particular ways. Human nature is plastic, but is so within limits. It exhibits preferences for the sequence in which capacities are developed—even though any particular culture will select, shape, and embody these capacities in distinctive ways. The plasticity means that logic and nature seem not to lay completely determining constraints on culture, but rather their constraining force is evident in general preferences or predispositions. My claim, then, is that this scheme is describing the forms and sequences of certain of these predispositions in optimally initiating people into our culture.

While I am clearly unable to characterize the nature of this predisposition precisely, my point here is to demonstrate why this claim is not straightforwardly empirical, open to straightforward empirical testing. This is not due to my wish to avoid such testing, but rather to indicate that this is not like a psychological theory, and that while circumstantial empirical and conceptual support can be amassed behind it, that support by itself is not its basis. Clearly, if any of my claims contravenes what we can show is logically or psychologically the case, then this would count as adequate disconfirmation. Logic and psychology define the constraints within which the scheme is composed. But there is considerable freedom within those constraints. It is in that area of freedom that the detailed specification of the layers is described, and those descriptions are derived from our cultural history and from empirical observations of students.

My claim for further circumstantial empirical support for this scheme lies in its offering a quite different explanation for why people at different ages find things easy or difficult to learn. It is different from the explanations presently most commonly accepted and it goes a long way towards accounting for what are anomalies to those explanations. It dispenses with simplicity-complexity, concrete-abstract, familiar-remote, and relevant-distant as adequate explanatory terms. They are obviously not irrelevant, or they would not have held sway for so long. But they simply focus on the wrong level or range of phenomena. What makes material easy to learn during the romantic layer of education is that it has the qualities I have outlined as romantic; what makes material difficult to learn during the romantic layer is that it is organized in what I call philosophic or ironic ways.

One achievement of this scheme is that it accounts for such anomalies as the apparently near-illiterate and dull student being, outside class, a fertilely imaginative Dungeon Master. Indeed, the scheme was in part composed from the study of precisely such anomalies. But its circumstantial empirical support must include the range of significant anomalies that are accounted for within it. And, it should be noted, these are not casual or marginal phenomena, but matters of crucial educational importance.

While the basis of the scheme itself is a complex fusion of the empirical, conceptual, and historical, it does nevertheless yield a whole range of straightforward empirical claims when it is worked out in practice. In general it yields the claim that when material is selected and organized according to the characteristics of this romantic layer, students will be more readily engaged by it, and find it more meaningful and comprehensible. When, for example, historical material about the Middle Ages is organized around some transcendent human quality, structured in a story form, and having other characteristics described earlier, it will be more easily learned and better understood than similar material organized and presented in ways that exclude the characteristics of the romantic layer.

The other straightforward empirical claim is the association of this layer with a particular age-range. This I take to be fairly uncontentious for this layer, though the association of the layers with ages will become more complicated as the scheme is elaborated. In the earlier chapters I have presented a range of observations supporting the connection of this layer in our culture with the middle-school years, up to about age fourteen—allowing a year or so either way for individual differences.

And how do we evaluate the desirability of this scheme so far? What does one say to the person who does not want the character of middle-school education to entail the stimulation of qualities of romantic understanding in students? If one's notion of education is the production of people skilled in the various ways required by the economy, then elaborating romantic capacities, stimulating imagination, and so on, may be useful for some people but not for most. Indeed, some features of imagination are seen as positively threatening to social and economic stability. This uncomfortably common position is just one of many whose conception of education, or of schooling, devalues certain of the capacities I am describing as fundamental to education. My arguments on behalf of the desirability of evoking, stimulating, and developing the capacities of romantic understanding are made extensively throughout the book. In general they support the principle that one ought to acquire as many sense-making capacities as possible. The scheme is to attempt to describe how one can do that, an important part being that one first acquire those capacities which are prerequisite to fullest development of other capacities. ("Prerequisite," again, in an educational sense—constrained by psychological predispositions and logical entailments acting through cultural recapitulation.)

The justification for following the path being laid down in this scheme, then, is that it characterizes the way to making fullest sense of the world and of experience in the terms available in our culture. The desirability of the scheme is tied to the desirability of making sense. "Making sense" is that combination of acquiring knowledge, of psychological development, and of imaginative fluency I have been trying to characterize.

And why—if we do not like "our" culture and its set of sense-making capacities—can we not choose another culture? And what does "culture" entail anyway? What are its limits and extent, especially in "multicultural" societies? Some of these questions raise issues that will have to wait for more of this scheme to be described before they can adequately be addressed. Some I will touch on in the next section. The option to choose another culture is, of course, not one that is open to us casually after we have been initiated into a particular language and society. To a large degree, fate commits us, but it is not an absolute imprisonment. I will return to this in the final volumes.

Characterizing education in terms of the acquisition of culturally constrained sense-making capacities allows us to focus on the ripening of childhood in the child and of adolescence in the adolescent while in no way losing sight of the ideal end. The capacities of mythic and romantic understanding are not steps to some distinct goal; they are constituents of the goal. Evaluating the desirability of this scheme will in part include assessing how adequately the aims both of traditional Platonic education into the forms of knowledge and the aims of the Rousseauian progressive ripening of each distinctive period of growth are accommodated. I think it is clear that discussing education in terms of the sense-making capacities I have focused on in this book does not obviate considering students' minds or knowledge. That great dichotomy of the traditionalist/progressivist debates is coalesced in sense-making capacities.

Whose Culture?

Most of the issues touched on in this chapter, concerning the nature and evaluation of this scheme, will become increasingly pointed as later layers are described. This is true also of what will be to some the most contentious feature of this scheme. Already those with highly developed ideological sensors will be detecting whiffs of the kind of "cultural imperialism" that has been identified by some (see Street, 1984) in the work of Havelock, Ong, and Goody. Goody, for example, who set out to break down the ethnocentric distinction between primitive and advanced cultures, in the end, it is claimed, only entrenched the distinction deeper under the labels oral and literate. He universalizes the particulars of our cultural history, to make the move from orality to literacy seem a necessary progressive move, and so more elaborately rationalizes the same old ideological viewpoint. This is an issue that belongs with questions about the desirability of this scheme.

The claim that an educational program is being designed to recapitulate "the" culture raises a number of ideological loaded questions. "Whose culture?" comes first. Then we might want to ask about the value of that culture and, indeed, what it comprises. If "our" culture is to be understood to include the whole panoply of largely middle-class "WASP" ideological assumptions, then this would be adequate grounds for some to reject the scheme out of hand. Defining cultures largely in terms of their sense-making techniques avoids obvious ideological pitfalls only to the point at which some kinds of sense are identified as better than others. I may seem already committed to astronomical theories being better sense-making techniques than astrological stories. The ideologically sensitive will see in this the adumbration of an argument that scientific cultures are better than oral cultures, and so just another culturally imperialistic attempt to use education to represent what are in fact contingent cultural forms as necessary, and to represent the difference between oral and literate and print and electronic cultures as hierarchical.

Cultural imperialism and cultural relativism are not exhaustive of the possibilities open to us, nor is either desirable or particularly coherent. One is not committed to believe that astronomy is absolutely better than astrology nor that they are, in their cultural contexts, equivalents. Both positions can be held only by refusing to observe a number of perfectly sensible distinctions between the social functions they perform and the kinds of sense astronomy and astrology make. The route I will take to undermining the vacuousness of the relativist position is hinted at in the distinction made earlier between astronomy and astrology. The route to undermining cultural imperialism lies in recognizing, first, that oral cultural capacities are foundational to subsequently developed capacities and, second, that the acquisition of the latter seems to entail losses.

"Our culture," then, is very widely interpreted here. It means the set of sense-making techniques accessible to us. Some of these are tied up in singing games, some are tied up in Virgil, some are tied up in technology, and so on. Whatever we *can* have access to is "our culture." So I am not using "culture" in a way that would distinguish middle-American culture from French dock-worker culture. For the time being I will continue to use it rather generally and vaguely. We live in a world culture and any individual can get access to a very wide range of the sense-making techniques generated throughout the world throughout history. Such access in practice, if not entirely in theory, requires literacy and print, of course, and literacy and print seem to require some loss of the sense of participation in nature that is possible in oral cultures, and, with the romantic tightening of our literal grasp on the world, some loss of our metaphoric grasp, and, with the growth of the sense of wonder, some loss of the sense of magic. The techniques of orality certainly can be extended to absorb capacities whose development we have come to associate with literacy (Feldman, 1988)—such as metalinguistic reflection and systematic scientific inquiry. But without literacy there will likely be severe limits on what can be absorbed. Here is, indeed, a value choice. And it is the value choice basic to this educational scheme—that certain sense-making techniques are worth the losses that accompany them. This is not true for all sense-making techniques—certain forms of religious fanaticism, ideologies, metaphysical schemes, are less valuable than what is lost in acquiring them. So there is no getting away from value decisions in constructing an educational scheme.

Nor is this scheme insensitive to social, class, and "sub-cultural" differences: "Children have to learn to select, hold, and retrieve content from books and other written or printed texts in accordance with their community's rules or 'ways of taking,' and the children's learning follows community paths of language socialization" (Heath, 1982, p. 70). This scheme is not intended as a universal homogenizer. It is sensitive to differences in different community forms of initiation, not to eradicate them, but to ensure that the set of sense-making techniques required to develop educationally are accessible to all children. Because different communities evoke, stimulate, and develop various of these techniques, or parts of them, differently, schooling will sensibly focus on attending to those techniques least well developed in particular forms of socialization.

I have raised a number of issues concerning the ideological implications of any educational scheme, especially one that rather casually refers to recapitulating "our" culture. I want, for now, only to indicate that I am not insensitive to these issues and even think I can avoid at least some of the ideological pitfalls. More than many issues, this cannot adequately be dealt with until more of this scheme is described, so I will put off this discussion to the final volume.

A. N. Whitehead's conception of romance

In "The Rhythm of Education" (1967), A. N. Whitehead discusses a "romantic stage" which lasts from about age eight to twelve or thirteen. It may initially seem that this book on romantic understanding is a kind of elaboration of his brief but richly suggestive comments. In this section I will note what I take Whitehead to mean by "romance," focusing on features in which my characterization could be seen as drawing from his. I will then touch on some aspects of his general theory, which I will compare and contrast with my scheme.

Whitehead's characterization of romance is given briefly. It is best simply to quote the salient parts:

> The stage of romance is the stage of first apprehension. The subject-matter has the vividness of novelty; it holds within itself unexplored connexions with possibilities half-disclosed by glimpses and half-concealed by the wealth of material. In this stage knowledge is not dominated by systematic procedure. Such system as there must be is created piecemeal *ad hoc.* . . . Romantic emotion is essentially the excitement consequent on the transition from the bare facts to the first realisation of the import of their unexplored relationships. . . . Education must essentially be a setting in order of a ferment already stirring in the mind: you cannot educate mind in *vacuo*. (Whitehead, 1967, pp. 17–18).

Romance is the vividness, the ferment, the excitement without which learning is barren. One may learn material and ideas, but if they are unleavened by romance they will remain "inert." A person can indeed pass most successfully through educational institutions gathering the approved knowledge but, failing also to develop the sense of romance, he or she is likely to turn out to be "the most useless bore on God's earth" (Whitehead, 1967, p. 1).

"The tremendous age of romance" is adolescence. "Ideas, facts, relationships, stories, histories, possibilities, artistry in words, in sounds, in form and in colour, crowd into the child's life, stir his feelings, excite his appreciation, and incite his impulses to kindred activities"

(Whitehead, 1967, p. 21). This "great romance is the flood which bears on the child towards the life of the spirit" (Whitehead, 1967, p. 22).

The implications Whitehead draws for the curriculum from his description of romance in the rhythm of education are perhaps rather less interesting to a modern reader than are the implications for teaching practice. His curriculum contents are very much those of a typical English boy's Public School; the differences from what are typical in such institutions lie in his proposals for how subjects should be organized and taught. The "essence" of proper teaching method, exemplified in part by the Montessori system, "is browsing and the encouragement of vivid freshness" (Whitehead, 1967, p. 22).

My work, then, may be seen merely as an elaboration of these remarks by Whitehead. Differences are largely matters of emphasis and the choice of rhetorical methods for laying out what is meant. If we consider Whitehead's theory in general, however, we will see quite radical differences despite the superficial similarities.

Whitehead's is of course an avowedly Hegelian theory. Romance, precision, and generalization are the terms chosen best to illustrate in educational phenomena the universal principle of the dialectical thesis, antithesis, and synthesis in operation. While Whitehead identifies adolescence as the great age of romance, it is only one of the periods when romance is dominant. In Whitehead's view, romance attaches to certain ages in particular, but also is properly dominant whenever new material is approached. (The great age of romance seems to be identified as such because it is the period when children begin to learn so many new things.) We constantly cycle through romance/precision/generalization. All should be present all the time; the cycle is of the sequential dominance of each one, determined by the stage of learning particular material. ("Towards the age of fifteen the age of precision in language and of romance in science draws to its close" (Whitehead, 1967, p. 23)).

Despite the differences between Whitehead's theory and the scheme I am developing, my scheme shares with Whitehead's an aspect of this image of domination by one of a set of "stages." I have mentioned that the capacities of the mythic layer coalesce with those of romantic, which in turn will coalesce with those to be described in the later volumes. Whitehead's stages are not characterized in terms of developing capacities, and the three "stages" are all present from the earliest years, but even so I share with him the notion that the "stages" are not things passed through, but (in my scheme, once acquired) each is used in distinctive ways in the mastery of new material. I will, then, argue for a similar pedagogical principle as that expressed by Whitehead: that access to a new subject at, say, the philosophic layer, will be gained more easily and meaningfully if guided through reformulated mythic and romantic capacities. The layers I am outlining, then, though more sequential in their acquisition, become the means for a pedagogical cycle not dissimilar in kind from that sketched by Whitehead.

The bases of Whitehead's scheme are relatively straightforward to identify, if rather harder to classify. We have first the metaphysical Helegian base. From that flow what seem like empirical and logical claims, but Whitehead seems uninterested in distinguishing between them. The rhythms seem at times to be determined by natural mental developments—("different subjects and modes of study should be undertaken by pupils at fitting times when they have reached the proper stage of mental development" (Whitehead, 1967, p. 15)—at other times to be determined by the subject matter being learned. ("The stage of romance is the stage of first apprehension. The subject-matter has the vividness of novelty" (Whitehead, 1967, p. 17). At times we have an interactionist view where the task is to work out what kind of knowledge environment best responds to and carries forward the developing child's mind. ("The environment . . . must, of course, be chosen to suit the child's stage of growth, and must be adapted to individual needs. In a sense it is an imposition from without; but in a deeper sense it answers to the call of life within the child" (Whitehead, 1967, pp. 32–3)). Furthermore, Whitehead is fairly casual in his use of "natural," which often makes matters even more confusing. ("Language is now the natural subject-matter for concentrated attack" (Whitehead, 1967, p. 22)).

What we see in Whitehead's essay, if we look at it through the main concern of this volume, is a similar recognition that during early adolescence there is a common development of a set of interests, energies, qualities, capacities, inclinations, sensitivities, forms of understanding—whatever we care to call them—that invite the description "romantic." Whitehead seems satisfied that, regardless of their causes, he has identified something qualitatively distinct about early adolescent students that is recognizable to anyone who deals with children and students in numbers. From the observation he moves to the general pedagogical principle that the design of curricula and the planning of teaching have to be powerfully influenced by such characteristics of students' thinking. What he succeeded in doing—along with Plato, Rousseau, and Dewey— was to make a complex and general observation about students' thinking in terms that lead directly to principles for designing curricula and planning teaching. What he left us with is a tantalizing sketch, inadequately worked out for us to be able to design for today a distinctively Whiteheadian curriculum. Rather, we have some profound insights to draw on, some principles sketched in outline, and some unclarity about just what bases the scheme actually rests on. His short paper is commonly described as "seminal." This is due, I think, to his having found a way of characterizing students' ways of making sense that combines the psychological and epistemological approaches that, pursued separately, are consistently disappointing and inadequate from an educational point of view.

Conclusion

The image of education that I am trying to articulate in these volumes is a layered one. There are, it seems to me, significant discontinuities in an effective educational program. It is not just that we learn particular content in particular sequences; we do, but that seems to me a relatively unimportant feature of education and the particular sequences are very largely contingent on particular circumstances. More importantly we learn different *kinds* of content at different ages and use it to develop different kinds of capacities which are and remain constituents of our mature forms of understanding. We often forget particular content, but the capacities developed in learning that content may remain parts of our very consciousness. It is one of these kinds of fundamental categories that I am trying to describe under the heading of romance. And I am trying to present an image of education as the progressive mastery of distinctive sets of such categories that coalesce to develop increasingly comprehensive understanding of the world and of experience during our education. Nor is it that enthusiasm and wonder, for example, are considered more important than learning facts about history or physics. Rather, the facts of history and physics can best be learned and can best further the educational process if they are in a romantic form, engaging and developing the sense of enthusiasm and wonder.

My general argument is that the sequence in which sense-making capacities have been evoked, stimulated, and developed in our cultural history has been constrained by logical entailments and psychological predispositions and that these play an equivalent role in shaping the sequence in which an individual can recapitulate those sense-making capacities. Metaphoric thinking and stories precede literal reflection and theories not as a contingent matter—we can program a computer to deal with the latter first (and the former hardly at all) but we cannot adequately educate human beings that way.

"If one changes the tools of thinking available to the child, his mind will have a radically different structure" (Berg, 1970, p. 46). This

Vygotskian view suggests a causal relationship between tools of thinking and mental structure. What I am calling sense-making capacities are the result of trying to find a way of characterizing considerations of minds and knowledge together to transcend, not simply avoid, the kinds of dilemmas that have plagued educational discourse this century. That is why the terms of this scheme, with its mythic, romantic, philosophic, and ironic layers, might seem rather odd, and the focus on the exotic, transcendent associations, imagination, and so on, in this volume are atypical. The oddity, of course, is no guarantee of correctness. But it is a necessary condition of generating a scheme that can bring together the great insights of the traditionalist and progressivist/modernist schools of educational thought.

9
A romantic curriculum

Introduction

There are many ways of being and becoming educated. In this and the following chapter I want to infer from the earlier discussions of romantic understanding a set of principles for designing a curriculum and for planning teaching during the middle-school years. In this chapter my first aim is to establish a set of principles that can lead to the selection of appropriate curriculum content, and then I will use those principles to outline a middle-school curriculum that can evoke, stimulate, and develop romantic understanding.

The principles allow a range of possible inferences, and the example I outline is just one among a set of legitimate romantic curricula. I would not like the particular curriculum outline I develop to be read as some authoritative instantiation of the principles. The range of legitimate interpretation is obviously restricted, and equally obviously, I think, my outline represents a central interpretation, but quite different outlines could just as well be inferred from the same set of principles. Different social and cultural circumstances from those within which I write would also influence the inferences made from the principles. The principles, then, are the first point of this exercise; the outline derived from them is intended primarily to show how one can move fairly easily from the principles to a particular curriculum.

In Chapter 10 I will be mainly concerned with planning teaching, but not in the sense of whether Inquiry or Didactic teaching methods are to be preferred in particular circumstances. There are numerous books on this subject, and teaching is well served by illustrative material on pedagogical techniques. It is less well served, I think, in the most important regard of how to select and organize material for teaching so that it will be most accessible and engaging to students. My aim, then, is to show how we can bring out for students at this age what is intrinsically most interesting and educationally useful about the chosen curriculum content.

I mentions this here because in both chapters my focus will be on the organizing principles that can be derived from romance. One effect of this will be a less sharp division than is usual between the criteria used to select curriculum content and those that determine methods of teaching. This seems to me entirely reasonable; what and how we teach are not the discrete concerns that their separate treatment by educational philosophers in the former case and by educational psychologists in the latter have tended to suggest.

Some principles of curriculum selection

First we must determine the criteria according to which we will divide up our curriculum. We cannot teach the universe of knowledge all together and so we have to decide what criteria, and indeed what kind of criteria, we will use to slice up the epistemological pie for pedagogical purposes. The first point that seems important to make in dealing with this question—a commonplace perhaps—is that the pedagogical uses of a discipline need not be identical with the scholarly objectives of a discipline. It would be odd indeed, of course, if the two were to be considered independent, but they should not be seen as identical. A conclusion from this is that an analysis of the nature of the knowledge and the purposes of scholars in any discipline at any particular time should not be seen as determining its pedagogical uses. For example, if philosophers of history and historians could actually get clear about, and agree on, the nature of historical knowledge and the objectives of historical inquiry, this should not prevent teachers from using history as a source of dramatic and engaging stories, as exemplifying heroic behavior, or even as teaching moral lessons. Whether any of these pedagogical uses of history is or is not legitimate has to be argued on educational grounds. None of them can be validated or rejected on grounds of a philosophical analysis of the discipline, or of the overall realm of knowledge.

This is an idle argument, not in the sense of engaging only "straw people"—there are many prominent educationalists who argue the opposite or proceed on the assumption that the opposite is true. Rather, it is idle because the disagreements among philosophers and practitioners of all discipline areas about the nature and purposes of each discipline are so great that the first requirement—some consensus established from which one might make inferences to education—is not met, or at least is not met with the clarity and unanimity that would allow one to design a curriculum as an entailment of such knowledge. The same is true of attempts to etch logical divisions among discipline. The philosophical disputes are certainly no less than the pedagogical disputes about the organization of subjects in the curriculum. We might more sensibly, then, stay at home and deal directly with the issues relevant to our practical problems, rather than make the somewhat implausible act of faith that we will be able to parachute in answers to our pedagogical problems from some area of greater epistemological security.

How we divide up disciplines, subjects, or topics for purposes of designing a curriculum, then, should be argued on educational grounds—on the basis of the educational uses of different knowledge and the kinds of understanding we think it is best to develop in students.

The most general principle being developed in this book is that we should look at the world as it is represented in our cultural tradition and select primarily those parts of it that stand out when viewed through the eyes of romance. Romance acts like a kind of lens which brings a certain range of things into focus. It is these that should form the romantic layer. To say that we will select for our curriculum the romantic aspects of things might seem like rather imprecise guidance. What might make it somewhat clearer is a more detailed consideration of how romance can be broken down into more particular principles. One way of doing this is to take parts of the earlier descriptive chapters in turn and consider what principle can be derived from each for the selection of curriculum materials.

In each case the principle will provide dual help. First, it will direct us to select content that is most appropriate for developing particular capacities of romance. Second, it will direct us to select aspects of that content that allow us to highlight what is most romantic about it. The general principle, for example, might direct us to select the Industrial Revolution as an example of human energy and confidence. Particular principles will then enable us to select aspects of the Industrial Revolution that can best present it in order to engage romantic layer students and help develop in them the capacities of romance. This dual guidance accounts for the degree of overlap between considerations of curriculum dealt with in this chapter and of teaching dealt with in the next. This duality will also be evident in each of the more particular principles outlined below. In each case, these principles point us towards the selection of particular content, but they also point us towards the selection of aspects of that content. I will thus consider each of these principles in two parts: first, in terms of the kind of content they guide us towards, and second in terms of those aspects of content that may have been selected on the basis of other principles to which they direct us.

What follows should not be read as some exhaustive set of principles that will enable us to determine a romantic curriculum. It is not exhaustive for one sufficient reason, because the principles are derived from a far from exhaustive description of romance. Once one has an adequate grasp on the nature of romantic understanding, that general and complex concept can serve as the principle that will select appropriate curriculum content. But clearly my attempt to elucidate it above is only a primitive sketch, and much more elaboration would no doubt enable us to infer further principles which could be of use in this curriculum building exercise. What follows, then, is an attempt to infer what principles I can from the sketch of romantic understanding given so far.

Each of the following principles, then, is taken directly from the discussion of romance in earlier chapters. The meaning of phrases like "the scale of reality" which might appear rather mind-boggling if taken literally should be read within the context of the earlier discussion.

Including knowledge of the scale of reality

This principle guides us to search for material that will give students a sense of the contexts within which the everyday world proportionately exists. Applying this principle leads us to look to the extremes of the real world: "Extremes" in the sense discussed earlier; in part a kind of *Guinness Book of Records* pursuit of extremes, but also extremes of emotion, of physical events, etc. Thus one might be led to a curriculum segment on "Disasters!"—the greatest man-made disasters, the greatest natural disasters, the greatest disasters to affect individual students, and so on, or to a segment on "Achievements"—climbing Everest, Helen Keller's story, Buoddacea's victory over the Romans, and so on. The great storehouse of knowledge about the extremes of human achievement is, of course, history and this principle alone will provide a prominent place in the curriculum for a romantic study of history.

Applying this principle to material that is included in the curriculum primarily on the basis of some other principle, we are guided to seek out dramatic features of that material and particularly those features that help to fix its boundaries. In the case of a topic like the Industrial Revolution, this principle guides us to select content about the Revolution and shows the extremes of human energy and courage and suffering, as well as the extremes of achievement and profit and the size of farms and the growth of mechanical power. Other principles will guide us to other content, of course, but the force of this principle constantly is to guide us to look for material that will engage and develop this key constituent of romance.

Including knowledge about the limits of experience

This principle clearly will overlap with the one above—the limits of experience are, after all, important indices of the scale of reality. We are guided by this principle largely to the lives of people. It might be used to justify a curriculum area called something like "People Past and Present." In such a curriculum area, possibly to be included three or more times a week for perhaps a quarter-hour each, students would become familiar with the "brief lives" of a wide range of real people. Partly, such a curriculum area could be supported by a textbook designed for it, partly no doubt teachers' ingenuity could devise a variety of methods for filling such curriculum time engagingly. Groups of students might be assigned a couple of weeks or a month in advance to decide on a person they would "research" and then introduce to the class at a given time.

In the case of content included in the curriculum on the basis of some other principle, this one constantly guides us to seek out aspects that can make the content more humanly meaningful by focusing on the limits of human experience within it. The focus on other lives and the extremes of experience is perhaps the most important way in which we begin to know ourselves. Constant focus on our own lives, thoughts, feelings and experiences tends to induce narcissism. Narcissism is a lack of proportion in estimating the value of our own experience. One purpose for focusing on the extremes of experience in the lives of others is to provide, again, a context and thereby a sense of proportion to our understanding of human experience—our own as well as others'. The insight that it is by "forgetting" ourselves that we come finally to know ourselves is not really so very mysterious.

These first two principles will be prominent in the way we search the world for material that can best engage and develop romantic understanding. They lead us to select the telling bright bits and pieces of the world that can vivify whatever content is to be learned. If in the curriculum area on "Ideas" (to be discussed below) we are studying Courage, these principles direct us to look for a variety of extremely courageous acts;

if we are studying logarithms we will search for extremes of dedication and ingenuity, opposed by ignorance and scorn perhaps, in their invention. In the case of the Industrial Revolution, they will guide us beyond noting new forms of pottery and the furnaces necessary to create them. Such facts will be made more humanly meaningful by having a context created for them by the story of, say, Palissy, whose obsession to create new glazes—about which no modern student can be expected to care unless they see them as a result of his obsession—led him to burn his garden fence and then his household furniture in order to keep up the furnace fire to create beautiful new enamel finishes. If we are considering the making of musical instruments, we will be guided to the extremes of confident mastery such as that expressed by Stradivari's "God could not make the fiddles of Stradivari without Stradivari."

Providing opportunity for detailed study

The problem with this principle is that it will seem so easy to apply. It does not so much guide us to particular curriculum areas as virtually all areas seem open to its application. It will come more prominently into play in the design of units and lessons. The trouble with this principle here is its apparent universality. The possibilities are so great that some constraining factor needs to be borne in mind. It is not enough simply to point in the direction of the library and tell students to explore some aspect of a topic in detail. This principle arose out of the discussion of students' obsessive hobbies and collecting. I suggested that students feel driven to get a sense of the scale of something, to master a set, to completely exhaust some area of reality. In identifying topics for detailed study, then, we should try to pick on those that have a potential for some kind of completion. We will want students to feel a sense of mastery, of having indeed exhausted some area, of having collected the whole "set." In the Industrial Revolution example we will not want to send students off to study the life of Isambard Kingdom Brunel. (That might satisfy the principle that leads us to the "People Past and Present" curriculum area.) The principle of exhaustive detail would seem to require us to limit the topic further, to something like a description of the major engineering projects of Brunel, or of a particular project. This principle will come into play once the general topic has begun to engage students' romantic understanding. That is a first condition. While the obsessive collecting may be directed to almost anything, there must first be a romantic association with the thing. Once that is made, then the second condition is that we select topics that are, in some clear sense, amenable to being completed. This principle points to a particular kind of satisfaction that needs to be felt by students, one that comes from completion of a task. This suggests also that such projects might be given special folders or boxes for the completed study to be housed in a finished form.

Selecting topics that can best be articulated on binary opposites

This principle by itself will provide little useful guidance in selecting curriculum content. Combined with either or both of the first two principles above, however, it suggests hat we should seek out those limits and those extremes that can be best articulated in binary terms. This again does not provide a great deal of guidance because almost any topics those principles guide us to can be articulated in binary opposites. A danger arises that this principle can become somewhat obsessive in that it is a fairly clear idea and seems easily applied. It will be recalled from the earlier discussion that it is a principle of organization of some importance in the earlier layer, and of diminishing importance during the romantic layer. While diminishing, however, I think it is still important in providing clear access to topics.

So while it can guide us in association with the first two principles to search for binary extremes, within which normality can be implicitly defined, its main use will come in organizing access to content which is selected primarily according to other principles. It guides us constantly to search for clear means of access to knowledge, as I will try to show by exemplifying its use for units and lessons in the next chapter.

Enabling students to form romantic associations

This principle guides us to select content that can best engage students' romantic associations. Along with some other principles, this can be used to support a curriculum area which we may call something like "Ideas." This particular principle will be useful in directing us to appropriate topics for such a curriculum area; topics such as precisely the kind of transcendent human qualities that most effectively engage romantic associations—Compassion, Courage, Power, Patience, and so on. Similarly this principle serves to support the curriculum area on "People Past and Present."

As with the previous principle, however, this one comes into play more prominently as a guide to the selection of aspects of a topic that has been chosen primarily on the basis of other principles. It directs us to seek out within a topic specific knowledge with which students can form clear romantic associations. To return to the Industrial Revolution example again, this principle will guide us to seek out, say, confident energy as integral to the Revolution and as a quality with which students can readily form a romantic association.

This principle can also come into play in deciding between topics which might appear equally desirable on the basis of other principles of selection. Other things being equal, one might simply ask which of them enables students to form the more vivid and engaging romantic associations.

Providing a strong affective component

This principle plays a powerful general role with regard to the romantic curriculum. It guides us to select content that is affectively meaningful to students in this romantic layer. This ensures that the emotional life of human beings is not excluded from the classroom but becomes a major feature of all aspects of the curriculum. It is through shared emotions and intentions that much of the world's knowledge can be made meaningful. This principle is also central to the aim of ensuring understanding rather than simply "learning." Understanding comes from knowing not just some content, but knowing its contexts and its human meaning. No area of our curriculum will be untouched by this principle. By "affective" I do not mean something that is a binary opposite to "cognitive," as it seems to be used in some books about curriculum. They are, in as far as the usual distinction between them makes sense, complementary aspects of understanding and meaning. This principle, then, directs us to consider why students should care about any content we wish to include in the curriculum.

The reason for emphasizing the importance of the affective is in part a product of the common assumption that we are made up of a cognitive part and an affective part, and that rationality, whose development is the point of education, is concerned with the cognitive part. I have argued extensively against this assumption and tried to point to the various kinds of damage it has caused in education. While we may distinguish between "affective" and "cognitive" for various purposes, it is a mistake to reify this distinction and deal with human thinking and understanding as though they have these distinct components. The two are always coalesced in human thinking and understanding, and rationality and education are matters in which coalesced cognitive and affective qualities work together. Henry James put it clearly:

> No education avails for the intelligence that doesn't stir in it some subjective passion, and . . . on the other hand almost anything that does so act is educative (James, 1913, p. 302).

This principle should not be confused with techniques that involve looking for an affective "hook" to a topic. Rather it is a matter of bringing to the fore inherent affective components. Some topics of course are more readily amenable to this treatment than others. In cases where all else is equal, we will let this principle determine which topics should be selected. It will guide us to material in which a strong affective component is more readily accessible and can more directly carry students to understand its central meanings.

Using the story form

During the romantic layer the students still inhabit a significantly story-shaped world. That is, experience and knowledge make sense more readily in story-forms. This principle guides us to select material that, other things being equal, is more amenable to story-shaping. It also guides us to shape material selected primarily according to other principles into story-forms. (I will give examples of how we can do this in the next chapter.) The call for the story-form follows from the analysis of how one can deal with an affective component in a manner appropriate to the romantic layer. It is within the story-form that one can clearly establish the affective meaning of a topic. The story-shaped world of the romantic layer, then, is a world in which feelings are prominent. The story-form can provide a human context which can make even theories and literal thinking more accessible and meaningful.

Stimulating wonder and awe

This principle supports those others that direct us to select content that exemplifies the extremes of human achievement and natural phenomena. But it can also direct us to bring out the wonder of the everyday world around students. Much of the world is so taken for granted that it is not noticed. This principle might lead us to a curriculum area called something like "The Technology of Familiar Things." In brief periods of time, perhaps twice each week, students would focus on the wonders of, say, nails and screws. (In the next section I will discuss the possible contents in more detail.) The aim would be to make the familiar strange, by sharing the human purposes that stimulated human energy and ingenuity to refashion the world, or even tiny parts of it. (In a trivial fashion some children's magazines do this by asking us to recognize familiar things when photographed from unusual angles, or when greatly magnified, and so forth. What I am suggesting is a kind of intellectual analogue of this, in which our understanding of the familiar is enhanced by recognizing familiar elements of our environment in new, wonderful contexts.)

Another sense of wonder could support a somewhat similar brief daily or weekly curriculum area dealing with a series of unrelated questions that students could raise and/or answer: are the stars round? how can birds fly? who built the Mexican pyramids? why are roads built higher in the middle? what good are mosquitoes? who made the first computer? must all things end? why are some people color-blind? and so endlessly on. The purpose here is not to teach physics, or astronomy, or history, but simply to raise, without pedagogical fuss, question after question about the world. And to answer them, without the kind of pedagogical fuss one sees in "discovery" strategies. Such strategies have their pedagogical uses, of course, but in this segment of the curriculum we are interested in raising questions and giving answers, directly, frequently, and in random order. The criterion for choosing questions and determining what kind of answer will suffice is to be derived directly from the principle of stimulating wonder and awe. One aspect of that stimulation comes from the exotic and dramatic, another, I am suggesting, should come from seeing the familiar as appropriately wonderful, and another aspect again by simply encouraging students persistently to wonder about the world, and to satisfy their wonder with a further wonder. Our questions, therefore, will make the student wonder about what may have been taken for granted; for example, how can birds fly? The answer, which need touch on only dramatic parts of the answer like hollow bones and the design and movement of feathers on wings, provides further things to wonder at. (This does not displace more detailed and systematic study of such questions in history, biology, mathematics, and so on.)

More commonly, however, this principle will direct us to select particular aspects of topics that are selected primarily according to other principles. It directs us to stop and reflect on each topic, bringing to the fore what is wonderful about it.

"Wonderful" is a word whose overuse has made it rather tired and empty. I am trying here to use it in a way that holds its proper meaning: of that before which we properly stand in wonder. Adolescence is a time when we can feel intensely alive. We need to meet this intensity with a curriculum that can adequately stimulate it and show it a world worthy of it. If the curriculum we offer students during this period lacks wonder and awe, and the associated constituents of romance, then we undercut important potential educational developments. If we do not stimulate their sense of wonder, we leave adolescent students victims of an intensity of boredom in schools, and the victims of any kind of sensation out of it. If this aspect of romance is not properly developed, students fall easily into various forms of cynicism.

The sense of awe is commonly seen as connected with religion. It is the human response to the sudden sense of a greater whole or unity in the world than our understanding can quite grasp. (Vico argued that this occasional flooding of our mind was the common intellectual state of early people (Vico, 1970).) We make sense of the world and of experience bit by bit, and sometimes the bits coalesce into greater wholes which permit more comprehensive understanding. I am trying, crudely, to describe some of these traditional coalescences in this scheme. We direct our pursuits of wisdom and certainty by intuitions and fleeting insights about greater wholes than our bits and pieces, our disparate disciplines, provide. A part of education at the romantic stage is to try to provide glimpses, hints, and guesses at what it is about the world and experience that properly evokes awe.

Focusing on human motives, intentions, and emotions

This principle overlaps with others that support a curriculum area such as "People Past and Present," and clearly overlaps with others above. It will be more influential, however, in guiding our selection of aspects of a topic included in the curriculum primarily on the basis of other principles. It will be seen in the next chapter to have a pervasive influence also on the planning of teaching. Subjects like mathematics or the sciences, which have usually been considered areas of the curriculum where human motives, intentions, and emotions play little or no part, will be most obviously altered if this principle is applied. The physics curriculum, for example, would be transformed to include a fuller human context for the material that properly forms its core. Instead of studying, say, Newton's Law of Motion in the abstract, or in the laboratory with the usual demonstrations, we would add to the curriculum knowledge about the character of Newton, about what he thought he was doing, why his study of nature mattered to him. One need not make an exhaustive study of Newton's metaphysics and beliefs here, but some notion of these are the appropriate context to make the Laws of Motion more humanly meaningful. This knowledge need not be a crude didactic introduction. One might follow the method described in the section on "The romantic classroom" in the next chapter, and come into class in an old wig and funny hat and introduce the Laws of Motion as though one were Newton. A plummy English eighteenth century accent and a bit of background material can work wonders. Until text-books are written in such a way to provide this kind of material, a bit of research into the human background of the knowledge to be taught is recommended by this principle.

Stimulating students' sensibility

This principle adds support for a curriculum area something like "Ideas." Apart from other uses for this area, which I will discuss below, it can include material directly intended to stimulate students' sensibility. We can embody ideas like Courage or Grief in vivid biographies, bringing out in the drama of intentions and events what those ideas can mean in real lives. In learning about others we can learn about ourselves. The teacher can in a number of ways deal with these ideas in students' lives. To have them write about their greatest grief, for example, and to share these anonymously with the class, can have a number of powerful and beneficial effects. We tend to treat classrooms a little on the model of institutions where the task at hand has a prescribed objective whose attainment satisfactorily ends the lesson. This industrial model tends to encourage us to suppress the individual humanity of each student, and of ourselves as teachers. An area of the curriculum which constantly confirms our common humanity and the emotional reality of our lives can help to make classrooms more humane social environments. Such a curriculum area can also stimulate students' sensibility.

But we should also consider the process by which this sensibility can be, and seems commonly to be, developed. We rarely find, initially, deep sensitivity to the suffering of others—indeed, typical cartoons encourage children to laugh at the suffering of the villain. Hecuba is nothing much to them, though sensitive children may exhibit a somewhat undifferentiated disturbance in response to strong emotion in a story or film. Early in the romantic layer we see the developing sensibility engaged mainly by the most dramatic and vivid events: the slaughter of innocents, dramatic self-sacrifice (as of Helen Cavel or at Thermopylae), the defiance of powerful injustice, and so on. Thereafter, most commonly with the help of literature, we can work to refine and elaborate students' sensibility, developing increasing "precision of the emotions." Sensibility grows with the perception that others feel and suffer as do we, or that events effect them no less than they effect us. It is something of a cliché to note that the pity we feel for others is proportionate, not to the amount of evil, but to the feelings we attribute to the sufferers.

The development of this sensibility can be seen, for example, in students' sense of patriotism. Often during the early part of this period we find that students develop a romantic association with their country. (Different governments work at achieving this end through schools with greater or less assiduousness and subtlety.) This romantic association leads to students seeing their country, as it were, as a bright and clear element contrasted with the relative dullness or darkness of the rest of the world. It stands out; it is the centre of their conception of the world, and the transcendent qualities that it embodies allow the student to understand that a country and its culture may be admirable and attractive. The heroes of the country, the ideals of its institutions, the qualities of its cultural life, and so on, all serve to engage emotions. The educational move, once this patriotic sense is established, is to begin engaging it to other countries and their heroes, institutions, cultural life, and so on. Once the association is made with the most readily accessible country, it can be elaborated and diffused to other countries, and it can be refined in its application to one's own. (One might begin with others, of course, but the paymasters of our schools are hardly ready for that.)

Apart from the particular curriculum content that this principle guides us to, concern with sensibility will have an effect on the selection of aspects of content chosen primarily on the basis of other principles. The most obvious curriculum content that can stimulate sensibility is poetry and literature, perhaps especially poetry. This is a tricky topic, as we can clearly make students uncomfortable and quickly make them powerfully antipathetic to poetry. Our choice of poems, and novels, then, is important. Below I will discuss what kinds of poems seem to me best able to stimulate and engage the romantic-stage student.

Providing knowledge of other styles of life

I will pass over the question of the cultural relativity of knowledge and arguments about our inability to understand other forms of life. What matters educationally is that we are constrained by our cultural presuppositions to varying degrees. This principle directs us to include in our curriculum material that will help students understand that their life style is one of a vast number of legitimate styles. The curriculum area of "People Past and Present" is supported also by this principle. The purpose must not be to show other forms of life as merely variants on the students' own; too often they are taken as more or less unfortunate perversions of the students' proper, natural way of life. Perhaps it does little harm to present them as various ways of fulfilling basic, common, human needs. A difficulty with this is that it tends to represent people as merely responding mechanically to environments, removing the creative aspects of individual cultures. Perhaps I am being unnecessarily scrupulous, but pedagogical method is crucial here. One needs to convey an understanding of the value of other life styles, while acknowledging that such understanding cannot be adequately achieved. This is also an area of considerable practical importance in a global village where one form of culture is dominating the transfer of information and knowledge. It is an area also in which piety and good intentions come easy, but practical solutions seem not to be coming at all. While this principle points to including in the curriculum knowledge about life styles that may be geographically and historically distant, or may be close at hand—as in studying the life of a film star, a bag-lady, a sailor, a member of some distinct religious faith, a stage-entertainer, a salesperson, etc.—other principles in this section might help the pedagogical task of developing understanding of the different, and also making the familiar come to be seen as "different" too. Important here is the careful emphasis on the values, worth, and dignity of each distinct style of life.

Here, too, we might acknowledge the common romantic rebellion or resistance, not in a well-meaning attempt to co-op it, but to show that it too has a long history of legitimacy, and values, worth, and dignity. Sympathy for rebels is relatively easy in cases like Galileo and the Inquisition, Socrates and the Athenian court, Ghandi and the British Army in India, and so on, but a little more difficult in the cases of those who rebel against the values held by the mainstream culture that the school represents. Education would seem to require us to include the latter too.

Stimulating the imagination and literal thinking

These two seem not to require particular discussion here. Stimulating imagination is involved in most of the above and stimulating literal thinking is the common focus of nearly all writing about education for the middle-school years. I add them here just as reminders that any set of principles that will guide our curriculum design during the romantic layers must attend to them. The requirement that we stimulate literal thinking in particular will justify the inclusion of mathematics, logic, and the sciences in our curriculum.

In concluding this section it is worth adding what I hope is obvious: that these are principles to guide us and they should not become obsessive requirements or rigid rules. We should not always insist that, say, binary opposites always be found and made prominent in structuring a lesson or unit, or that the story-form become an absolutely essential component in all curriculum or pedagogical planning. Sometimes we may find it convenient to ignore some of these principles; some content may just prove intransigent to being organized according to them; sometimes the insistence on binary opposites may prove counter-productive due to other inherent structures of a topic being more engaging; and so on. Obviously I think these principles can provide important guidance in the selection of curriculum content and its organization into accessible and engaging units and lessons. But it would be a mistake to see them as the complete set of romantic principles; the rigid insistence that they are could get in the way of the application of others that I have not thought of.

Curriculum structure

In this section I will move "down" from the level of principles to a discussion of the ways one might structure a curriculum derived from those principles. I will distinguish a number of curriculum areas that could be formulated for dividing up the timetable. Each of these divisions could be taken as a subject to be scheduled according to the amount of time we want to give it. But, as there are many ways of being and becoming educated, so there are many sensible ways of designing a curriculum derived from these principles. What follows is just one way.

A general point about the curriculum outline I will sketch in this chapter is that the divisions do not comprise a coherent set each member of which is exclusive of others and each of which represents a similar kind of category to the others. They are a disparate, overlapping set. "People Past and Present" will obviously overlap with the "History" area, and both will overlap with some parts of the "Ideas" area. I don't think we need to struggle to coordinate these, to ensure, for example that we look at ancient Roman people while studying ancient Rome in history and examining the idea of Empire. Romantic understanding, as explored above, seems not overly concerned with systematic coherence across its intellectual inventory, but rather establishes associations directly with a diverse array of knowledge. Systematization becomes more central in the next, philosophic, layer. This is not a plea for diffusion of meaning and a random, chaotic curriculum structure, but rather an observation that the rather disparate and overlapping curriculum areas outlined below should not be considered as obvious flaws in need of sorting out, but as appropriately mirroring something about romantic understanding.

To those who have read *Primary Understanding* it will be clear already that the structure of the romantic curriculum is going to be significantly different from that outlined in the earlier volume. Unlike most currently dominant curriculum structures, this one will affect a significant discontinuity between the year three curriculum and the one to be sketched below. To mitigate the potential difficulties of too sharp a transition, and given the typical range of differences among any group of children at about age eight, I will designate year four as a transition year. Its purpose will be to introduce elements of the romantic layer and specifically to stimulate the development of romantic capacities. It will be easier to describe the year four transition curriculum briefly after describing what it is a transition to. I will also designate year nine as a transition year with a somewhat different curriculum designed to stimulate philosophic capacities, and will describe it in the next volume. What follows below then is designed for years five to eight inclusive.

The overall principle at work in moving to the curriculum recommendations that follow is that we want to introduce students to the various means that have been developed in, or are accessible to, the Western tradition to make sense of the world and of experience romantically. The aim is to ensure that students develop an adequate sense of the tradition to which they belong and to the traditions that confront them, when "an adequate sense of tradition manifests itself in a grasp of those future possibilities which the past has made available to the present" (MacIntyre, 1981, p. 207).

It might be useful to begin discussion of the middle-school curriculum by considering some of the more unfamiliar curriculum areas that will make it up:

Ideas

It will be evident from the discussion of principles above that I am proposing a curriculum area focused on ideas. Apart from the reasons given above, or rather as another dimension of the reasons give above, this curriculum area is supported by a certain practical urgency. One of the major failures of our present educational efforts is that so many school leavers have little sense of what ideas are or how to use them and control them. They are consequently at the mercy of the few submerged ideas that dominate the mass media and of political manipulators of simple ideas. The development and manipulation of ideas are central to rationality, to romantic understanding, and to the Western intellectual tradition. "The unexamined life is not worth living," Socrates said near the beginning of this tradition—no doubt an overstatement, and anyway one wonders how he would have known. Still, reflection, the capacity to think about one's thinking, the ability to know oneself and keep within one's bounds, the capacity to distinguish between the world and what we think about it, are all aided by the development of fluency in dealing with ideas.

All disciplines have ideas, of course, and all disciplines will be able to contribute to this aim. And while one may consider Courage as an idea and examine it through a dozen examples of different forms of courage and use these to reflect on the nature of courage, or courages, this obviously in no way hinders the students' considering the courage of, say, Ghandi while studying India in history. On the contrary. Seeing ideas embedded in different content is just one of the ways in which that content becomes enriched and engaging, and the ideas become more flexible.

To Piagetians and others who are concerned that these ideas may be "formal" or abstract concepts beyond many students' grasp especially during the earlier years of the romantic layer, a number of responses might be made. First, it need not be assumed that the ideas will be dealt with abstractly. No doubt in each case "concrete" examples of the idea will be dealt with. Indeed, part of the point would be to consider a number of disparate examples in order to show its complexity and enable students to manipulate the idea flexibly. The purpose of this curriculum area is not to give definitions of ideas but to help students flexibly to grasp their complexity by multiple examples. Second, understanding does not come because students are "ready" for it. As we do not wait till babies are "ready" to talk before talking to them, so waiting for students to be "ready" to deal abstractly with ideas will not stimulate and develop that capacity. Third, the inferences that have been drawn to education from Piaget's theory seem to me mostly unwarranted, and rarely sensitive to the insecurity of the theory itself. (Egan, 1983, ch. 3). And I might add here that I consider this curriculum area important in preparing the ground for, and leading towards, philosophic understanding.

This curriculum area would seem appropriate throughout the middle-school years, dealing with a wide set of ideas. It would continue into the transition year nine, emerging in the philosophic layer playing a somewhat different and more dominant curriculum role. Students might consider ideas such as Justice, Courage, Grief, Patience, Authority, Knowledge, Liberty, Hope, Beauty, Space, Altruism, Fear, and so on. I would also include as variants proverbs and parables: brief forms that embody ideas in readily graspable ways. Collections of proverbs and parables drawn from all over the world are available to support this aspect of the Ideas curriculum. Teaching through parables is familiar in the West through the Judeo-Christian Bible, though much more extensive and varied use of the brief parable story is common in the Islamic tradition. Perhaps the proverbs and parables might be the more common way of introducing ideas in the earlier part of this layer, moving on to exemplifications of more "abstract" ideas later.

I imagine that the purpose of this curriculum area can be achieved in relatively brief time segments, perhaps fifteen minutes, about three times each week. The relative brevity seems appropriate because detailed elaboration and didactic teaching is not the point. These quarter hours are intended as stimulants to a particular form of mental life; that at later leisure the student can ruminate on the ideas, can play with them, can come to feel at ease with them. What is needed is sufficient time to introduce the idea, by telling a parable or proverb or by asking how students understand or can give examples of a specific idea. Discussion should be encouraged and the "lesson" can be concluded once it is clear that the idea has been launched with enough description, explanation, contexts of use, and meaning that students can take it away and do what they want with it.

People past and present

A number of principles from romance support a distinct curriculum area such as this. A useful resource for this area would be a text-book of brief lives, in which the focus would be on the romantic qualities of the subjects. Each life story would be selected to exemplify the extremes of courage, endurance, villainy, or whatever, showing them in terms of vivid events and in conflict with opposing forces. This need not become a stale formula. Obviously it could if approached without imagination, but equally obviously it need not. As with the Ideas area, these brief lives might take no more than fifteen minutes each, perhaps four or five times each week. The same life may be revisited on a number of occasions. The lives need not appear in any particular sequence, topical or chronological. Indeed random ordering seems more desirable: Napoleon today, Mother Teresa tomorrow, Ramon Lull yesterday, Marie Curie last week, Jesse Owens next week. As I indicated above, this curriculum area does not displace history nor the more systematic attempt to study people's lives in the context of their times and places.

Students in groups can be given a couple of weeks notice to select and present a brief biography of someone whose human qualities seem to transcend the everyday world around them. The aim is not to organize a systematic life-story in appropriate diversity and chronological order, filling in as much background detail as possible. Rather, the focus is on very specific events which exemplify transcendent human qualities in peoples' lives. Historical and contemporary famous characters provide one obvious source of such lives. But a significant feature of this curriculum area is to help students to see everyone, including themselves, as embodying transcendent human qualities. Consequently, a significant research activity for students might be to engage in interviews with people in their community—in the old people's homes, in offices, wherever people can be found to talk about their lives and memories. In such cases tape recorders can be useful tools and from what may be elaborate "oral history" case-studies, students can learn to abstract particular incidents that exemplify the transcendent hopes, achievements, fears, events, of people's lives.

The technology of familiar things

I would not include an area for this topic in the curriculum as an attempt to deal with the familiar as a basis for expanding "outwards" to the less familiar. In fact the organizing principles for this curriculum area would be opposite to that familiar concern. The aim might be better seen as making the familiar strange and wonderful. A common theme would be discovering, in general terms, how familiar things in our environment are made and/or work. Subjects might include clothing, tools, nails and screws, glass, salt, automobiles, books, light bulbs, pottery, cardboard, the plastic hardened laminated surfaces of their desks, and so on.

The romantic purpose for this curriculum area is similar to that for "People Past and Present." It is not to teach technology; it is not designed to come with tests to see whether students can recall the details that were used to convey the sense of wonder that can be evoked by what we most take for granted. In the case of screws for example, the aim will not be to classify them and have students learn their different names, but to show the ingenuity and precision of their varied designs for different purposes. Our purpose might again be best achieved in fifteen-minute segments, perhaps once or twice a week. This is a case in which the technology of the video-disk might serve a useful purpose. To be able to access immediately clear demonstrations of the relative gripping power of different screws on different materials would support the aim of this topic wonderfully. It is also a curriculum area that would be most hospitable to visitors to the classroom. Experts on light bulbs or on carpets or glass-making, and so on, could add to the effectiveness of this curriculum area, particularly if the visitors are encouraged to bring out what is dramatic, unexpected, strange, or wonderful in their topic of expertise. An enthusiastic plumber proud of his or her expertise with faucets or taps and their subtle intricacies can make turning on water into a momentary wonder.

Making and doing

This continues a curriculum area from the previous layer, but within it I would like to include much of what is now included in woodwork, clothes making, metalwork and other areas commonly seen as preparatory to, or a part of, vocational education. I mention it here not to propose it as a distinct area but to propose moving it under the heading of "Arts," which I will discuss separately below. The main purpose for this is to emphasize the aesthetic dimension that is educationally a necessary part of the practical arts.

The universe, animal and plant life, other countries and ways of living

These are three further curriculum areas that might be introduced. Each of them would follow the basic pattern laid out for the areas above.

Each would require no more than about fifteen minutes a few times in the week. These involve explorations of the extremes of the contexts within which we live. They will overlap with more systematic studies, but their purpose is a little different from those. Here we are gathering material of particular romantic appeal. This is the time for exploring the extent of reality, for locating the bright bits and pieces, for trying to exhaust particular engaging areas of knowledge. The curriculum during these years is to be packed with information and ideas of the kind I have been describing. Some classification and ordering will go on willy-nilly, but this is not the primary focus of our curricular concern here. Nor is evaluation of what is learnt; the prospect of a "test" at the end would undermine the purpose of these explorations. The focus rather is on engagement with the wonders of the world and human experience and, as a consequence, the extensive amassing of considerable and diverse knowledge about them.

A prerequisite to the development of adequate philosophic understanding is the accumulation of a considerable quantity of diverse knowledge during the romantic layer. During this layer, then, it is educationally important that students simply learn a lot. By making knowledge "romantically" engaging, this requirement should not lead to the strains we see when bodies of knowledge arranged in logical schemes are impressed into students' memories. I hope it is clear by now that the principles of romance and the characteristic ways in which students' imaginations can be engaged by knowledge indicate how a considerable range of what might be somewhat less systematic knowledge than is usually striven for during these years of schooling can be achieved.

Each of the above curriculum areas is intended to take relatively small blocks of time. Some flexibility in allotting curriculum time will be more desirable for this scheme, much of which will less easily accommodate to the typical equal time blocks that are currently the norm. In addition to these briefer areas, five curriculum topics will require larger blocks of time to achieve more systematic purposes. The five are history, the sciences, language, the arts, and mathematics/logic/computing.

I will discuss each of these briefly, not with the aim of providing a comprehensive curriculum outline for the middle school years, which would require a book by itself, but rather so that I can try to indicate what would be some distinctive characteristics of a "romantic" curriculum. I will deal with history first, as one feature of the romantic layer curriculum is that it will be more historically oriented in general than is common at present. That is, one impulse derived from the principles inferred from romantic understanding is towards seeking knowledge as a product of the lives and social conditions in which it was first generated. So mathematics, for example, will be seen as far as possible in historical context. This will have two effects: first, to embed the particular mathematical manipulation in a meaningful social context showing it as a product of comprehensible human purposes, and, second, to add a little to the students' expanding bright circles of familiarity with other times and conditions.

Before going on I should perhaps consider why the notion of cultural recapitulation does not compel me to an even more radically historical curriculum. Why do I not propose that all subjects should be studied and "recapitulated" in the sequence of their historical invention or discovery? The belief that such schemes are required by a recapitulationist theory is true only if the theory ties itself into knowledge. My argument that it is kinds of understanding that are recapitulated frees me to build the curriculum from any content that seems best able to evoke, stimulate, and develop those forms of understanding. So one can attend to current social utility in this scheme, in a way that was problematic for the radical recapitulationist theories of the late nineteenth century.

History. During the history curriculum of the previous layer, students will have learned the history of the world in general terms as the "great stories" of human cultures. They will have recycled through the whole of human history as a continuous and continuing struggle for freedom against oppression, for knowledge against ignorance, for security against fear and danger, and so on. In each cycle, through the overall historical story, different events and characters will have been highlighted. Such general accounts would work on the "cliff-hanger" principle, as a story constantly moving towards a resolution that is constantly undermined or hindered or changed. This is neither an improper nor necessarily inaccurate way of representing history; it catches a particular "layer" of the human story comprehensible to the child because the struggles have direct analogies in children's own lives. "Human life has a determinate form, the form of a certain kind of story . . . it is not just that poems and sagas narrate what happens to men and women, but that in their narrative form poems and sagas capture a form that was already present in the lives which they relate" (MacIntyre, 1981, p. 117). There are many layers of historical understanding—four of which I am trying to excavate in these volumes—and in the romantic layer the focus is on a kind of narrative that is not merely our imposition but also reflects one layer of how the people we will study made sense of their own lives.

So we begin this layer with students having already in place the broad story of human history, in a number of its more dramatic dimensions. During the romantic layer students will explore particular events in more detail. They will examine particular vivid instances of the struggles for freedom, the victories of oppression, the temporary gains of security, the recurrent dangers, the expansions of knowledge and persistence of ignorance, and constantly the people caught up in these events, and their hopes, fears, intentions, strengths and weaknesses.

I have perhaps already written enough for my notion of an appropriate romantic history curriculum to be clear. It need not be organized on the basis of chronological sequence, but could be thematic, structuring events on strong narrative lines and using causal connections internally. The causal connections among themes need be only sketchily drawn. The exotic and dramatic will be prominent in this history; it is the time for gathering up the bright bits and pieces. Thomas Carlyle characterized history as "the essence of innumerable biographies." We might reasonably be wary of that "essence," but for the romantic layer this catches an important feature of history and what makes it engaging, meaningful, and of educational value to students. Our central focus will not be on mass movements or institutions rising and falling or diplomatic shifts or national policies, or on any of the depersonalized concepts that have been developed to describe and explain historical change. The romantic history curriculum may include all of these but as incidentals to the packed lives of lots of people acting in particular ways in response to their hopes, fears, intentions, and so on. And in further particular it will be the transcendent actions, the transcendent events that will be the focus of attention. Institutions, policies, and so on, become accessible to the degree that they are seen as the products of people's emotions and intentions and the transcendent actions these stimulate.

This may be seen as simply a return to a discredited kind of "great man" approach to history. Such an inference would be mistaken. Apart from the distinctive romantic characteristics, it might be observed that it also coincides with what is becoming recognized in a new way as the value of biographical studies for the understanding of history (cf. Le Goff, 1989). As Bernard Guenée puts it:

> a biography enables one to take a first look at the overwhelming complexity of things. What is more, the study of structures seems to give too much prominence to necessity . . . . But "it is only through men that things happen." And the story of a life helps us to understand better how fragile and uncertain the destiny of these men is . . . . A biography makes it possible to

pay more attention to chance, to the event, to chronological
sequence; it alone can give the historian a sense of the time
through which people actually lived (cited in Le Goff, 1989, p.
394).

Establishing our cultural identity requires that we learn about and
make some kind of distinct association with, what is now popularly
called our roots. One aspect of this is fulfilled by learning about our
family tree, our ancestral origins as far as these are known, the places
our ancestors lived, and the kind of work they did. These roots, however,
are largely a social matter. There is a similar sense in which the exploration of reality, the association with the transcendent, and the perception
that all our knowledge is a response to human needs and purposes which
we share, is a part of a wider establishment of our roots as cultural
animals.

As we learn history during the middle-school years and come to
understand the actions of particular people as motivated by their courage,
or fear, or anger, or love, or whatever, and examine the results, we are
also exploring ourselves. We begin to discover our individual selves in
those cultural roots to which we attach romantic associations. We do
not just learn about, say, Alexander the Great or Florence Nightingale
and then admire their courage and energy. Rather, we recognize them
as a reflection of our own developing courage and energy. We recognize
them as a couple of our cultural roots, and by learning about their
struggles, campaigns, adventures, the oppositions they faced, and their
characters, we give some definition to ourselves as cultural beings.

This is also the time for the more exotic features of history, which
can trespass into what is more commonly considered anthropology. If
we study the ancient Greeks, we will want to consider their alienness,
rather than the domesticated Victorians in fancy dress that are the normal
textbook staple. We will explore their curious rites and rituals. The
romantic approach to history will be very ready to move off into the
byways of the past that tend to be little explored in the regular history
curriculum. Later in the layer, to prepare for the philosophic concern
with our use of "structural amnesia" in recalling the past, we will
increasingly consider what kinds of people write history and for what
purposes do they do it, and what kinds of people are most commonly
written about and what kinds commonly ignored.

This layered scheme is not a kind of "spiralling" curriculum in which
we constantly return to topics at a different level of sophistication.
Rather, in each layer students will be looking at history through, as it
were, different lenses which bring a different level of historical phenom-

ena into focus. The contribution of the romantic layer is to provide much diverse knowledge of historical events and to stimulate and develop the basic concepts of intelligible action in history, particularly those which give meaning to narratives built from people's intentions and emotions. The more varied and diverse the topics studied the more likely is the student to develop sophisticated ways to make sense of their own and other people's actions and experience.

The sciences. What does science look like when considered "romantically"? During the previous layer the curriculum was designed to encourage an imaginative participation in nature and an exploration of various particular features of the natural world. It aimed to develop knowledge of science and technology by seeing inventions and discoveries in narrative accounts of, say, the story of flight from Daedalus to space probes, of locomotion on land from the wheel to the hovercraft, of the discovery of the universe from mythic accounts of the stars to black holes and pulsars, of the exploration of the earth from African beginnings to satellite mapping, of measuring time from the sun to quartz crystals. During the romantic layer, the sciences are to serve as one of the main agents in stimulating and developing literal thinking and rationality. One means to this will be an increasing concern with theories and experiments as students grow through this layer. Theories and experiments will be usefully introduced, again, through the lives, hopes, and intentions of those who first designed and constructed them. The purpose for this is again to connect the particular knowledge being learned with the romantic imagination. The reasons for *this* are the pedagogical ones addressed throughout the book, which aim to discourage "disembedded" science teaching, because such disembedded teaching of disembedded science also tends to convey a false view of science. It represents it too simply as a smoothly and regularly expanding objective truth breaking through clouds of ignorance and superstition. By contextualizing topics of the sciences curriculum we emphasize that scientific knowledge has been made by people in particular times and places for particular purposes. The particular knowledge may transcend those circumstances, but access to its meaning seems much easier during this layer if students know something of the context of its invention or discovery.

The approach to science that I am recommending during this layer fits quite easily with that which was common in the Romantic period, when it was known as Natural History, and found its fulfillment less in large-scale theory building and rather more in the labelling of minutiae, of listing, categorizing, classifying, searching out and bringing under some kind of order the variety of phenomena relevant to the different branches of science. It is a form of scientific activity that developed along with the realization that the world around us is not static and unchanging but is itself a part of a narrative which we can come to understand. Nature too is seen to have a kind of history, which with ingenuity we can persuade it to tell us. Nature was perceived as having "secrets" which, by careful observation, we can "unlock." We can learn much about the exploration of nature and the requisite skills needed to "unlock" its "secrets" by learning about how particular individuals established scientific knowledge bit by bit, and how this forced the constant reformulation of theories. So, rather than seeing the sciences as bodies of fixed facts to be learned, we can encourage students to see it as a peculiar adventure in which people have, with infinite patience, ingenuity, and persistence tried to pin down some things securely.

The principles I have inferred from romance do not seem necessarily to lead to a science curriculum made up of different content from what is presently common. Rather, using the lens analogy again, it encourages us to bring into focus a particular layer of scientific invention, discovery and knowledge. The principles do suggest the inclusion of a couple of areas not usually associated with the sciences curriculum. One of these is cosmology. In this layer it would pick up from the curriculum of the previous layer and study its extent, scale, and more dramatic features, perhaps in the manner used in the Carl Sagan *Cosmos* book and T.V. series. The more uninhibitedly romantic features of that series embarrassed some critics, but they would seem to me to fit quite well with this layer of understanding. The second area I would include in the sciences in geography. At present it tends to have a rather precarious existence, certainly in North America and Australia, attached to history within social studies. Clearly it will remain appropriate to learn some geography, if only incidentally, while studying history, but the systematic study of geography I think might be better pursued in the sciences.

Language. Under this heading I want to include, what might be expected, the study of literature, the performance of drama, learning additional languages, and also a couple of less common topics, rhetoric and humor.

The use of poetry, plays, and novels is, as William Empson pointed out, that they show you what it is like to have feelings other than your own. No doubt that is too simple a way of putting it, but it suggests the way in which literature adds to our capacities and adds to our sensibility.[1] Literature, and particularly poetry, can enrich the rhythms of one's language and one's ability to make richer, more abundant sense of the world and of experience. One might add Northrop Frye's observation that "It's clear that the end of literary teaching is not simply the admiration of literature; it's something more like the transfer of imaginative energy from literature to the student" (Frye, 1962, p. 55).

The kind of poetry that can best support the development of romantic understanding is not necessarily that produced by the major poets of the romantic movement. What makes them major poets is that their poetry engages many layers of understanding. Much of Wordsworth's poetry, for example, is likely to be beyond the grasp of students during this layer because his poetry is rarely simply romantic; it is, in the senses to be elaborated in later volumes, philosophic and ironic as well. This is often the case for his simpler poems that are often anthologized for schools. Simplicity of diction in this case is confused with accessibility of meaning. When aspects of a poem are beyond students' grasp, they have a power to disturb and cause a diffuse resistance. Students cannot then easily respond to them, except with groans, abuse, or some self-protective dismissal. This is too often the fate of poetry read aloud to students during this layer. While it is important for some poetry to be read aloud, preferably by someone who does it well, in order that the rhythms and play of sound get a clear airing, a significant amount of time should be allowed for browsing and silent reading, so that students can discover privately what they respond to. A staple for recitation, however, should be poems with strong rhythms and powerful and clear narrative lines, whose content focuses on extremes of human achievements and on transcendent human qualities, with highly charged emotions confronting—what is for students newly discovered—the transience of things.

The kinds of literature that best supports romantic understanding can be readily inferred from the earlier discussion of romance, as so much of the discussion has been in the context of literary sensibility. Perhaps I need to make clear that romance, as I am using it, should not be associated with the "Teen-Romance" books published in such vast numbers for females at middle-school years of the "Teen-Omnipotent-Rebel" stories consumed in lesser numbers by males. These qualify as junk

---

[1]Sensibility is sometimes associated or confused with moral education. They seem to me distinct, if not entirely so then very largely so. If literary sensibility were a major contributor to moral education we would expect professors of English to be among the more moral people in society. This is an example of the logical form *reductio ad absurdum*.

literature and do for the sensibility and intellect pretty much what junk food does for the body. There is clearly nothing much wrong with the occasional junk food meal and no great harm in the occasional "Teen-Romance" or "Teen-Omnipotent-Rebel" story. Some teachers and parents seem happy to encourage such reading, as it will help reading "skills" and may lead on to better literature. A diet of such stories seems as likely to lead on to nourishing literature as junk food leads on to nourishing food—that is, not much. They more commonly seem to lead on to more of the same, as their commercial exploiters well know. Perhaps this is too grumpily pessimistic a view. These kinds of stories have an attraction because they do draw on some of the features of romance considered earlier.

What one looks for in literature classes, however, are stories that share these, and also include other, romantic qualities. A story such as L.M. Montgomery's *Anne of Green Gables* has some of the characteristics of Teen-Romances, but has in addition a range of other romantic qualities; Anne being something of the typically romantic, noble, but beleaguered heroine, we get a sense of rebelliousness and indomitable strength in the face of adversity that allow transcendent associations with a range of experience distinct from the everyday routines of the students. By the middle of this layer, if students have adequately accumulated the capacities of the mythic layer and the early romantic layer, then Charles Dickens's great novels come within their "zone of proximal development"—to use Vygotsky's insightful term for what students can be helped to understand by a teacher which, by themselves, they would have too much difficulty grasping. An education in a modern English-speaking culture that does not provide students with a considerable diet of Dickens must be considered pitifully inadequate—as empty as an ancient Greek ignorant of Homer. Of all the great romantic writers, Dickens is accessible to students in the romantic layer, without obtrusive philosophic and ironic hurdles. (Of course, I should add, there are also alternatives to Dickens!)

Given the earlier observations about memory and the imagination and the close relationship between them, such that one can see the imagination as a part of the ever-active human memory working in another dimensions,[2] I infer that memorization of literature is educationally

---

[2] A point given another dimension, relevant to history in romantic understanding by Sir Lewis Namier's:

> One would expect people to remember the past and to imagine the future. But in fact, when discoursing or writing about history, they imagine it in terms of their own experience, and when trying to gauge the future they cite supposed analogies from the past; till, by a double process of repetition, they imagine the past and remember the future (cited in Gross, 1983, p. 322).

very important, particularly during this layer. This is one of those unfashionable conclusions this scheme leads to. We are often surprised by the subtleties of ancient Greek psychology, embedded in the relationships among the gods. As we make what seem to us new psychological insights, we find them prefigured or adumbrated in Greek literature, as Freud for one pointed out so forcefully. Mnemosyne, the goddess of memory, for example, gave birth to the Muses, the personifications of the highest intellectual and artistic aspirations, her daughters by Zeus thus demonstrating the close relationship that the Greeks thought prevailed between memory and human imaginative activities. We will not, of course, want to build a significant recommendation for the language curriculum on a reading of a Greek myth, but the Greek myth helps to support the inferences made from the earlier observations about memory and imagination, and is supported also by informal observations we can make about the values of memorizing poems, drama, and prose passages. Such memorization will often involve hard work, though perhaps less hard for students who have retained oral capacities from the mythic layer than for the typical student today. But, if the material to be memorized is well chosen, it can greatly expand the rhythms of our language and the range of our articulate grasp over the world and experience. I should perhaps add, in the face of the contempt in which "rote-learning" has been held during the whole period in which progressivism has been influential, that I do not see this memorization as an occasional imposition, but as a regular part of the language curriculum: perhaps a weekly homework assignment will require poems or prose passages to be memorized. Recognizing that this recommendation will run harshly against some people's ingrained assumption, I would like to defend it at greater length. Perhaps I can refer readers to Volume 1, Chapter 2 where differences between human and computer "memories" are discussed, in which I emphasize the fact that, unlike books or computers or other storage devices, human memories are ever-active matrices of meaning and that they can work only with what they know. It is for this reason—that the imagination can work only with what is known—that this scheme emphasizes the great and persisting educational importance of students learning much and diverse knowledge. Knowing where to find knowledge and "learning how to learn" have their clear educational values, but they become enemies of education if they are used as justifications for reducing the amounts of knowledge that students should memorize; the mind and imagination can do nothing with the library of knowledge one knows how to access when "needed."

Drama can help release the constraints of conventions on students and encourage imaginative exploration of other lives and feelings, and consequently enlarge their own. There is place here for the usual drama plays and the most improvisational explorations of the kind well exemplified in Dorothy Heathcote's work (see also Levy, 1987).

The earlier discussion and principles lead to the promotion of rhetoric from an occasional or minor role in the language curriculum to a central activity. In Chapter 2 I discussed the role of rhetoric as being one of the main agents that preserved many of the capacities of orality into a literate culture, and this recapitulation scheme suggests it can help to perform much the same role in the individual's educational development. There is now a growing educational literature on rhetoric, though much of it is aimed at the college years. I would like here to add just a few points particular to my theme.

In rhetoric classes students might usefully learn dialects, with accents, of their native language, exploring what such dialects permit one to articulate, and studying the force or subtlety or vividness that they permit, which may be difficult to achieve in one's native dialect. Similarly, students should be encouraged to explore what Walter Ong has called different "grapholects," different forms of writing language in addition to the proper forms that are approved. The grapholects might experiment with the dialects. One of the great losses common with literacy is the inadequate mastery so many students achieve with the dominant writing techniques of their culture. This means for *most* people that they never learn to write what they can think, feel, and say. *Most* people's writing is a grey ghost made up of empty conventional forms, such that they cannot communicate anything that carries emotional force through writing. And this constriction, I fear, reacts back on thinking and talking, and stifles imaginative outlets. Well, this is a criticism common to the point of boredom. Is this not just an effect of writing that we should accept, and not dream of some unrealizable ideal of expressive writers? I think the ideal is far from unrealizable, and the problem is clearly caused by our conventionalizing and constraining of writing to a very limited norm. The writing of literate but largely unschooled people very often has an emotional power that we find only in the major writers of our tradition of schooled high literacy. One sees it now also in old people in the West, who learned the alphabet and how to write, but then went out to work before they were fully schooled in how to write "properly." One sees it also more frequently in the third world countries today, where people are taught simple literacy and no more. What frequently happens is that these people use literacy to "talk" with. Their spelling, syntax, grammatical constructions are not at all like those of this book. But their writing has a directness and force that we high literates have largely lost the power to achieve. I think that exploration of "grapholects" would at least hinder the decay of our oral capacities as literacy becomes increasingly internalized. Relatedly, this seems to me the time for explorations in etymology (an argument for which seems to me well made in Temple and Gillet, 1989).

In rhetoric, students might explore and study the variety of language uses around them, in advertising, newspapers, comics, prayers, scientific articles, politics, and so on. In each case, the surface and structure of the language should be studied and related to its purposes. Students might also experiment with copying such styles, and copying, say, formal eighteenth-century prose, and reflect in each case on how the forms of language affect their thinking and feeling. (Again, I recognize that to the teacher struggling to achieve marginal literacy, these will seem like exotic and hopelessly unpractical suggestions, but I am addressing what seems to me realistic if students have been taught the curriculum of the mythic layer adequately and have made a successful transition to romantic understanding.) In addition to the above, students might be encouraged to keep diaries in which they can be helped to explore their daily experience and feelings, elaborating a sense of "I" as a separate, private, distinct, and secret viewpoint. All the above rhetorical activities have among their effects stimulation of thought about language itself and what has been called "metalinguistic awareness." This by itself seems to have clear benefits on students' language use and literacy generally (Herriman, 1986).

A further aspect of the rhetoric curriculum that I think is important but rarely addressed in educational writing is humor. The wise-crack and the abusive joke are the main examples one finds among typical males and more or less subtle pretend jokes seem more prominent with females. Much middle-school humor seems to be of a defensive, "put-down" kind. Students need such defenses of course against the institutions, especially the school, that hem them in. Rhetoric can be used to move from the rather limited examples of humor that abound in the direction of much greater elaboration of forms and range. By range I mean intrusion beyond the confines of word-jokes into the world—more elaborate pretend jokes. One example, more male-oriented perhaps, is the *Monty Python*-ish skit. At their best, such skits create a consistent, logical world, so wildly at variance with everyday reality because a single metaphor is taken literally and explored well beyond the range of its applicability. I think the use of humor to keep metaphoric capacities working at maximum fluency is one of the great defences against the tyranny of convention.

"A metaphor might be regarded as a calculated category-mistake . . . in which a set of terms, or alternative labels is transported; and the organization they effect in the alien realm is guided by their habitual use in the home realm" (Goodman, 1976, pp. 73–74). Both rhetoric and drama might be more deliberately used to stimulate and develop metaphoric capacities and, connectedly, our capacity for humor. I think we generally underestimate the importance of humor in education; because it is a serious business, too many educators think it must therefore be a grim business. But human life at its most serious has a hallowed place for humor (as William of Baskerville argues (Eco, 1983)). Intellectual development seems to require a flexibility and fluency that are tied in with the continued stimulation of our capacity to use metaphors, and I know of nothing better than humor to achieve this. An incidental benefit of such developments is the range and subtlety of jokes we can get pleasure from: something whose educational importance seems again to be greatly underestimated.

Another topic within the language curriculum is that concerned with second-language learning. This does not seem something that needs much argument, as utilitarian interests tend to coincide with those of education. The difference tends to lie in the relationship of the language to forms of thought and cultural assumptions. Utilitarian interests are served by learning to translate the second into the native and to negotiate one's way around the foreign culture. Educational interest, on the other hand, require the native to grow into the second language and its distinctive forms of thought and to be invaded in turn by the foreign cultural assumptions. Learning a second language, then, requires the enlargement of students' perceptions and sensibilities, and contributes an enhanced ability to make sense of the world and of experience.

More contentious is the place of "classical" languages, for Western students, Latin and Greek. They no longer have any shred of utilitarian support, and in a curriculum that gives itself very largely over to utilitarian criteria, classical languages largely disappear. William Hazlitt in the nineteenth century expressed one sharp view of the curriculum then in place in the major private schools of Britain: "Anyone who has passed through the regular graduations of a classical education, and is not made a fool by it, may consider himself as having had a very narrow escape" (Hazlitt, 1951, p. 147). Today, however, one may meet, particularly in England and particularly in academic circles, a somewhat bewildered regret at the decay of the classics in schools. It seems self-evident to such people that this decay has resulted in a perceptible reduction in analytic keenness in students and an unquestionable inability to make sense of vast areas of their cultural experience. In North America, the large scale abandonment of the classics in schools earlier in this century was, and as far as one can see generally still is, taken as a self-evidently progressive move away from the uselessly "ornamental" towards dealing meaningfully with the everyday world around the student. Of the North American assumption about the irrelevance of the classics one must ask what replaced them in the school curriculum that has borne such obvious educational fruit. There is not space here for any elaborate argument on behalf of the classics for the middle-school years, but I do want to note that a number of the principles of romantic understanding would clearly support an expansion of their presence in the middle-school curriculum.

The arts.   Romanticism bequeathed to us an idea of the importance of the arts and of artists that would have likely shocked even the more assertive Renaissance artists. Coleridge's sense of the imagination being the nearest earthly embodiment of God's creative power expresses the hallowed role artists and their admirers accepted for artistic creations in society. Creating works of art came to be seen as the most heroic activity open to human beings, and a sacred duty for those whose creative powers were widely recognized. So while many young people died of "consumption," the disease was seen as especially tragic when it justified Keats's fears that he should cease to be before his pen had gleaned his teeming brain. And it was perfectly comprehensible that Beethoven should forego committing the suicide to which his deafness inclined him because, as he wrote to his brothers, he felt a duty to give to the world the music he knew was still within him. The romantic sense of the arts, then, is one in which artistic activity is generated in a mysterious center of the self and can be expressed in any of the myriad of forms which seem suitable to the kind of truth and sense of reality found within. The arts curriculum is the place where students can explore this dimension of human experience in their own experience; it is a time when they can do things which may or may not have any practical utility but which certainly have value.

This curriculum area is generally well served by insightful writing on music and art relevant to romantic understanding, and one in which the principles of "the romantic imagination" lead relatively straightforwardly to curriculum implications, so I will dwell here only on what might seem the oddities I would want to include under "the arts." Perhaps oddest is my wanting to include what are usually considered the "vocational subjects" of woodwork, metalwork, clothes-making, food-preparation—what may be called practical arts—and also what is usually included as a distinct area, physical education.

The development of manipulative skills in making or repairing things has both utilitarian and aesthetic justifications. The aesthetic dimension has been long recognized if only too rarely practiced when such skills are seen as "vocational," and primarily for those students who are not "academic." The tradition of arguments for the educational value of such skills for all students has been rather forcefully put by Rousseau in *Emile*. That materials and machines can be seen from a distinctly aesthetic dimension in no way need to detract from a concern with practical utility. Aesthetic concern with machines or tools focuses on their fitness, their functional excellence, design, and ingenuity—overlapping with the Technology of Familiar Things curriculum area. The value of taking apart and rebuilding old clocks, televisions, radios, typewriters, and so on can be considerable both from a practical and from an aesthetic perspective or, rather, by coalescing the two, can be seen as a part of students' aesthetic education. Making art objects from the residue of broken or useless machines, converting to aesthetic use what no longer has practical value, can help further this romantic exploration of the "made" world. The romantic engagement with reality seems incidentally to be given a further dimension when we learn techniques whereby reality can be effectively manipulated by tools and machines.

The purpose for putting these practical "shop" and "vocational" activities under "the arts" is to emphasize the aesthetic dimension of such practical activities, and to emphasize their human value. There are extensive arguments to support such a position, of course, perhaps most notably those of John Dewey.

There is also a tradition in which Plato is prominent, that argues that aesthetic concerns should be influential in physical education, and it is on such arguments that I justify including this area in the Arts curriculum. This would not aim to change from team sports to dancing for all but, rather, to emphasize the aesthetic dimension of any physical activity. Team sports, for example, have tended to lose much of the aesthetic quality that *participation* in them should provide, largely no doubt due to the professional exemplars for whom winning money is pretty well the exclusive purpose of their activity. The placing of physical activities within the Arts is easily justifiable: it might lead to deemphasizing the almost unbelievably crude conceptions of sporting activities encouraged by their commercialization; it might increasingly emphasize the aesthetic delights in the kind of grace that comes from strength and discipline in movement.

The Arts in general are at the heart of the education enterprise. In engaging in artistic "making," we step outside the utilities of our physical needs, and come to understand a little, why, in the face of all the pettiness of daily life, of all the horror, stupidity, bloody wars, mindless destructiveness, small-mindedness, and inevitable death, people have gone on and on making things of beauty, and trying to express something that is the best they can locate within themselves. Some sense of this is the purpose of the Arts curriculum in the romantic layer.

Math/Logic/Computing. I would put logic and computing in with mathematics in order to explore the ways in which the assumed certainty or security of mathematics has been extended towards human affairs. As in the mythic layer curriculum, so here I would explore mathematics and logic to a significant degree historically. That is, I think the technical manipulations of both these areas, that can seem so stark and meaningless to students, can be given a human and meaningful context by showing each new manipulation in the lives and purposes and social activities of its initial inventors.

I have recently asked a number of students of middle-school age what mathematics is, and none of them was able to come up with even a faint glimmer of an answer. At best they gave examples of the manipulations that have constituted their mathematics curriculum. The students reported that none of their teachers has ever discussed at any level at all what mathematics is, though some have pointed out that they need to know various manipulations to deal with life in general or particular jobs. Not one, of course, knew that "Al" is the Arabic for "the" and "gebar" is the verb "to set," and that even today in Spain, one residue of its Moorish past, "Algebrista," is used to designate a bonesetter or kind of chiropractor. But an approach to mathematics, and to algebra, that put them into their historical context would likely give students some idea of what these enterprises are about, some foothold of meaning for them in their minds, other than as seemingly endless rules to remember and apply. While textbooks that support such an approach are largely lacking, there are some resources for teachers wishing to give students a sense of mathematics in human social and historical contexts. The most interesting I have found is Tobias Danzig's *Number: The Language of Science* (of which Albert Einstein wrote: "This is beyond doubt the most interesting book on the evolution of mathematics which has ever fallen into my hands" (Danzig, 1967)).

The "romantic" mathematics, logic, and computing curriculum area may not necessarily involve significantly different content from what is normal at present, though the approach to that content and the contexts in which it would be embedded would be significantly different. An unsystematic knowledge of some aspects of Greek, Arabic, Medieval and Enlightenment history, and individuals' lives in these times, would be an incidental by-product of a "romantic" approach.

I have put computers into this curriculum area because of some obvious overlaps. I do not want to discuss computers as a distinct topic for one sufficient reason: that is, I imagine various applications of computers being used in nearly all curriculum areas, and conforming in those to the principles outlined above.

In schematic outline

This attempt to infer a curriculum structure from the principles inferred from the discussion of romantic understanding gives us five curriculum areas that will take the bulk of timetable space:

— History
— The Sciences
— Language
— The Arts
— Mathematics/Logic/Computing

In addition we have a variety of areas, each of which will take up a relatively brief amount of timetable space and each of which may overlap in irregular ways with the above areas and with each other:

— Ideas
— People Past and Present
— The Technology of Familiar Things
— The Universe
— Animal and Plant Life
— Other Countries and Ways of Living

I envision the five larger curriculum areas taking up larger blocks of time, being concerned with ensuring a mastery of particular content in a deliberate way, and being more systematically organized. The smaller areas will be somewhat "freer." They will be concerned with "browsing" in Whitehead's sense, in exploring the variety and wonder of the world of human experience, in following interests in detail wherever they might lead, in just rambling around. That this free rambling around will overlap time and again with areas where more systematic work is going forward seems to me beneficial rather than the reverse.

The romantic principle I have discussed under "details" implies that we might consider breaking up the regular timetable routine a number of times during the school year. We might involve particular groups, classes, or the whole school in explorations of a single theme. Such themes could be enormously varied: light and its sources, ferrets, the Mendicant orders during the Middle Ages, eggs, the contents of the Solar system, beetles, castles, and so on.

An alternative implied by the same principle might involve individual or small group projects negotiated with teachers that would involve a long-term commitment of two or three years. Some times would be scheduled for these projects, for reporting and consulting, and perhaps making trips for "field" research or major library searches. The range of possible topics for such projects could be as diverse as the themes above. The aim would be to encourage in a more comprehensive form than is usually available in regular class time that romantic impulse we see in obsessive hobbies, satisfying in projects such as these the desire to know everything about something as exhaustively as possible.

Many other kinds of learning activities, and curriculum structures might be inferred from the principles drawn from romantic understanding. A teacher put together some elements of the curriculum outline from a draft of this book and built a week-long theme on castles, about which she claimed to know little. Here is Sandy Chamberlain's "Medieval Castles" outline, reproduced with permission, and thanks.

The principles outlined earlier imply that the universe of knowledge and experience can be organized meaningfully in many different ways in this romantic layer. My purpose here, I repeat, is not to provide an "authoritative" interpretation of these principles. Many different curriculum outlines may be equally valid interpretations of the principles, especially as there are no doubt important romantic principles that I have not identified. This is not to suggest that anything goes, however, so much as that there is clearly a degree of latitude for interpretation. Interpretations may vary depending on personal preferences and understanding but they will also vary significantly depending on the cultural circumstances of the curriculum developers. The focus on Australian aboriginal societies will likely be a less urgent topic in France, say, than in Australia.

My reluctance to draw up a detailed curriculum outline for the whole period of the romantic years is, however, only partially a result of my wish not to try to restrict other legitimate interpretations of romantic principles. It is also due to two other causes. Less constraining is the huge amount of space that would be required, and more constraining is my ignorance. I *could* not draw up a detailed science curriculum based

Monday	Tuesday	Wednesday	Thursday	Friday
History —the development of the castle in early medieval society; purposes, and responses to social needs and forms.	*Art* —arts in castles, study and practice. *Music* —as Arts above mix two and extend through week.)	*Animal and Plant Life* —around the castle; rats and disease; herbs and healing; herb gardens.	*History* —castles at the height of their power; numbers and placement around Europe.	*Science* —the physics of undermining a castle's walls. *History* —the decay of castles and their destruction in order to build the town around them.
Math —geometry of castle construction, and defensive angles of fire, etc.	*People Past and Present* —hierarchy of Kings, Barons, Minstrels, Jesters, etc.	*Logic* —the logic of aggression and deterence in castle dominated societies.	*Art and Music* —extend Tuesday's work; world of the minstrel, songs and instruments.	*Language* —oral and literate influences on cultural life of castles.
Language —folk tales about castles; effects of castle life on our language	*History* —increasingly sophisticated castles as technology of attacking escalated.	*Language* —medieval castle games and their rhymes.	*People Past and Present* —minstrels and artists	*People Past and Present* —toolmakers in the castles.
		People Past and Present —functionaries in castle life, the jobs that kept the daily life going.	*History* —the growth of villages and towns around castles.	

People Past and Present
—famous people in the development of castles; major builders and planners.

Science
—building walls; using catapults and other weapons.

Technology of Familiar Things
—the wheel and its uses in castles, drawbridge, supplies, etc.

Ideas
—justice in medieval castle culture.

Science
—dynamics of drawbridges; moats, and their maintenance.

Technology of Familiar Things
—eating utensils and their development; toilets in castles.

Science
—instruments for measuring time in castles.

Ideas
—feudal protectionism.

Celebrate
—constructed model castle, medieval songs, stories, and games.

Making and doing
—Construction of a model castle continues through the week.

247

on these principles without learning a great deal more science, for example. If these principles are found persuasive to groups of people with varied curriculum development expertise, then it is impossible that curricula will appear in practice in schools and will be described in appropriate documents.

The transition-year curriculum

I can now indicate quite briefly how the year four transition-year curriculum would differ from the mythic layer curriculum on the one hand and the curriculum sketched above on the other. The purpose of this transition year is to stimulate the development of the initial romantic layer capacities. The mythic curriculum was designed to encourage gradual movement in the direction of romantic understanding and this fourth year is designed to ensure that the engagement with a "romantic" reality gets properly underway.

The main curriculum change from the year three curriculum would be the introduction of "People Past and Present" area described above. I would also move from the very general stories of history to more particular events in more detail, choosing topics at least in part on the basis of what children wanted to explore, but taking a distinctively "romantic" approach to them. Similarly the "Mathematics and Logic," "Sciences," and "Language" curricula would be deliberately moved from their year three focuses in the direction of what has been sketched above. I would leave the "Ideas" and "Technology of Familiar Things" and the other brief areas till year five.

In general, the purpose of the transition year is to work deliberately on engaging students with those characteristics of romantic understanding, and with the features of the romantic imagination, discussed in the earlier chapters.

Conclusion

One feature of this curriculum that may seem most in conflict with current assumptions is the absence of anything deliberately focused on the social world around the child. "Social studies," introduced by John Dewey to the very center of his curriculum, is entirely omitted; there is no "civics," no detailed study of state, provincial, regional, or national constitutions, and so on. The reason for this is entailed in my arguments against the "expanding horizons" form of curricula, captured in the lines from T.S. Eliot's "Little Gidding," that it is at the end of all our exploring that we arrive where we started and know the place for the first time. One cannot prevent some intellectual engagement with the everyday world around students, and their socialization will go forward willy-nilly, but there is an important sense in which their social world cannot make proportionate sense to students until they have some secure hold on a context which can give it meaning. The central aim of the romantic layer, the central feature of romantic understanding, is that it sets in place the context which can make the everyday world and everyday experience meaningful. "Civics" and "social studies" tend to appeal most to those who feel an ideological mission, who want to tell students the truth about the world even before students have in place a context that might provide some means of evaluating the asserted truth. Such curriculum areas, for similar reasons, tend to form the focus of politicians' interest, along with the utilitarian aspects of mathematics and language. The absence of civics or social studies is a product of my concern here being educational, rather than ideological or propagandist or indoctrinatory or even socializing. Some compensation for this lack during this layer is provided by such topics becoming educationally central in the next, and in the year nine transitional curriculum, where "Society and Politics" will be a core topic taking considerable time.

There is always a danger that comments about seeking out the exotic and dramatic aspects of a topic will be interpreted as trying to replace education with entertainment. My concern is engagement with knowledge and access to meaning, not entertainment—though it is hard to see why schooling should not be generally more engaging than is commonly the case.

There are at the moment few ideal texts to support teaching this romantic curriculum. The materials that publishers provide in such numbers at present are rarely of a kind that encourage romantic understanding. Teachers can of course gather their own resources to support this kind of curriculum, but this is easier in some areas than in others. It would be asking a lot to expect physics teachers to do for themselves all the research that would be necessary to design a curriculum according to these principles. Again, if these principles are found persuasive, we may expect to see appropriate support materials being written and published. That we lack such materials at present does not, however, mean that we cannot begin to move in this direction. Even if we cannot change the curriculum overnight, we can begin by changing our own teaching to better embody these principles. How we can do this in the planning of lessons and units is what we turn to now.

10
Romantic teaching

Introduction

What remains now is to consider what implications may be derived from the characterization of romantic understanding for teaching. I will do this in two parts. First I will consider some general principles that should lead to the more effective teaching of romantic-layer students. My aim in this section is not to provide some novel ideas about teaching so much as to clarify what kinds of practices seem best suited to evoking, stimulating, and developing romantic understanding.

Second, I will draw on a number of the major characteristics of romantic understanding and build from them a framework which might prove useful in planning teaching. At present the planning models taught in pre- and in-service courses for teachers are largely derived from that proposed by Ralph Tyler (Tyler, 1949). This requires that planning begin with the precise statement of objectives, and on the basis of these, move to the selection of appropriate content, then to the choice of methods, and finally to the method for evaluating whether the objectives have been attained. While this model has been important in bringing structure and order to the planning process, it is a pity that it is virtually the only planning device evident in standard educational text-books, especially so as it is derived from principles of industrial productivity (Callahan, 1962) which are not perhaps more in tune with the process of education. As an alternative or supplement, then, appropriate for romantic-layer students, I will develop a romantic framework or model for planning teaching, and will give a few examples of how it might be used.

The romantic classroom

What are the distinctive characteristics of the romantic classroom and of the teacher's role within it? I think one significant characteristic can be derived from the earlier discussion of "rehumanizing knowledge." Central to this was the "reconstitutive" metaphor: the teacher's role being to reconstitute living knowledge from inert symbolic codes. Teachers in the romantic classroom, then, have to play a literally vital role; they have to raise the dead daily.

Another implication from the discussion of romance leads to a view of the classroom that is somewhat discordant with common assumptions: assumptions that are a part of the inheritance of progressivism and "modern education" that have become almost invisibly taken for granted. In North America, as Cremin has argued in some detail, "by the 1950s the more fundamental tenets of the progressives had become the conventional wisdom of American education" (Cremin, 1976, p. 19). One of the tenets of progressivism, that was reinforced by the neo-progressivist writings of the 1960s, was the importance of opening up the classroom to the "environment" outside. The aim was to eradicate the stagnant artificiality of so much classroom life and inject into it something of the "real world" intensity and meaning of life outside of schools.

While engagement with, and activities in, the environment outside the school can obviously fit in with the aims of developing romantic understanding, and may indeed be indispensable to some of them, there is nevertheless an implication in the discussion so far that important features of romance can be better brought to life by emphasizing the separateness of the classroom from the everyday world outside the school. Rather, it is a special place that is a connecting point with an infinite set of "environments," of which daily life outside the school is only one. The romantic classroom transcends its local environment and is like a staging point from which students can move readily to many other environments in time and space. We might imagine entering a classroom as a little like entering Dr. Who's time/space kiosk. Once aboard and underway, we might take off to any time or place.

Clearly such imagining does not transform the usual desks and windows and floor coverings, but adopting a romantic conception of the classroom can transform our sense of what is appropriate and possible in such a place. A teacher, and students, might have fun organizing lessons that take such a conception half-way literally. The teacher might begin lessons by inviting the students to pull over them their protective suits, and then to close their eyes. The techniques of Guided Imagery can be used to stimulate images appropriate to the topic of the next lesson: "You are slowly rising into the air. . . . You are safe. . . . Let us slip into the stream of time. You can feel its soft wind in your hair and on your face. The wind of time is warm and sweet. See below you. . . ." And so on. Three or four minutes can suffice to set students into a medieval mathematics class in Pisa, or in an African village, or in Edison's or Curie's laboratory, or in Shakespeare's London, or wherever and whenever one wishes. One can go to some lengths supporting the illusion with appropriate equipment, pictures, props and disguises, or one can be satisfied with stimulating students' imaginative transformation of the regular classroom in such a way that the lesson to follow will be more meaningful and engaging. Whether or not a teacher goes to the extent of consciously suggesting the notion of the classroom as a place from which one "takes off" into other environments, the implication of romance is that some sense of the classroom as a time/space machine, or as a great memory device, or as a stage is more appropriate than is its common acceptance as a straightforward extension of the local environment with everyday conventions, forms of behavior, *mores*, expectations, and so on.

I referred earlier to Richard Eakin's method of rehumanizing knowledge for his introductory classes at college. This is one way in which any teacher can inject life into inert symbols. A very few props can carry one a long way. If teachers will see the classroom as a place apart in which they have to play the magician's role of bringing to present life the distant and long dead, then they can reconceive their role a little. They may usefully conceive the classroom as, in part, a stage. We all have some acting skill, but the prevailing image of the prosaic classroom, and "teaching for the real world," inhibits the teacher from, simply, hamming it up a fair amount of the time.

This is not a recommendation, such as some have made recently, that teacher-training should be based on Stanislavsky and "method" acting. But it is a recommendation that teachers feel freer to conceive of the classroom as a distinct environment in which the norms of the everyday world do not hold. One cannot constantly sustain the illusion of an enchanted place, nor play the actor. But one can reconceive the classroom as a place in which one can try much more varied forms of behavior; it is the place in which teachers work whatever magic they can to bring the dead to life and make contact with a transcendent world culture of infinite richness.

There is a danger of letting the rhetoric—"magic," "dead to life," "infinite richness"—seem to remove the recommendation from anything practical. Rather, the choice of rhetoric is intended to suggest that what is being recommended is a reconception of what the classroom is and what its relationship to society is. The reconception is important because it more readily leads to different forms of behavior—a different sense of what it is appropriate to do. It is a conception that makes appearing in class in a wig or headscarf and cane, or whatever minimal props are available, and talking in a funny voice, less odd. No doubt such a conception, if it catches on, may loose the frustrated thespian in some teachers with terrifying results. I must admit I suspect that, even in the bizarre extremes, such teaching will likely be of more educational value than the most conventional kind that encourages such soul-destroying boredom. Perhaps, if such a conception catches on, we may see some small amount of schools' money going to a Teachers' Props Room. A mask, or any indication, such as a wig or a false beard, that normal expectations should be suspended, provides surprising release from the normal constraints on our behavior. If the middle-school classroom is to be romantic ground, then masks that release the teacher from behavioral norms proper to the unromantic ground outside the school are appropriate. The change need be only small, but the effects can be magical.

Apart from this very general romantic conception of the classroom and of the teacher's role within it, we can derive from the earlier chapters a number of lower-level principles of teaching. I indicated that in this scheme the principles guiding the curriculum and those guiding teaching would have much in common. We might then simply echo a number of the principles articulated in the previous chapter. So in romantic teaching we will expect teachers to search out knowledge of the extremes of whatever aspect of reality is the subject of a lesson, and include some sense of the limits of human experience relevant to it, and provide opportunities for detailed study within it and of wider contexts within which it is situated, and encourage students to make romantic associations with transcendent qualities evident within it, and provide a strong affective component, and use the story form in organizing the lesson or unit, and stimulate students' wonder and awe about it, and focus on human motives, intentions, and emotions, and stimulate students' sensibilities, and so on. Now, no teacher will likely set out consciously to incorporate each of these one by one in teaching, but, insofar as teachers grasp what romance is and seek to stimulate romantic understanding in students, each of these in greater or lesser degree will likely play some part.

I will try to incorporate a number of these principles into the planning framework in the next section. But, even in this kind of stark list, they may serve as useful reminders of some ways in which teaching might be made more engaging to romantic-layer students. Let me take a few at random and consider what effects they might have on the way we might teach physical geography—a topic that may initially seem less than hospitable to a romantic approach.

Study of the physical geography of an area might be introduced less by the usual maps and symbols and more through the transcendent qualities of those who first discovered and settled it. So we might "discover" North America through the hopes and fears of people who came across from Asia in the north into what is now Alaska, and who spread down through and across the continent. We need to see the physical features through their eyes, but also through their emotions. We can similarly follow European settlers and explorers, focusing again on their hopes and fears, their expectations and plans, and see how they responded to the landscape bit by bit. In such an approach, we can expand our maps slowly, using first our own invented symbols for the physical features our explorers or settlers discovered. Such maps might be inaccurate at first, representing what people expected, and become gradually refined as further exploration clarified what was actually there. So with Europe, where such a plan might be easier as there are so many records, both narratives and early maps. The early maps should not, following this scheme, be seen as a set of gradual improvements to the present, but rather in the context of the emotions and expectations that provided the information for them. The increasing accuracy then becomes not some necessary progress, but a response to particular hopes and intentions. England and Australia could be similarly explored through the eyes and emotions of the earliest discoverers, invaders, and settlers. If we think of physical geography less as a given thing to be taught, and more as an adventurous process of discovery, we might be able to make it more engaging and meaningful.

One might introduce or close, or both, one's geography lessons with a "geographical records" quiz, asking about some extreme or exotic feature of physical geography. A book or chart can be compiled—the class book of geographical records. After a few weeks of this, students can be given the task of discovering some extreme or "record" that they can present at the beginning or end of a class a couple of weeks hence. In a while, this feature can be completely left to the students, and they will be ransacking geography books and maps in order to discover some "record." What will become clear after a while is that one can find something unique or exotic about almost anything anywhere. On what point of land are you standing from which, if you set off in a straight line, you would cross the greatest distance on water before touching land again? (To answer this involves discovering that maps of the world are deceptive and globes are required—a useful introduction to how the familiar Mercator map of the world is an ingenious way of representing features of a globe but necessarily distorted.) How many lakes are there in Canada? (Would you guess 50,000, 250,000, 1,000,000 or more than 30,000,000?) What are the three smallest countries in Europe? What is the largest island in the world that at no point is wider than 80 miles?

And on and on. At the end of a year one will have conveyed a surprising amount of what may seem random geographical information, but it is information that is gradually building an image of the extremes of the physical world, within which more systematic geographical instruction can become more meaningful.

Another way of humanizing the physical geography of an area is to find stories, myths, or adventures that are located in the area and let students feel the importance of the landscape through the story. The simplest example of this is to find engaging fictional stories set in the particular places being taught about. Alternatively, one may turn to historical mysteries, such as Alexander's lost fleet. Before Alexander the Great died, he had brought together a great fleet which was to be used in a conquest of the east, to compensate for his previous disastrous overland attempt to conquer Asia. We have no record of the fleet's dispersal, nor any record of what happened to it. There are, however, some remarkable traces of Greek games and other suspicious traces around the Arabian peninsula, and on the coast of India and through Pacific islands to the west coast of South America. One of the reasons Cortez and the Conquistadores had such an easy time conquering Central and South America was that the Americans were expecting the return of white faced "gods" (see Margaret Irwin's *White Gods and Stone Faces*). Or in studying the lands around the Mediterranean one might tell of the mythical adventures of Jason or Ulysses, and perhaps use the attempts by Tim Severin or Thor Hyerdahl to reproduce past supposedly-mythical voyages. In the process of such accounts, students will almost incidentally learn much physical geography, particularly if the teacher highlights the emotional meaning of the various physical features.

When studying maps, students might be asked to think in terms of which places they consider the happiest, and why, which the saddest, which the safest, which the most dangerous, and so on. Well, one could take the earlier principles one by one and with very small ingenuity spin a number of engaging ways of making physical geography, or anything else, meaningful to students and interesting to learn.

Another general point about the principles of teaching arises from this discussion of romance and the inferences I have drawn about students at this stage. This concerns what we ask them to do either to give evidence of what they have learned or to encourage them to learn. It may seem imaginative to ask students to write, say, what it would have been like to be present at some significant event, such as the driving of the last spike into the rail-lines across Canada or the United States. A good principle for teachers to bear in mind is to stop and ask themselves how they would like to do that. Does it engage your imaginative energy, or is the thought of sitting down and writing something like that about as engaging as washing the car or the dishes or painting the picket fence again? I think a lot of the tasks given to students are deadly to the imagination. As a useful guideline, I recommend that teachers not ask students to do things that the teachers themselves couldn't get any imaginative sustenance from. This principle needs to be very clearly distinguished from the notion that students should be asked only to do things that are entertaining and cannot be asked to work hard. Hard work and imaginative stimulation can be close companions. Some teachers seem to think that dull work is necessary to learning, because that is how they learned what it is they now teach. That that is how they learned it, alas, seems to be the reason they cannot without great difficulty understand how to make work imaginatively engaging. I saw a videotape recently of a class that had been asked, in groups, to deliver their reports on their social studies projects in the form of rap songs. They were taught the various beats, each selected one, eagerly organized their information, and made their presentations in ways that they enjoyed enormously and which conveyed a lot of information in a memorable form to the rest of the class. Clearly one need not go to such lengths, but teachers might at least ask themselves how they might get some imaginative charge out of reporting something they have learned, and allow students similar possibilities.

I should perhaps emphasize that my focus here is on the teacher, not the student. The potential danger is to suggest that suddenly my earlier active students "imaginatively reconstituting knowledge" have become passive observers of dressing up, play-acting, dead-raising teachers. I hope it is clear that teachers active in the ways I am suggesting here do not require or create passive students. The reverse should be the more likely case. The kinds of intellectual capacities in students that I have discussed earlier are precisely what the teacher's activities are designed to stimulate. The result should not be a theatre with one actor and a passive audience, but rather a workshop in which the teacher's activity stimulates the students' and vice-versa.

A romantic planning framework

I will begin by setting up the framework and then I will discuss and elaborate it by exemplifying how it might be used in planning a unit on the Industrial Revolution. Thereafter I will consider some further examples more briefly.

A romantic planning framework

1. Taking a romantic perspective:
    What images are brought into sharpest focus by viewing the topic romantically? What transcendent human qualities with which students can form romantic associations are prominent and accessible?
2. Organizing the content into a story form:
    2.1 Providing access: What content with which students can associate most vividly exemplifies the romantic qualities of the topic?
    2.2 Organizing the unit/lesson: What content best articulates the topic into a developing story form, drawing on the principles of romance?
    2.3 Pursuing details and contexts: What content can best allow students to pursue some aspect of the topic in exhaustive detail? What perspectives allow students to see the topic in wider contexts?
3. Concluding:
    What is the best way of resolving the dramatic tension inherent in the unit/lesson? How does one bring the romantically important content of the topic to a satisfactory closure that opens to further topics?
4. Evaluating:
    How can one know whether the topic has been understood and the appropriate romantic capacities have been stimulated and developed?

Rather than elaborate on each section in the abstract, I will take the example of the Industrial Revolution and show how using this framework can shape the topic for teaching. In the process of exemplifying its use, I can discuss it and its limits. Laying out a model like this may make it seem a little formidable, as though it requires teachers to master a complex planning procedure in place of the more familiar (and thus simple-seeming) procedures they use at present. I hope it will become clear that this model is not so complex as it may at first appear, and that it is in fact a much less artificial way of organizing a topic than is required by the presently dominant procedures. This model encourages us to approach a lesson or unit as a good story to be told rather than as a list of objectives to be attained.

First, then, we are to take a romantic perspective on the Industrial Revolution. In doing this, we will think about the value of a romantic understanding of the Industrial Revolution for students' education. Any relatively recent social and historical change is infinitely rich in records of events, personalities, artifacts, theories, literature, and so on, and so a major problem for teaching is selection. Traditionally this has stimulated two distinct questions: What bits matter most? What bits will be most meaningful to the particular students? This requires the teacher to be constantly looking in two directions—at the content and at particular students. I have argued earlier the inadequacy of the epistemologist's approach to knowledge and the psychologist's approach to the student as contributions to solving the educational problem. This bifurcation, which shreds the phenomena of education, is mirrored at the classroom level by approaches which attend excessively either to the content of a topic like the Industrial Revolution or to the needs and interests of the students. Nor is it a matter of trying to answer both questions and bringing them together in a balanced way. Two wrongs don't make a right. The first question of this model is designed to see these usually distinct questions together. It transcends the divisions that have generated arguments about whether one teaches knowledge or children. In asking what constitutes a romantic understanding of the Industrial Revolution, one does not separate knowledge and the students' interest.

So what *is* brought to the fore by viewing the Industrial Revolution romantically? What transcendent human qualities are most prominently embodied in the topic? Most generally, it was a burst of confidence and creative energy such as the world had never seen before. It represents an enormous gamble, hurling us into vast material transformations, an experimental science generating constant technological innovation, and profound changes in literature, philosophy and economics, that have transformed the face of the earth and cultures all over the world. Viewed romantically, what is brought to the fore is the sheer energy and confidence that have flung the world into a new, and perhaps increasingly terrifying, adventure; and its cost in human suffering. It was a volcanic outburst of energy, power, will. It was the creation of the modern world; we are still living in its wake, still trying to get some control over the titanic forces it unleashed, and still trying to make sense of it and evaluate it.

This is a romantic perspective. What is in the foreground are the transcendent human qualities of energy, courage, power, will. Throughout our planning, this perspective must be held firmly in mind. It is, however, merely a perspective; it is not *the* truth, even though it is a constituent of the truth.

Taking a romantic perspective should allow us fairly easily to identify those aspects of the topic that can most engagingly attract students' romantic associations. The transcendent human qualities with which such associations can most readily be made are prominent—energy, confidence, will, power.

This first phase of planning is sketched out formally here, even if briefly, but after some practice it should become almost automatic. Once one develops a clear sense of romance, or learns to distinguish romantic from other forms of understanding, then one will be able simply to switch on, as it were, one's romantic perspective, looking at any topic through romantic lenses. What may seem an academic exercise initially can become a perfectly straightforward, virtually instantaneous, ability.

With any complex topic, there will be a wide range of perspectives one could take and a wide range of transcendent human qualities on which one could focus as potential sources for romantic associations. One could, for example, choose to focus on the compassion and dogged persistence, as embodied in the great humanitarian figures of the Industrial Revolution period who worked to ameliorate the sufferings of the exploited classes and to stimulate the consciences of the exploiters. One might focus on technical ingenuity, as embodied in the inventors and developers of the tools and machines that provided an evident engine for the Revolution. One might focus on almost any human quality and allow it to lead us to the particular content that best embodies it. This taking of a romantic perspective, then, is an important first step which will largely determine the range of content to be chosen. The better our knowledge of the Industrial Revolution, the better choice we can make of transcendent qualities that will best illustrate the most important features of the revolution for students at this stage. But there is nothing in these questions that determines the perspective we will choose. We can choose to present the Industrial Revolution as a great triumph of human achievements, or as a vast human disaster, setting us on a destructive course that is poisoning the earth, water, and air and threatening to blow all life and the earth into dark and silent death. This model, then, is simply a tool to enable us to make whichever view we choose to present more meaningful and engaging to students. (The principles that have led to this model, however, also play a role in the selection of content and in guiding the choice of view we will present.)

Let us focus on the quality of confident energy and see how this can help us in the organization of the content into a story-form. The first task is providing clearest access to the topic. We will want to engage students with some essential aspect of what the Industrial Revolution is about. From our romantic perspective, remember, the Revolution is about an outburst of confident energy. In the opening class we will, then, want to form an association between students and some essential aspect of the Industrial Revolution that embodies confident energy. The danger is to look for a "hook," something that is engaging but may be unconnected with an organic plan for making the whole unit meaningful. Commonly such a "hook" is found in details of children working in coal mines. This indeed can be engaging and memorable. What it does not do is show the Industrial Revolution as an outburst of confident energy. (Indeed, children in coal mines could provide access to the Industrial Revolution if we had chosen to present it as a vast exploitation and the cause of endless human degradation.)

A further characteristic of romantic understanding, and one that runs somewhat counter to the "expanding horizons" principle, is that things strange and remote from students' everyday experience can often be most engaging. So we might choose our opening content from among the more remote and exotic content. This also makes sense if we want to expand their understanding to new content by means of transcendent human qualities to which they have direct access.

And in addition we must bear in mind here, and throughout our planning, the persistent attraction of the story-form. We use principles derived from the story-form not simply to entertain students but rather to communicate the meaning of the unit with maximum clarity and force. We do not have to tie the unit into a simple story-form with the tightness appropriate during the mythic layer, but we do need to remember the main principles that give stories their engaging power. Prominent among those principles is the articulation of the content between polar opposites. Again, these need not be so prominent and determining as at the earlier layer, and during the romantic layer the opposites will usually be extremes of some aspect of reality. Our introductory segment, then, will set up a dramatic conflict between the embodiment of the transcendent human quality of confident energy and whatever opposes its exercise.

In the abstract this perhaps begins to seem impossibly complicated, like keeping four or five balls in the air at once. Let us move back to our example and see how, at the concrete level of planning, things are much more easily dealt with.

Let us begin our first lesson by showing students a picture of Isambard Kingdom Brunel. There are posters available made from photographs taken in 1857. Brunel appears in these pictures as distant indeed from today's students: a small man in a dusty black crumpled suit, a tall top hat, high collar and Victorian bow tie, dangling watch-chain, dirty boots, cigar stuck in the corner of his mouth. He might as well be a Martian as far as modern students' understanding goes. The task is to form a romantic association between our students and Brunel's confident energy.

Behind Brunel in the poster are enormous chains. They were forged to launch his ship, the *Great Eastern*. Previously the largest iron steamship had been a few hundred tons. Brunel's *Great Eastern* was about 24,000 tons. The first attempt to float it was a disaster. Like all of Brunel's schemes, it bordered on the impossible. It was indeed the limits of the possible that attracted him. These were the great days of romantic engineering, and none was more romantic or daring than Brunel. At twenty, he took charge of building the first tunnel under the Thames for the underground railway. Half way through, he cleared out the debris and held an enormous banquet for the great and famous of London, and further down the tunnel, typical of Brunel, he held an equally grand banquet for his labourers.

He built the Great Western Railway (G.W.R.—God's Wonderful Railway) from London, England to Boston, United States. Well, the railway went out to the west coast of Britain and from there the *Great Eastern* could carry anything on to America. Every mile was a drama. Brunel designed and built some of the most daring and beautiful bridges—including the Clifton Suspension Bridge and the Saltash Bridge. He established the principles that engineers followed for a hundred years, and that formed the model for the Brooklyn Bridge, among so many others. One of the impossibilities he achieved building the G.W.R. was the amazing Box Tunnel—two miles long, on a gradient, half of it through solid rock. It cost many lives and he saw many disasters, but he drove the railway through it. On his deathbed, Brunel steamed over the Saltash Bridge. He frightened investors at the time, and often had difficulty financing his wild and daring projects. We might, after a brief discussion of Brunel and his near-impossible engineering feats, invite the students to look again at the portrait and more carefully at his eyes and see something of the confident energy that might reasonably frighten any one of us. He was the embodiment of the Industrial Revolution.

With a few facts and a picture of a dusty little Victorian we can achieve our first step of providing access to the Industrial Revolution by forming a romantic association between our students and the transcendent quality of confident energy as embodied by Brunel. One could of course find many other examples to start from. What is important is that the transcendent quality that is to be our key to understanding the Revolution is vividly and dramatically embodied in the opening association. Different teachers might choose a variety of ways of vivifying Brunel's achievements. (Anything from straight exposition, to a scripted television "interview" with Brunel, to an Eakin-like autobiographical presentation, to a dramatization of one particular clash between Brunel and an opponent of some daring scheme, etc., could suffice.) What also needs to be made vivid is the opposition to Brunel's confident energy, from investor timidity to natural obstacles.

Now we have to organize the rest of the unit. We have a number of romantic principles to help us in selecting and organizing the content. Overall, we have the requirements of the story form to satisfy. The most prominent binary opposites are given clearly in our opening—between the confident energy of Brunel and the human timidity or nature's intractability that opposed the realization of his aims. The main general requirement of the story form is that we must never in our unit simply describe achievements or list statistics or indicate technical innovations without showing them in each case as products of individuals' confident energy and as having overcome particular obstacles in being realized.

In addition we have drawn on the other principles derived from the discussion of romance in planning our unit. We will include the opening up of the vast United States prairies and their production of meat and grains. This is often presented as sets of statistics with maps indicating increasing cattle range and arable land. There is obviously nothing wrong with the statistics and maps, but without a context of vivid, personalized human motives, they tend to remain for the romantic-stage student sterile and rather meaningless, and perhaps worst from an historical point of view, inevitable. Applying just a couple of prominent romantic principles will direct us to finding out about particular ranchers and farmers. (An appropriately written textbook will have such examples readily available.) The expansion of meat and grain production are commonly presented as wonderful achievements, but the abstract statistics are expected to carry the wonder to the students. The romantic students will find it much easier to understand the statistics if they see them as products of transcendent human qualities. Individuals exercising those qualities in particular contexts against particular oppositions can better carry the wonder of the achievement that the statistics embody in an abstract way.

The initial access to an essential feature of the Industrial Revolution through Brunel does not end the personalizing. The machines, the meat and grain production, the legislative changes, all need to be seen through the intentions, hopes, fears, and, particularly, through the confident energy of individuals. Huge ranches and farms did not just happen as though a part of some evolutionary "progress." They were made by individuals against considerable opposition, through their exercise of confident energy, ingenuity, courage, ruthlessness, and so on.

Whatever content we select to describe the Industrial Revolution needs to be shaped further by applying romantic principles. In the case of the principle applied above, this does not mean that our history has to be organized as a sequence of biographies. Rather, it suggests that whatever content we want students to understand should be presented in the context of individuals' intentions and their exercise of confident energy in the face of natural, institutional, or personal opposition. While this constant personalizing of history may seem an unfamiliar way of presenting the subject, it should not be seen as artificial. The romantic perception of history, as of anything else, is a constituent of a rich and sophisticated understanding. It is not the whole truth, but it is an important constituent of the truth. It is especially important during this stage to understand history as the product of individuals' actions. In more sophisticated ways of studying history, we sometimes forget that historical abstractions are built from the reality of endless individual lives and their intentions, hopes, fears, etc. At the romantic stage it is this basic reality that needs to be grasped clearly.

We do not need to admire all these people, even though students' contact with them is through their exercise of confident energy. We may indeed want to teach admiration of the value of confident energy, but we can distinguish this from what it is used for. This is not a distinction difficult to understand: one may admire a beautiful vase but not admire its use to break someone's head open.

Another romantic principle leads us to seek out content exemplifying extremes of human achievement and suffering. The achievements will be dealt with both in the heroic materialism of the age and in the new humanitarianism that developed during this period. We need also, however, to see the opposite pole, and consider the extremes of poverty, misery, and exploitation that the Revolution created. Early on there were great humanitarian hopes for the Revolution, but it produced, among much else, enormous human suffering. It is important to show these polar opposites not as simply co-incidental, but as necessarily tied together. The creators and beneficiaries of the Industrial Revolution can easily be presented as merely callous about the suffering they caused, or permitted and benefited from, and no doubt many were. But at the romantic stage we need to be realistic also in the sense of increasingly "mediating" between the poles of good and bad. It is important to present also the economic and social beliefs that guided the typical industrialists' behavior. Malthus' and Ricardo's influential ideas persuaded many that increasing wealth and expanding population *necessarily* caused poverty. For many, therefore, it was a difficult choice: the general improvement and progress of society involving the suffering of some, or no general improvement and progress. For others it led to struggles to ease the suffering of the poor. For others it was a matter of indifference—the price to be paid—and perhaps casual gratitude that the price for one's benefits was being paid by others. (Perhaps I need to add again that when I talk above about the teachers "showing" "presenting", "mediating," and so on, I am using such terms for economy's sake. Needless to say these need not be teacher-centered exposition, but can come as a product of students' explorations or inquiry processes or whatever method seems best able to engage students' understanding.)

Each of the principles of the previous chapter can provide us with guidance in planning units and lessons. The interest in extremes, for example, can suggest a class display, or a booklet of Industrial Revolution Records. Students could add records that their research uncovers: the deepest mine, the largest ranch, farm, bridge, etc., the most influential invention, the biggest engineering project, the greatest transformation of land, the greatest humanitarian achievement, the biggest disaster, the most workers killed on a single project, and so on.

While organizing the body of the unit according to romantic principles we need to bear in mind the value for romantic-layer students of pursuing some aspects of the topic in exhaustive detail. The teacher might gather resources that would allow this in areas where students might be most readily engaged. Some exhaustible aspect of the lives of Elizabeth Fry, James Watt, or Brunel; the design of steam engines or spinning-jennies; making guns with standardized parts; changes in clothing styles; gas-lamps, their styles and care; the lifestyle of lamplighters; dyes and the coloring of the world; and so on. Taking less time, probably the teacher will also want to step back and help the students to "contextualize" the Industrial Revolution as a stage in the human pragmatic control over the environment, or compare its transformations with those of other revolutions, religious, political, and cultural.

How should one conclude a romantic unit on the Industrial Revolution? The story line has been the dramatic conflict between confident energy applied to the material world and those forces that opposed it— timidity and fear, the sometimes intransigent world itself, the forces of conservatism, the skeptical and horrified observers of disrupted social life. The story form requires some kind of resolution of this conflict. It need not be so clear a resolution as at the previous stage.

We might present an image of the world as it has been changed by the Industrial Revolution. Look out of almost any window. This world is a kind undreamed of by those who made it and those who resisted it. Students should understand this. It is neither the Utopia expected by some nor the nightmare predicted by others. We might shape our conclusion, then, by focusing in turn on the utopian expectations and the degree to which these have been realized, and then on the nightmare predictions and the degree to which they too have been realized. Our conclusion then may seek a mediation between these, of a more complex world that can be seen as both better and worse than it was when the Industrial Revolution began.

We can consider what benefits confident energy has brought about in terms of the technology that gives us greater ease, security, and power. We can show how the humanitarianism of the Revolution has had pervasive beneficial effects on society. We must stress the value of these. We will stress also the value of confident energy. A part of our unit will seek also, in Frye's words quoted in the previous chapter, some transfer of this confident energy to the students. It is important for people growing up into our rapidly changing society, driven by technological innovation, that they feel in control of it, at home with it.

In contrast, we can present a Blakean vision of the devouring barbaric technological monster spawned by the Industrial Revolution. We need to convey the aesthetic and moral horror, expressed neatly in Robert Burns's little verse, scratched on a window-pane after viewing the Carron Iron Works in 1787:

> We cam na here to view your works,
> In hopes to be mair wise,
> But only, lest we gang to Hell,
> It may be nae surprise.

In this view, also partially true of course, we are caught hopelessly in a dehumanizing process in which institutions are dedicated to the accumulation of wealth above all else, and against this institutionalized greed nothing is effective. The Industrial Revolution is precisely caught in the image of Frankenstein's monster: human beings made it to further their purposes but it has run amok, cannot be controlled, and terrorizes us.

Various methods may be employed to help students achieve some mediation between these polar views. Not least effective would be formal debates, with proponents of each view making their case as vigorously as possible. In conclusion, one might even draw up a crude list of pros and cons, and consider how one might try to weigh one against the other.

And how are we to evaluate such a unit? Evaluation is an area of education that is rich in methods and techniques and that is undergoing rapid development and increasing sophistication. This area of education is among the most generously served by an extensive literature, and there are many suggestions for how one might go about evaluating a unit. I have nothing much to add here, except perhaps a *caveat*.

It is most important to make sure that we evaluate what we set out to teach. In this case our purpose is to teach a romantic understanding of the Industrial Revolution. The *caveat* might be made by reference to the old joke about the man poking around under a street lamp at night. His friend comes along and asks what he is looking for. "A quarter." The friend looks with him for a while. "Are you sure you dropped it here?" "No. I dropped it at the dark end of the street in the long grass." "Then why are you looking here?" "Because it's easier to see here." We know that students forget a great deal of factual detail within, say, a year of having studied a topic. The study may yet have resulted in developing some of the capacities of romantic understanding. There is not a lot of point measuring only how many facts students can recall immediately after the unit, if what we want is some index of their development of romantic understanding. This is, of course, a point commonly made, but also commonly ignored. The administrative imperatives of grading and sorting tend to be impatient with this fundamental objection to their most common evaluation procedure because they do not have a range of equally easy alternative forms of evaluation to draw on.

Securely identifying indices of romantic understanding may be very difficult, but there is no point looking under distant street lamps instead. Evaluation instruments appropriate to romantic understanding will need to focus on the particular capacities we want to develop. The fact that a crucial core of these involve the skills of rationality may lead to the temptation to focus on these as relatively easy to get at. But the skills of rationality in this scheme are not adequately measured distinct from the sense of romance that gives them life and meaning. Evaluation, then, should focus on what students' make, compose, or construct, and should seek evidence of their imaginative engagement, their originality, their skilled effectiveness and, so, their romantic understanding. These are, again, not distinct elements that we can seek to evaluate separately— forty percent on the imaginative engagement tests on Tuesday and ninety percent on the skilled effectiveness tests on Wednesday, or thirty percent on skilled effectiveness, two percent on originality, ninety-seven percent on imaginative engagement, yielding a romantic understanding score of forty-three percent. Perhaps this looks silly, but sillier things are done daily in schools in the name of educational evaluation.

Well, this is rather tedious preaching perhaps, but it seems important to underscore that this scheme is designed to stimulate and develop a particular kind of understanding as educationally important, and that evaluating the development of this kind of understanding is not easy nor can we reasonably expect very great precision in doing so. Evaluation tends powerfully to influence what kind of teaching goes on. If the evaluation instruments employed measure something other than romantic understanding, then that something will tend to replace romantic understanding as the goal of teaching. People who want degrees of precision in education that are inappropriate to the phenomenon begin to replace education with something else. And this has been going forward on a massive scale, one symptom of which I have considered above in the trivialized sense of "learning" that has become ubiquitous in school-related discourse.

So, forms of evaluation should mirror the kinds of activities recommended earlier for stimulating and developing romantic understanding, and should seek indices of how energetically students deploy romantic imagination in their rational construction, organization, and application of knowledge. We will want, in the case of the Industrial Revolution, some index of whether or not the degree to which we have succeeded in engaging students' romantic associations with some aspects of the Revolution, and some index of what they have come to understand about it.

Some more examples

Rather more briefly, I will sketch four more examples using the framework. (For those particularly interested in the use of these "romantic" principles in teaching, the companion book to this one [Egan, in press] might be worth a glance.) More or less randomly I will take topics that appear in my local curriculum guides for mathematics, science, and social studies.

A mathematics topic that receives prominent attention is Pythagoras' theorem. If we were to use the romantic planning framework how might we go about teaching it?

First, we are to take a romantic perspective on it. I have suggested that one way of doing this is to see the topic, in this case the theorem, in the context of the human purposes and emotions at first discovery. This again suggests a more historical and biographical approach to mathematics than is at present adequately supported by textbooks. Students who have been through the mythic-layer mathematics curriculum will already be familiar with the magus Pythagoras. They will know of his departure from the Greek island of Samos and his founding of a kind of monastery in Crotona in southern Italy. Pythagoras founded and led a sect devoted to the pursuit of knowledge and to a life-style that included vegetarianism, secrecy, elaborate rituals, and a worship of Apollo, in his guise of guardian of the Greek ideal of moderation—"nothing too much." Pythagoras cultivated philosophy, in the sense that has come down to us, as the use of observation and reason to make sense of the world and of experience.

We might begin taking our romantic perspective on the theorem by discussing Pythagoras' idea of the *cosmos*. It seems it was Pythagoras who first used this concept for an orderly, harmonious, beautiful, and moral whole that encompassed everything. The cosmos was taken to be an organized structure of parts in harmony, and the key to that order, the key to understanding the universe, was number. In other areas of the curriculum, such as music, and in earlier mathematics, something will have been learned of the Pythagorean harmonies and explorations of the relationships among numbers. The romantic perspective leads us to Pythagoras' excited perception of musical harmonies and the blazing conviction that "number rules the universe," and that the universe could be understood through number. This passionate belief drove the community on Crotona to intense study of the relationships among numbers. Our romantic perspective, then, is on this community, surrounded by a world that considered them crazy and worse—as their subsequent history shows. We might stress the weirdness of this monk-like community, leading very strict and disciplined lives, somehow focused on what we consider elementary mathematics, but which they saw as the key to the cosmos. The driving ambition of Pythagoras was to show the power of numbers over the world.

Opening the lesson, we might provide access to this romantic perspective, first, simply by discussing it, and then by showing some of the relationships that fascinated Pythagoras. In the process we will show how the belief that abstract number could help to make sense of the concrete world might be supported. One way of moving from integers to the world was by making numbers with dots, and building shapes on them. Consider the progressions involved below:

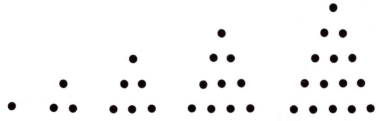

If one built squares on the base numbers and compared those with the triangles, further interesting relationships become apparent. A few minutes of this would be useful. If certain sets of numbers are put into particular shapes, yet more remarkable relationships become apparent. Consider a triangle whose sides are built on a ratio of 3, 4 and 5:

Now build a square on each side:

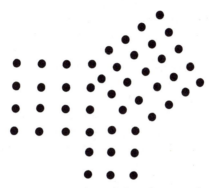

It becomes clear that the number of dots that constitute the square on the hypoteneuse are equal to the number of dots that constitute the squares on the other two sides. 9 on the base, plus 16 on the perpendicular, add up to the 25 on the hypoteneuse.

This was triumphant proof to the Pythagoreans that number thus governed geometry, and was a step in their plan to show that number governed the universe.

The further organization of the lesson might involve joining up the dots into lines and exploring other and more conventional proofs of the theorem. Having embedded discussion of the theorem in a romantic context, we can organize the central part of the lesson in a way that teaches the necessary geometrical understanding of Pythagoras' theorem, but in a way which refers back to what was initially so exciting about it. The opportunities for detailed exploration might be given as homework assignments to explore some of the Pythagorean harmonies, perhaps especially the *tetractys* and why the number 10 was considered sacred by the Pythagoreans. These are now commonly esoteric topics in the history of mathematics, but they are clearly accessible to romantic layer students, and can help them to understand what mathematics is.

We can provide a choice of two conclusions, or both. One concerns the general triumph of Pythagoras' vision, the second its particular failure. The triumph is that we take for granted what were in one sense mystical faith and magical discoveries. The mad sect of Crotona was right and the sane, scornful, hostile world around them was wrong. Mathematics is one of the bases of our civilization and is the most useful of all sciences. All explorations of the *cosmos* rely on mathematics to a greater or lesser extent. The failure was in the search for harmonious relationships between geometrical shapes and numbers. The proof that the diagonal of a square would not form harmonious relationships with the sides was a severe blow. Pythagoreans referred to this knowledge as "the unutterable." It was a kind of heresy which caused much confusion and distress. We can display this disharmony quite easily with dots, particularly when they can be placed with precision, as on a computer.

Evaluation of such a lesson should include evidence that students understand the theorem and its proof, and also that they understand its importance to the Pythagoreans and how it was a crucial step in applying abstract number to the real world.

One might design a rather similar lesson or two for the logic curriculum based on Eubulides of Miletus' paradox of the liar, and its impact on applying abstract logical reasoning to real events. We might begin with the paradox: "A man says that he is lying. Is what he says true or false?" One can have fun with this, leading through its history to Paul of Venice's set of attempted answers in the fifteenth century, pointing in the direction of Bertrand Russell's attempt to deal with it, for later in the logic curriculum.

As a second example I will deal with how one might plan a unit on the Middle Ages in social studies or history. I choose this only because a student-teacher, who had been taught that it was necessary to begin with content that was a part of students' everyday experience, recently complained to me that it was very hard to make the Middle Ages "relevant" to students today. She had worked hard and conscientiously looking for "hooks" to modern everyday experience, and in the end came up with the fact that this was the period during which high-heeled shoes for women were invented. She had difficulty finding much else of "relevance." The romantic planning framework, to say it again, directs us to find relevance not just at the level of content but rather at the level of students' imaginative lives.

First, then, we are to take a romantic perspective on the Middle Ages. This invites us to consider the Middle Ages romantically— not in the vulgar sense, but in the sense of highlighting the characteristics sketched earlier. The first step suggested is that we focus on whatever transcendent human qualities are most prominent in the topic. What, in romantic human terms, were the Middle Ages all about? We might sensibly focus on what is increasingly being called the Renaissance of the twelfth century and its aftermath—the High Middle Ages. This succeeded centuries of political chaos, social disruption, large scale migrations of people, relieved briefly by Pepin's and Charlemagne's empire, which fell apart after Charlemagne's death. The main unstable order came from the varied forms of the crude protection racket vaguely referred to as Feudalism. Gradually out of this crude chaos emerged a remarkable civilizing force that created and held together a unique kind of civilized life in Europe for more than a century. During this period the feudal protection rackets gave way to written, law-regulated, political units and over them developed one of the strangest powerful organizations that Europe has ever seen. The engines of this civilization were monasteries, the leading power was the papacy, and among the most influential characters who caught the popular imagination was Francis of Assissi. The transcendent human quality that we can identify as central to the Middle Ages is the ideal of a spiritual life, whose appeal is more powerful and important than the secular powers that have control over our bodies. The papacy's authority was based on its claim to represent this spiritual power, and on its near monopoly on literacy and the powers of organization that that allowed. The Middle Ages, then, can be seen for our unit in terms of the rise and dominance of this spiritual power and it conflicts with the physical, worldly power of kings, princes, and emperors. It was a curious period of history when the powers of the church and those of states were very distinct, in a way not known before or since in Europe. We might focus on the transcendent vision and courage of popes like Gregory VII and Innocent III and their attempts to keep alive the spiritual ideal and its authority in the face of the warring secular powers, and their civilizing of those secular powers in the process.

In organizing the content of the topic, we are directed by the model to select first content that is distant from students' everyday experience which will nevertheless be accessible because it allows students to associate with the transcendent qualities central to our theme. We might begin with three vivid stories: first of the emperor Henry IV's refusal to acknowledge Gregory VII as pope and Henry's being eventually forced to cross the Alps and stand waiting in the snow until Gregory pardoned him and lifted his excommunication; second, of Henry II at the tomb of Thomas à Becket doing penance for his part in Thomas's death, while being whipped by monks (no doubt fairly gently); and third, how the tough and wily emperor Barbarossa was brought to heel by the pope— almost literally—being forced to kiss the pope's feet in repentance for encroaching on the church's property and prerogatives. These can be told, shown, enacted in whatever way seems best to individual teachers.

They are vivid and powerful stories when fleshed out in their dramatic detail, and they make clear to students that a spiritual organization with, at that time, virtually no armed resources could exert its power across Europe against the mightiest of kings and emperors.

In organizing the unit we are directed to select the content which our romantic theme brings to the fore. The High Middle Ages are about, for example, the energy and sweetness of St. Francis of Assissi, who had within a few short years an immense influence on Europe simply by renouncing all wealth and material goods and trying instead to help those in greatest need. Every time you see a crib at Christmas, you see something that was first invented by St. Francis. He was helped by Innocent III to found an order of priests and brothers and, with St. Clare, of nuns who were to put into practice his vision of how best to live. No doubt a century later St. Francis would have been burnt at the stake as a heretic by the papal authorities of that time, as were his "spiritual" followers, but, during the expansive years of the High Middle Ages, the Franciscan spirit was a part of the great Renaissance of civilized life. It also added a new flavor of its own to civilization of course, helping even to civilize the barbarian knights with ideas of chivalry. Through the careers of various individuals, such as Peter Abelard, we can see old dogma attacked (and the schools of Paris emptying as the students followed the expelled Peter across France), and the clerical skills in literacy helping to bring law and order to the kingdoms of Europe. We would also fill out such a unit, perhaps with a two minute session at the beginning or end of each lesson, with a kind of *Guinness Book of Records* of cases of the most strange, exotic, wonderful events, characters, inventions, of the period.

The options for pursuing some element of the Middle Ages in exhaustive detail seems endless: castles or cathedrals (perhaps using David Macauley's superb books (Macauley 1973; Macauley 1977) to begin with), and here we could indeed bring in high heels and dress in general, the simple Rule St. Francis wrote for his followers, eating utensils, and typical foods eaten by lords or peasants during a typical day, and so on.

Our conclusion can try to bring together all the elements of the unit to show how people could think of themselves first and foremost as members of Christendom and less significantly as members of a particular state. Our conclusion might also focus on the waning of this spiritual ideal and the narrowing vision, the corruption of the papacy as the power-hungry struggled for it or to control it, the schisms, the effects of the plague, the Inquisition, and the fading of an institution and set of bright ideas that for a while seemed to work and have a remarkable civilizing effect on Europe, until the usual thugs, the money-hungry and power-mad types who usually rule, became more powerful again in secular states and in the church itself. Our conclusion might stress that, for a while, something strange and wonderful happened in Europe that brought art, literature, and architecture to new levels of achievement and made the likes of Francis of Assissi the pop-heroes of the age.

Now clearly, this is not the whole truth; it is a simplification. But it is not false; it catches something important and true about the Middle Ages, and it organizes it in a romantic way that can catch the imagination of the typical early adolescent.

Evaluation of such a unit might proceed using informal observation, the traditional kinds of assessment techniques, but also this approach clearly calls for something in addition. It requires that we ensure that the students' romantic capacities have been stimulated and developed. One might approach this through assignments that elicit from the students evidence of enthusiastic engagement and a sense of wonder. Such assignments might include a project on some aspect of the Middle Ages that stimulates their interest, or some model construction of a castle or cathedral, or recreation of the dress or games available at the time, or the re-enactment of some crucial event, or something similar. The important point is to provide for some kind of activity that allows the students' romantic engagement to be exhibited, to find an outlet, and to be further developed at the same time.

Finally, I will adapt a couple of examples designed by Scott Sayer and Pierre Blouin, two teachers who have been working with this framework. From a series of science units they have planned I will first, with their kind permission, provide an abbreviated sketch of their plan for "Hunters of the night," on owls. They take a romantic perspective by focusing on the associations of owls with mystery and magic and their prominence in lore to do with witches and secret knowledge, and also on their deadly prowess as swift and silent hunters. They would begin by discussing briefly the place of owls in cultural lore and their long association with wisdom, including their connection with the Roman goddess Minerva who was a patron of intellectual activity. Perhaps owls were seen as wise because of their great eyes which face forward as human eyes do. This discussion would be accompanied by a film or video showing the dramatic characteristics of the owl as hunter—the size of the Great Horned Owl, its silence, speed, sudden strikes, and remarkable hearing and vision. The romantic quality that the unit builds from and on, then, is the sense of the owl as embodying mysterious power.

The body of the unit would focus on the various adaptations that make the owl so powerful a hunter, seeing each in terms of its ability to suggest mysterious power. Considering its ears, for example, would be in the context of their size and sensitivity to high pitched sounds such as their typical prey makes, and their remarkable accuracy in locating the source of the sound. Similarly, they would focus on each distinctive feature of the owl, eyes, talons, beak, feathers, and see them as contributors to the mysterious power of these huge birds that can travel so silently and with such deadly effect at night. They would focus also on the pellets produced by owls, and show how a large bird needs a lot of energy and so it gets rid of those parts of its prey that are least easy to convert to energy. Thus it compresses fur and bones and spits them out as hard pellets. They would conduct a field study, searching out pellets from at least two different locations and see whether dissection can tell about the owls' sources of food in each area.

Possibilities for detailed study are numerous. They suggest, among many other topics, a study of the various kinds of owls, the forms of control that affect the owl population, including the first hatched eating the later hatched if a sufficient supply of other food is not provided, the distinctive nature of owls' feathers—suited for silent flight, and so on. They would conclude their unit with a visit to a nearby owl rehabilitation center, where injured owls are cared for.

Their evaluation would be conducted from observation of student participation, comments, and questions, from their design of an "animal challenge"—in which the animal must be able to survive in a particular kind of environment—from their examination of student reports that the "owl data bases" they would be required to keep, and from students writings, tape recordings, films, or whatever, displaying what they had learned from the unit.

Finally, let me simply transcribe Scott Sayer's sketch plan for a chemistry unit on water. I will leave it as he designed it. Instead of following the romantic framework exactly, he has adapted it, and incorporated a section from the mythic-layer framework.

Romantic Association. Water as the rebel substance that does not conform to what people expect it to do.

Binary Opposite. Expected/Unexpected

Access. Using any surprising experiment involving water that children can do. This should immediately engage their imagination and will be used to characterize water as a "rebel," forming the basis of the main romantic association. An example might be the circle of broken toothpicks—put water drop in center. Follow up with water flowing down a slanting string, perhaps.

Development. The story of water as a rebel substance might be told mainly through activities or teacher demonstrations. These would be chosen not to exhaustively characterize water, but rather to show the rebel nature of the substance—to examine ways in which it behaves unexpectedly and properties it possesses that are unique and different from other substances in the world. It might be useful to consider Thales' idea that everything in the universe is made of water and to recall that early chemists thought there were many kinds of water— aqua fortis, aqua regia, aqua vini, aqua valens, etc. There are many interesting and surprising things that could be developed using the idea of the "rebel." I think that the story might best be developed through activities or (in the case of somewhat dangerous substances) demonstrations. As the story progressed and students became more aware of the properties of water, "unexpected" events would become more "expected" but since some of these things are rather unique to water, it would still be a "rebel" in a sense.

Conclusion. If possible, show how life as we know it would not exist but for some of the odd, "rebellious" quirks about water. For example, water has the odd characteristic of contracting normally as it cools, as any normal substance does, but at 4 degrees C, it begins to expand. Thus ice floats. What would happen to life in lakes and ponds in the winter if this were not so? There are no doubt other better examples, if one were only more knowledgeable. Perhaps even just making strongly enough the point that, as Primo Levi writes, "we too are liquids," and one of the great problems of life on land is packaging that liquid.

Conclusion

What I have tried to show in this chapter are some of the ways that the principles outlined in the previous chapter can affect teaching practice for the better. The main effect will be not so much on the style of teaching as on the choice of material and its organization. I am assuming that teachers will use the variety of styles and models of teaching that best suit them. There are a number of excellent books about pedagogical methods, or ideas for how to present material in the context of the normal classroom, and there is a rich teachers' lore that intersects with these books but also is carried on in discussions in staffrooms and teachers' professional organizations and conferences. I see my recommendations here as complementary to all of that, except perhaps in as far as the planning model I outline conflicts with the more "technological" models that have become prominent particularly in teacher training programs.

What I have tried to stress is that it is the characteristics of romance that need to predominate in planning for teaching. The teacher, I have argued, should conceive of the task as telling good stories about real things, focusing on their limits, establishing clearly where reality ends, and thereby the contexts within which reality can be understood.

A number of popular books based on T.V. programs which are successful at organizing complex knowledge romantically, are Kenneth Clark's *Civilization* (1969), James Burke's *Connections* (1978) Jacob Bronowski's *The Ascent of Man* (1974), John Romer's *Testament* (1988), and the one I have mentioned a few times already, Carl Sagan's *Cosmos* (1980). Some are perhaps not suitable for the normal "romantic" classroom because they contain other elements as well as romance— gentle irony in Clark's case and general philosophic schemes in Burke's. But they are successful at taking subjects that are usually inaccessible in their normal scholarly textbook environments and making them romantically engaging. The characteristics of romance are constantly evident in them.

Much of this chapter can be seen as addressing an aspect of what is usually discussed as "motivation." My focus in planning teaching is not just on how to engage students' interest but also on how to stimulate and develop their sense of wonder. I have stressed the need to focus on the extreme and the exotic. This may be all very well at times, but it can be a tiresome nuisance to have students eager to engage only the exotic and wonderful if the task at hand is one that requires painstaking and precise measurement, or mastery of certain basic information. I have argued that this problem too can be mitigated by using various romantic principles, particularly by creating dramatic contexts within which the detail and precision can themselves become the focus of romantic association. This, of course, is a counsel of perfection, requiring constant energy and imagination. Published lesson and unit plans derived from these principles and textbooks designed for romantic-stage students would make it all more realizable. But no one can be expected to sustain a vivid romantic presentation all the time.

Teaching, after all, is impossible. The principles outlined here might enable us to educate students better, and engage their interest more profoundly, but they will not make teaching one of the possible jobs. Being president of a multinational corporation, or a clockmaker, or an auto-mechanic, or President or Prime Minister may be more or less difficult jobs, but they are all possible. Teaching is impossible in that no one can be expected to engage and successfully teach fairly large groups of disparate children hour after hour, day after day. This book is supposed to be a guide to educating students better during the middle-school years, and it provides I think some practical principles that can ease some of the impossibilities of teaching. But I do not imagine that these few principles provide a panacea for teaching in the typical classroom. (I would be less modest in my claim for their value to the individual parent or tutor with the individual child.)

Clearly the kinds of historical material I can draw on, sitting in a study full of reference books, for a lesson on Pythagoras' theorem can hardly be at the finger-tips of teachers for all the lesson they have to teach every day. There are two points related to this that I have mentioned above a number of times but which bear repeating. First is the simple one that current textbooks are typically not organized in a manner particularly hospitable to encouraging romantic understanding. But this can be relatively easily remedied. The second is that teaching is a tough job and, when done conscientiously, can be gruelling. It has its rewards of course. But the kind of technologizing approach to education that has seeped in from industry has led increasingly to the view of the teacher as the somewhat de-skilled deliverer of a curriculum designed and developed by "experts." This conception of the teacher's role is contingent on a distorted conception of education. In this book the teacher is conceived as our culture's primary story-teller, and the stories to be told during this romantic layer are primarily those in which rationality provides sense-making capacities in alliance with the romantic imagination. To be able to conceive of curricula content romantically, teachers need to know a lot about the topics they teach. Teaching in this view, then, is properly a learned profession. At present this is not as generally recognized as it might be, and this is a problem not so easily remedied as the textbook problem. Time and resources need to be provided to encourage teachers' scholarly development throughout their careers. And this costs money.

Conclusion

Perhaps I should call this "Conclusions" as I want to make a few points that require some shifting of gears. First I will echo, with a few small changes, the conclusion of Volume 1 that remains appropriate here. Then I will step back and draw an implication about the role of schools, and finally I will make a few smaller points that I think bear some brief elaboration.

Education is being characterized here as the process wherein the individual recapitulates the accumulation or development of the sense-making capacities invented and discovered in our cultural history. "Sense-making capacities" are a product of knowledge accumulation and psychological development working together along with a generative element, which may be a product of their joint working or may involve something independent. Cultural history can enlighten our study of education because we can see in it the effects of these forces in shaping the sequence in which sense-making capacities have been and can be generated.

The space shuttle was possible only after the invention of the vacuum flask, the machine gun similarly required the clock, the representational style of Leonardo required the technical developments of Giotto, the historiography of Thucydides required the forms articulated by Herodotus, Boolean algebra required Pythagorean harmonies and so on. The causal sequences in these processes are complex and very difficult for us to pin down, but the sequences are not arbitrary or accidental; Thucydides's history could not have preceded Herodotus', nor could Leonardo's style have preceded Giotto's, nor the space shuttle the vacuum flask, and so on. In writing histories of technology, or painting, or various forms of inquiry, we try to pinpoint necessary prerequisites of later developments and locate the causal dynamic. In some cases, such as mathematics, we tend to rely on a sense of an unfolding logic in the subject. In others, such as technology, we find a logic in the sequence of inventions tied in with social purposes and occasional psychological quirks of inventors. In cases like historiography and the arts, the logical element tends to take a subsidiary place to social environments and the psychological make-up of the writers and artists. In the sciences, it is claimed that, if Darwin or Rutherford or Einstein had not made the discoveries associated with their names, someone else very soon after would have. In the arts, if Leonardo or Beethoven or Joyce had not produced the works they did, no equivalents would have appeared. There is considerable opaqueness about causal dynamics in cultural history but what is evident is the effects of these shaping dynamic forces. Regardless of our ignorance about causes and our imprecision in defining the constituents of these dynamic forces, we can see and describe the sequences in which they permit the sense-making capacities that constitute our culture to develop. These same forces—logical, psychological, and generative—constrain the sequence in which any individual may develop the sense-making capacities available in our culture. The logic of subjects does not let up, nor is the human psyche released from its bounds.

It has long been obvious that education involves in some fashion a recapitulation of cultural history, but it has not been clear how we could find a basis for describing whatever may be common to the two processes nor how we could locate a dynamic that would point up some causal sequence that they share. The bifurcated ramifications of Plato's and Rousseau's insights have encouraged in the study of education separate focuses on knowledge accumulation and on psychological development, assuming that separate advances from philosophical and psychological research will somehow be brought together. Clearly, recapitulation does not make much sense in terms of knowledge accumulation or psychological development separately. Even if it were possible, there is no good reason to recommend that the child should recapitulate the accumulation of knowledge as it was invented or discovered in history. How, for example, would one teach geography or history in such a scheme? Similarly, any scheme that sees the individual as recapitulating an historical process of psychological development faces the bizarre need to characterize Euripides and Plato as somehow psychological equivalents of modern children. What I am trying to do in this essay is describe, in terms of sense-making capacities, what cultural history and education share, and so what the latter recapitulates of the former, and locate, if only imprecisely, the dynamic that points up the causal sequence that they have in common. The focus on sense-making capacities enables us to bring concerns with knowledge accumulation coherently together with psychological development and it allows us to transcend the Platonic and Rousseauian, the traditionalist and progressivist, conflicts by designing a curriculum that stimulates the ripening of childhood in the child while putting in place the foundations for later layers of education.

The category of "sense-making capacities" is intended to bring together what we have been accustomed to think of as appropriately distinct, or at least as meaningfully distinguishable. The distinct studies of epistemology and psychology have had difficulty coming together in education, I have argued, because we cannot give an adequate account of how they are to interact. Clearly, psychological development and accumulating knowledge, if considered separately, have to interact in the process of education. One problem this creates is identification of where the dynamic of the educational process lies. Does accumulating knowledge drive psychological development, or does psychological development drive accumulating knowledge? Or, in terms of the Piagetian/Vygotskian dispute, does learning drive development or development drive learning? Perhaps they drive each other, dialectically? This last is a convenient but unfortunately vacuous solution, in that it fails to deal with the problem at all. A similar dilemma appears in education when "learning" is separated from what is to be learned. The content to be learned is left to the philosophers or curriculum specialists while "the process of learning" is investigated separately. Again, these separate forms of inquiry have not been brought together with any notable success. Once we are engaged with the practical task of helping children to understand mathematics or Chinese or history, the promise that learning theories make to enlighten "processes" of learning vanishes away. My argument has been that one cannot meaningfully separate minds and knowledge, "processes" and "content." The category of "sense-making" resists being artificially broken apart; we are not inclined to look for abstract processes of sense-making distinct from what is being made sense of. Nor are we inclined to consider accumulating knowledge apart from the psychological uses it is put to. If we think of education in terms of increasingly elaborate sense-making, we will contain the insights that education requires accumulating knowledge, on the one hand, and psychological development on the other; we will transcend the artificial problem of their interaction generated by holding those two separate; and we will avoid the *impasses* into which identifying the dynamic of education in either one or the other runs.

The use of "sense-making capacities" is not itself an ideal term, of course. For one thing, "capacities" suggests some abstract structures of mind or something that can be distinct from particular knowledge.

Similarly, "techniques of thinking," a phrase I have used occasionally, carries a similar implication of a distinction between abstract techniques and what is thought about. The trouble is that the language we have available has been generated presupposing the value of the distinctions that I am suggesting are educationally dysfunctional. In the previous volume I resorted to the term *bonnes à penser*. "Good things to think with" catches both the knowledge and psychological components we need to keep together. If the accumulation of knowledge goes forward with too little concern for psychological development we get, in Michel de Montaigne's rude phrase, "asses loaded with books;" if psychological development is pursued with too little concern for the accumulation of knowledge, we get skilled, confident, ignoramuses.

The area of study that this scheme finds most useful for education, then, is cultural history. Rather less, it follows, should be expected from the presently dominant research traditions, concerned with knowledge and with psychological processes than their considerable scale seems to promise. Education seems unlikely to be improved by some dramatic new findings about children or learning, development, motivation, or the nature of knowledge. Education seems likely to benefit more, to echo Wittgenstein, not by getting new information but by rearranging what we have known all along. The sense-making capacities this scheme focuses on were not generated, to use Walter Ong's nice phrase, "in the hollow of men's minds but in the density of history" (Ong, 1971, p. 7). Similarly, their recapitulation by children is not a matter of learning abstract "thinking skills" but of making sense of their social and cultural circumstances in the density of their history and of their experience.

I have perhaps dwelt a little too much on oral cultures and the oral foundations of our forms of knowledge for some people's taste. It has seemed useful as a means of emphasizing the central point that rationality, if it is to develop richly, must keep in contact with its oral foundations. Our sophisticated forms of rationality are not the result of "breaking away" from myth and from the forms of thought most evident in oral cultures; the result of breaking away is desiccation, sterility, and inhuman(e) technocratic, directionless thinking. Mythic understanding is, I have argued, a foundational constituent of any rich rationality; it is the connection of thinking to life and to our hopes, fears, purposes, and so on. A well developed mythic understanding is the grounding for romantic understanding, and becomes a constituent of it. Only if we remain well-grounded can our thinking—Anteus-like—grow strong and effective. To "break-away" from these oral foundations leads to the pathological autisms of thought that are unfortunately common in our society. Perhaps the kind of technocratic thinking that invades social and political policy-making and loses sight of the varied purposes of human societies is a common example of such autism (Wilson, 1979).

It may appear odd to some that this discussion of education for the middle-school years has had so little to say about jobs. Let me, for a few pages, indulge in a rhetorical shift to a kind of analysis of education and schooling that is more common in the public media.

I am writing during a period of national reports on education, politicians' and business demands for improvement of schools, and a general ferment of dissatisfaction about the achievements of nearly all educational institutions. Prominent in all of these are concerns for the appropriateness of what schools are doing to students, given the kinds of jobs that are or are likely to be available and given the demands of modern and future "citizenship." And prominent in these concerns is the problem of literacy. All Western nations, and no doubt others, have conducted major studies of literacy among their populations and, using even very lax criteria, the results in countries with universal schooling for at least ten years of students' lives are, shall we say, disappointing. Large numbers are illiterate. If we exclude books of cartoons and self-help or how-to-do-it books, only a small minority of people read a book after leaving school. If we further exclude pulp romances, science-fiction, and detective novels, then only a tiny minority of Western populations can be considered book readers. That is, what we mean by "Western culture," which is in significant part encoded in books (along with other equally minority activities) is engaged by only a very few people.

In the relatively recent past, a large number of jobs in Western economies could be successfully done without even "functional" literacy. With the advent of robots and computers, these jobs are disappearing. The visibility of the "literacy" issue comes about as the sectors of the economy that could happily absorb illiterates or the marginally literate no longer do so. We can clearly no longer afford the proportion of illiterates that our schools have been accustomed to produce.

Teaching any child, except the severely mentally damaged, to read and write is easy. It takes just a few weeks, then practice to pick up fluency. Teaching thirty children to read and write when they live in an environment in which literacy is not valued, is difficult. Very many children lack a background of encouragement to read, any clear reason to put in the required effort, the opportunity for individual help, and sustained assisted practice.

But even if schools were successful in achieving the kind of functional literacy that seems to be the focus of much media attention, it is far from clear what social value that would have. The evaporation of jobs for illiterates is equalled by the evaporation of jobs for the just functionally literate. What society seems willing to pay for is a relatively high level of technical efficiency in a wide area of economically useful skills. The prospect for significant improvements in literacy, let alone this much more ambitious aim, seems certainly to most media commentators and political decision-makers dim. The vast investments of the 1960s failed to produce the promised results, and no politician can responsibly support that extent of investment in so unpromising an enterprise.

One role of schools is what we may call "acculturation." During the middle-school years students on the whole become integrated into the mass-culture outside the school. In the main, in the West, this is dominated by and reflected in television, radio, and a few mass-circulation magazines and papers (not really in *news*papers, but those filled with "factoids" about television and film stars and amazing discoveries, cures, and weight loss diets)—low level romantic/mythic structuring. But this integration with mass-culture seems to take place largely without the schools' help and, as far as one can see, often in the face of the schools' efforts to combat it. Many teachers identify television as an enemy. But schools only half-heartedly seem to feel they have the influence to combat the acculturation performed so successfully on middle-school students by television, radio, etc. The residual commitment of schools to a culture that transcends that available in the daily environment is evident in the common claim that students should be "exposed" to selected parts of this transcendent culture. The result of largely context-less exposure is of course to create hostility to such boring stuff. The occasional attempt to transcend the kind of narrow patriotism that tends to be a part of media acculturation seems to meet with no more general success. That is to say, the acculturation of students seems to be adequately performed by other social agencies and the schools either conform with this marginally or, if they try to combat it, seem largely unsuccessful.

One of the other promises of the schools was that they would help to eliminate social inequalities. "Equality of opportunity" was a slogan that promised something the democratic societies were willing to support. But here again schools have largely failed. The rich remain rich, the poor remain poor, and schools seem to have little discernable effect on social mobility. (Some argue that the reproduction of class divisions is one of schools' covert functions, see, for example, Bourdieu (1989).)

With potential increases in long-term unemployment for significant proportions of young people, schools, in promising to instill the values of good citizenship, offer to prevent what seems to many a fearsome scenario. That is, gangs of illiterate "dispossessed" young people roaming the streets of a society which everywhere displays and advertises goods to which they have no access except by crime. It is clear that politicians on the whole have concluded that the schools have failed to fulfil their promise here as well. Compare the relative salaries of police and teachers over the last decade or so, and the relative increase in numbers of police to teachers in nearly all Western societies. Society has apparently concluded that the prevention promised by schools is not worth the money, and the kind of containment and control offered by increasingly well-armed police forces is the better investment.

The "crisis in schooling" we read so much about concerns what role schools can adequately perform that is worth their enormous cost. As suppliers of appropriately skilled labor to a rapidly changed job-market they are doing poorly; as social equalizers they are even worse; and as producers of people who, if unemployed, will turn to socially approved or at least undisruptive activities, they are poor. What do they do that is worth their cost? They are successful in what is sometimes called their "custodial" role. For significant amounts of time they keep gangs of teenagers off the streets and they keep children out of the home. This latter has allowed large numbers of women to enter the workforce over the last two decades, but these women moved overwhelmingly into precisely the kinds of jobs that are now being eliminated by the microchip.

Well, this kind of analysis is what we are accustomed to see when the topic of "education" appears in the media, or is the subject of reports intended for informing political action. And here I am writing about recapitulating in students important parts of the Western cultural tradition. It will perhaps seem that my scheme is addressed to a minute proportion of the population, a proportion which is anyway catered to by private schools. I think, rather, that I am addressing what it is worth the state paying its schools to do.

My claim is that if this scheme is followed, if curricula and teaching are revised to conform with these principles, nearly all children and students will achieve higher levels of literacy, they will become much better informed and more fluent thinkers, they will be more sensitive and sensible, and they will make better sense of their world and of their experience as inheritors of a cultural tradition.

When people hear the word "culture" these days they are less likely to reach for their guns as feel overcome with lassitude. "Culture" is the boring bits we switch television channels to avoid. The implication of this scheme nevertheless is that the job of the schools should be seen primarily as a cultural one—not socializing, nor crime prevention, nor job preparation. If the Western school becomes more single-mindedly an educational institution and the classroom a distinctive place, apart from an everyday society, in which contact is made with a cultural tradition, then the schools will be performing a role well worth paying for. This might seem a slightly incredible claim, but may appear less so if one considers what seem to be me incidental but inevitable corollaries of success at this narrower ambition. If schools become more successful at educating, in this narrower cultural sense, they will incidentally provide the kinds of flexible intellectual skills that are required by our radically changing job-markets, they will give people more satisfying ways of using leisure than trashing the neighborhood, and they will produce more responsible, intelligent, and imaginative citizens. A problem for schools in the West during this century is that they have become increasingly agents of the expanding control of centralized states. Their educational role, always a small part of what the state has paid them for, has survived with eroding influence into present times. An irony of the history of Western schools during the past century is that the aims of their political paymasters might have been better met had they been content to expand schools' educational role and not pay them to produce peaceable patriots well prepared to supply the manpower needs of the economy. Schools just are not very good institutions to achieve these ends because of the constant conflicts between them and the cultural aims of education—of which schools have never fully let go. An implication of this scheme is that the school should more firmly adhere to its cultural role and seek consciously to reduce the influence of socializing, ideologizing, job preparation, psychotherapy, and so on, in its daily activities.

Many students leave school these days, even those who are not unsuccessful in the school's terms, feeling cheated. So many assignments, so many tests, and somehow the richness of the world and experience beyond their everyday experience, which they sense is there, has eluded them. The sheer knowledge of the dimensions of the world, the range of human experience, are not a part of what they understand. What I am arguing for here as at least a partial solution to this problem is a sense of romance, and its agent is the imagination. In this I am in part echoing Whitehead's point made earlier. "romantic emotion is essentially the excitement consequent on the transition from the bare facts to the first realizations of the import of their unexplored relationships" (Whitehead, 1919, p. 18). It is the imagination that can carry us beyond the bare facts and that can hint at the wonder of their unexplored relationships.

One shouldn't, of course, make too sharp a distinction between everyday experience and imaginative life, as the one continually must feed the other. But we can forget that "experience isn't necessarily a window on to meaning" (Wills, 1988, p. 254), or as T.S. Eliot put it compactly in the *Four Quartets*, "We had the experience/But missed the meaning." The current half-hearted sense in which so many teachers feel they cannot bring so much of the students' cultural heritage to vivid life but rather are responsible only to "expose" them to it, perhaps provides the experience but, without imaginatively engaging students, misses the meaning. I fear that one of our main concerns with schools at present, despite the heroic efforts of so many teachers, ought to be that they provide so little for the imagination.

Having tried to clamber onto the giant shoulders of Plato and Rousseau, and keep a grip on both, it would be well to finish by repeating what has been a constant theme of these two volumes so far. One of the central educational concerns addressed by Plato and Rousseau was that of how to overcome the apparent inevitability that people simply ceased thinking after the fantasy of their earliest years and their minds become dull mirrors of the ideas, opinions, confusions, bigotry, and general stupidity that passed for adult thinking according to the conventions of society at large. How can one keep the mind awake, and not have it sink into an ossified slumber—mashing metaphors—reflecting back whatever are the conventions of the time? Whitehead described all Western philosophy as merely footnotes to Plato. I am in danger of representing modern educational thought at its best as merely footnotes to Wordsworth. The same problem he expressed rather more vividly: "And custom lie upon thee with a weight,/Heavy as frost, and deep almost as life!" The socializing that custom and conventional ideas performs on us is of course crucial to making us social beings, able to get by among our fellows. But, if we are not careful, that weight of convention and custom seeps through our whole lives, heavy as frost, and that distinctive Western enterprise we call education is frozen at the start and cannot get adequately underway. Wordsworth's and Romanticism's answer, which I am drawing on, is for the middle-school years a particular energetic kind of understanding which begins to build rational thought through the activity of our romantic imagination.

Bibliography

Abrams, M. H. (1953), *The Mirror and the Lamp: Romantic Theory and the Critical Tradition*, New York: Norton.

Allott, Miriam and Super, Robert H. (eds). (1986), *Matthew Arnold*, Oxford: Oxford University Press.

Apple, Michael W. (1979), *Ideology and Curriculum*, London: Routledge and Kegan Paul.

Ashton, Rosemary (1989), "Faking a Winning Formula," *Times Literary Supplement*, March 24–30.

Auerbach, Erich (1955), *Mimesis*, (Willard R. Trask, trans.), Princeton, New Jersey: Princeton University Press.

Barzun, Jacques (1961), *Classic, Romantic and Modern*, Boston: Atlantic-Little, Brown.

Bayley, John (1988), "The Lost Instructors," *Times Literary Supplement*, February 12–18.

Benjamin, Walter (1969), *Illuminations: Essays and Reflections*, (Harry Zohn, trans.), New York: Schocken Books. (Cited essay first published 1936).

Bereiter, Carl and Scardamalia, Marlene (1989), "Intentioned Learning as a Goal of Instruction" in L. B. Resnick (ed.), *Knowing Learning, and Instruction: Essays in Honor of Robert Glaser* Hillsdale, NJ: Erlbaum.

Berg, Edward E. (1970), "L. S. Vygotsky's Theory of the Social and Historical Origins of Consciousness," Ph.D. thesis, University of Wisconsin. (Cited in L. S. Vygotsky's, *Mind in Society*, 1978, q.v.).

Bloom, Harold (1982), *Bridges to Fantasy*, (eds. George E. Slusser, Eric S. Rabkin, and Robert Scholes) Carbondale, IL.: University of Southern Illinois Press.

Bloom, Harold (1971), *Visionary Company*, Ithaca, NY: Cornell University Press. (Revised and enlarged edition).

Bloom, Harold (1973), "Emerson: The Glory and the Sorrows of American Romanticism," in D. Thorburn and G. Hartman (eds.), *Romanticism: Vistas, Instances, Continuities*, Ithaca, NY: Cornell University Press.

Bossy, J. (1985), *Christianity in the West*, Oxford: Oxford University Press.

Bourdieu, Pierre (1989), *La Noblesse d'état: Grandes écoles et esprit de corps*, Paris: Minuit.

Bovet, P. (1923), *The Fighting Instinct*, London: Allen and Unwin.

Bowen, Elizabeth (1964), *The Little Girls*, New York: Knopf.

Bowra, C. M. (1961), *The Romantic Imagination*, Oxford: Oxford University Press. (Cambridge, Mass.: Harvard University Press, 1949).

Brinton, Crane (1965), *The Anatomy of Revolution* (revised and expanded edition), New York: Vintage Books. (First published 1938).

Bronowski, Jacob (1974), *The Ascent of Man*, Boston: Little, Brown.

Brown, T. S. (1954), "Herodotus and His Profession," *American Historical Review*, LIX, 4.

Bruner, Jerome (1988), in D. Cayley (ed.), *Literacy: The Medium and the Message*, Toronto: Canadian Broadcasting Corporation. (Transcript of *Ideas* programs February 1st and 8th).

Bruner, Jerome (1986), *Actual Minds, Possible Worlds*, Cambridge, MA: Harvard University Press.

Bruner, Jerome, and Olson, David (1977/78), "Symbols and Texts as Tools of Intellect," *Interchange*, 8 (4), 1–15.

Bullock, Alan (1985), *The Humanist Tradition in the West*, London: Thames and Hudson.

Burk, Caroline Frear (1907), "The Collecting Instinct," in Theodate L. Smith (ed.), *Aspects of Child Life in Education*, Boston: Ginn; Rpt. Arno Press, 1975.

Burke, James (1978), *Connections*, Boston: Little, Brown.

Burke, Kenneth (1969), *A Rhetoric of Motives*, Berkeley: University of California Press.

Burke, Peter (1985), *Vico*, Oxford: Oxford University Press.

Butler, Marilyn (1981), *Romantics, Rebels, and Reactionaries*, Oxford: Oxford University Press.

Butler, Marilyn (1987), "Revising the Canon," *Times Literary Supplement*, Dec. 4–10, 1349, 1359–60.

Callahan, R. (1962), *Education and the Cult of Efficiency*, Chicago: University of Chicago Press.

Cayley, David (ed. and presentor) (1988), *Literacy: The Medium and the Message*, Toronto: Canadian Broadcasting Corporation.

Clark, Kenneth (1969), *Civilization*, London: BBC and John Murray.

Coe, Richard (1984), *When the Grass was Taller*, New Haven: Yale University Press.

Cole, Michael, and Griffin, Peg (1980), "Cultural Amplifiers Reconsidered," in David R. Olson (ed.), *The Social Foundations of Language and Thought*, New York: Norton.

Cole, Michael, and Scribner, Sylvia (1974), *Culture and Thought: A Psychological Introduction*, New York: Wiley.

Coleridge, S. T. (1907), *Biographia Literaria* (J. Shawcross, ed.), (2 vols.), Oxford: Oxford University Press. (First published 1817).

Coleridge, S. T. (1960), *Shakespearean Criticism*, (Vol. 2), London: Dent. (The Eighth Lecture from Lectures on Shakespeare and Milton, 1811–12).

Cooper, David E. (1986), *Metaphor*, Oxford: Blackwell.

Cornford, F. M. (1957), *From Religion to Philosophy*, New York: Harper and Row. (First published 1912).

Cox, Jeffrey (1988), *In the Shadow of Romance*, Athens, OH: University Press of Ohio.

Cressy, David (1980), *Literacy and the Social Order: Reading and Writing in Tudor and Stuart England*, Cambridge: Cambridge University Press.

Danzig, Tobias (1967), *Number: The Language of Science*, New York: Free Press. (First published New York: Macmillan, 1930).

Darbishire, Helen (1958), *The Poet Wordsworth*, Oxford: Clarendon Press.

De Garmo, C. (1895), *Herbart and the Herbartians*, New York: Scribner.

de Kerckhove, D. (1986), "Alphabetic Literacy and Brain Processes," *Visible Language*, XX, 3, 274–93.

de Kerckhove, D. (1987), "Writing Left and Right," *Interchange*, 18, 1/2, 60–77.

de Kerckhove, D. 1988), in D. Cayley (ed.), *The Medium and the Message*, Toronto: Canadian Broadcasting Corporation. (Transcript of *Ideas* programs February 1st and 8th).

de Sousa, Ronald (1988), *The Rationality of Emotion*, Cambridge, MA: MIT Press.

Detienne, Marcel (1986), *The Creation of Mythology* (Margarete Cook, trans.), Chicago: University of Chicago Press.

Dewey, John (1916), *Democracy and Education*, New York: Macmillan.

Dewey, John (1938), *Experience and Education*, New York: Macmillan.

Dodds, E. R. (1951), *The Greeks and the Irrational*, Berkeley: University of California Press.

Donaldson, Margaret (1978), *Children's Minds*, London: Croom Helm.

Doddy, Margaret Anne (1989), *Frances Burney: The Life in the Works*, Cambridge: Cambridge University Press.

Drews, Robert (1973), *The Greek Accounts of Eastern History*, Washington, DC: Center for Hellenic Studies.

Durkheim, Emile (1965), *The Elementary Forms of the Religious Life*, New York: Free Press.

Eakin, Richard M. (1976), *Great Scientists Speak Again*, Berkeley: University of California Press.

Eco, Umberto (1983), *The Name of the Rose*, New York: Harcourt Brace Jovanovich.

Eco, Umberto (1984), "Science Fiction and the Art of Conjecture," *Times Literary Supplement*, Nov. 2nd.

Egan, Kieran (1983), *Education and Psychology: Plato, Piaget, and Scientific Psychology*, New York: Teachers College Press, 1983; London: Methuen, 1984.

Egan, Kieran (1988), *Primary Understanding: Education in Early Childhood*, New York: Routledge.

Egan, Kieran (in press), *Imagination in Teaching and Learning*.

Egan, Susanna (1984), *Patterns of experience in autobiography*, Chapel Hill: University of North Carolina Press.

Eisenstein, Elizabeth L. (1979), *The Printing Press as an Agent of Change: Communications and Cultural Transformations in Early-Modern Europe* (2 vols.), New York: Cambridge University Press.

Eisenstein, Elizabeth L. (1983), *The Printing Revolution in Early Modern Europe*, Cambridge: Cambridge University Press.

Eliade, Mircea (1959), *Cosmos and History*, New York: Harper and Row.

Ellis, Annie Raine (ed.) (1889), *The Early Diary of Frances Burney* (2 vols.), London: Bell.

Enzensberger, Hans Magnus (1987), "In Praise of Illiteracy," *Harper's Magazine*, October, 12–14.

Erikson, Erik H. (1962), *Young Man Luther: A Study in Psychoanalysis and History*, New York: Norton.

Erikson, Erik H. (1963), *Childhood and Society* (2nd ed.), New York: Norton.

Fauvel, John, Flood, Raymond, Shortland, Michael, and Wilson, Robin (eds.) (1989), *Let Newton Be!: A New Perspective on His Life and Works*, Oxford: Oxford University Press.

Feldman, C. (1988), in D. Cayley (ed.), *Literacy: The Medium and the Message*. Toronto: Canadian Broadcasting Corporation. (Transcript of *Ideas* programs February 1st and 8th). (This theme is elaborated in her paper "Oral metalanguage," presented at the Conference on Orality and Literacy, University of Toronto, June 1987.)

Finley, John H. J. (1966), *Four Stages of Greek Thought*, Stanford, CA: Stanford University Press.

Fox, Susan (1977), "The Female as Metaphor in William Blake's Poetry," *Critical Inquiry*, 3, 507–519.

Freud, Sigmund (1938), "Totem and Taboo," in A. A. Brill (ed.), *The Basic Writings of Sigmund Freud*, New York: Modern Library.

Frye, Northrop (1962), *The Educated Imagination,* Toronto: CBC Learning Systems.

Gardner, John (1972), *Grendel,* New York: Knopf.

Gardner, Martin (1982), *Logic Machines and Diagrams,* (2nd ed.), Chicago: University of Chicago Press.

Gearhart, Suzanne (1984), *The Open Boundary of History and Fiction,* Princeton: Princeton University Press.

Gombrich, E. H. (1960), *Art and Illusion,* Princeton: Princeton University Press.

Good, Graham (1988), *The Observing Self: Rediscovering the Essay,* London: Routledge.

Goodman, Nelson (1976), *Language of Art* (2nd ed.), Indianapolis, IN: Hackett.

Goody, J. (1977), *The Domestication of the Savage Mind,* Cambridge: Cambridge University Press.

Goody, J. (1986), *The Logic of Writing and the Organization of Society,* Cambridge: Cambridge University Press.

Goody, J. (1987), *The Interface Between the Written and the Oral,* Cambridge: Cambridge University Press.

Goody, J., and Watt, I. (1968), "The Consequences of Literacy," in J. Goody (ed.), *Literacy in Traditional Societies* (pp. 304–345), Cambridge: Cambridge University Press.

Gough, K. (1968), "Literacy in Kerala," in Jack Goody (ed.), *Literacy in Traditional Societies,* Cambridge: Cambridge University Press.

Gould, Stephen Jay (1977), *Ontogeny and Phylogeny,* Cambridge, MA: Harvard University Press.

Gowin, D. Bob (1981), *Educating,* Ithaca, NY: Cornell University Press.

Gross, John (1983), *The Oxford Book of Aphorisms,* Oxford: Oxford University Press.

Hall, G. Stanley (1904), *Adolescence: Its Psychology and Its Relations to Physiology, Anthropology, Sociology, Sex, Crime, Religion, and Education* (2 vols.), New York: Appleton.

Hall, G. Stanley (1907), *Aspects of Child Life and Education* (Theodate L. Smith, ed.), Boston: Ginn. Rpt. Arno Press 1975.

Hall, G. Stanley (1921), *Youth: Its Education, Regimen, and Hygene,* New York: Appleton. (From Hall, *Adolescence,* 1904).

Hall, Nigel (1987), *The Emergence of Literacy,* London: Hodder and Stoughton.

Hallpike, C. R. (1979), *The Foundation of Primitive Thought,* Oxford: Clarendon Press.

Hamlyn, D. W. (1978), *Experience and the Growth of Understanding,* London: Routledge and Kegan Paul.

Hanson, Karen (1986), *The Self Imagined,* New York: Routledge and Kegan Paul.

Hanson, Karen (1988), "Prospects for the Good Life: Education and Perceptive Imagination," in Kieran Egan and Dan Nadaner (eds.), *Imagination and Education,* New York: Teachers College Press.

Hartog, François (1988), *The Mirror of Herodotus* (Janet Lloyd, trans.), Berkeley: University of California Press.

Havelock, Eric (1963), *Preface to Plato,* Cambridge, MA: Harvard University Press.

Havelock, Eric (1980), "The Coming of Literate Communication to Western Culture," *Journal of Communication,* Winter.

Havelock, Eric (1986), *The Muse Learns to Write,* New Haven: Yale University Press.

Hazlitt, William (1951), "On the Ignorance of the Learned," in W. E. Williams (ed.), *A Book of English Essays,* Harmondsworth, Middlesex: Penguin.

Heath, Shirley Brice (1982), "What No Bedtime Story Means," *Language in Society,* 11 (1), 49–76.

Heath, Shirley Brice (1983), *Ways With Words,* Cambridge: Cambridge University Press.

Herriman, Michael (1986), "Metalinguistic Awareness and the Growth of Literacy," in S.

de Castel, A. Luke, and K. Egan (eds.), *Literacy, Society, and Schooling*, Cambridge and New York: Cambridge University Press.

Hirsch, E. D. Jr. (1987), *Cultural Literacy: What Every American Needs to Know*, Boston: Houghton Mifflin.

Hirst, Paul (1974), *Knowledge and the Curriculum*, London: Routledge and Kegan Paul.

Horton, Robin (1982), "Tradition and Modernity Revisited," in Martin Hollis and Steven Lukes (eds.), *Rationality and Relativism*, Oxford: Blackwell.

Hughes, Ted (1988), "Myth and Education," in Kieran Egan and Dan Nadaner (eds.), *Imagination and Education*, New York: Teachers College Press; Milton Keynes: Open University Press.

Hume, David (1888), *A Treatise of Human Nature* (L. A. Selby-Gigge, ed.), Oxford: Oxford University Press. (First published in 1739).

Innis, Harold (1951), *The Bias of Communication*, Toronto: University of Toronto Press.

James, Henry (1913), *A Small Boy and Others*, London: Macmillan.

Jowett, B. (1937), *The Dialogues of Plato*, New York: Random House.

Kames, Lord Henry Home (1782), *Loose Hints Upon Education, Chiefly Concerning the Culture of the Heart*, Edinburgh: John Bell.

Karier, Clarence J. (1986), *The Individual, Society and Education*, Urbana: University of Illinois Press.

Karier, Clarence J. (1986), *Scientists of the Mind: Intellectual Founders of Modern Psychology*, Urbana: University of Illinois Press.

Kelly, A. V. (1982), *The Curriculum: Theory and Practice*, London: Harper & Row.

Kendon, Adam (1989), *Sign Languages of Aboriginal Australia*, Cambridge: Cambridge University Press.

Kuhn, Thomas S. (1962), *The Structure of Scientific Revolutions*, Chicago: University of Chicago Press.

Lancaster, A. (1897), "Psychology and Pedagogy of Adolescence," *Pedagogical Seminary*, 5, July.

Lankshear, Colin, and Lawler, Moira (1988), *Literacy, Schooling, and Revolution*, Sussex: Falmer Press.

Larkin, Philip (1988), *Collected Poems*, London: The Marvell Press and Faber and Faber.

Le Goff, Jacques (1989), "After Annales: The Life as History," *Times Literary Supplement*, April 14–20.

Lévi-Bruhl, Lucien (1985), *How Natives Think* (Lilian A. Clare, trans.), Princeton: Princeton University Press.

Lévi-Strauss, Claude (1966), *The Savage Mind*, Chicago: University of Chicago Press.

Levy, Jonathan (1987), *A Theatre of the Imagination*, Rowayton, CT: New Plays, Inc.

Locke, John (1961), *An Essay Concerning Human Understanding*, London: Everyman. (1690).

Lodge, David (1975), *Changing Places*, London: Secker and Warburg.

Lodge, David (1984), *Small Worlds*, London: Secker and Warburg.

Lovejoy, Arthur O. (1936), *The Great Chain of Being*, Cambridge, MA: Harvard University Press.

Luke, A. (1988), *Literacy, Textbooks, and Ideology*, Sussex: Falmer.

Luke, A., de Castell, S., and Luke, C. (1983), "Beyond Criticism: The Authority of the School Text," *Curriculum Inquiry*, 13 (2), 111–128.

Luria, A. R. (1979), *The Making of Mind*, Cambridge, MA: Harvard University Press.

Macauley, David (1973), *Cathedral*, Boston: Houghton Mifflin.

Macauley, David (1977), *Castle*, Boston: Houghton Mifflin.

MacIntyre, Alisdair (1981), *After Virtue*, Notre Dame, IN: University of Notre Dame Press.

Malinowski, Bronislaw (1954), *Magic, Science and Religion,* New York: Anchor.

Mays, John Barron (1965), *The Young Pretenders: A Study of Teenage Culture and Contemporary Society,* New York: Schocken.

McGann, Jerome (1983), *The Romantic Ideology: A Critical Investigation,* Chicago: University of Chicago Press.

McLuhan, Marshall (1962), *The Gutenberg Galaxy: The Making of Typographic Man,* Toronto: University of Toronto Press.

McLuhan, Marshall, and McLuhan, Eric (1989), *Laws of Media,* Toronto: University of Toronto Press.

Melling, David J. (1987), *Understanding Plato,* Oxford: Oxford University Press.

Monroe, W. S., De Voss, J. C., and Reagan, G. W. (1930), *Educational Psychology,* New York: Doubleday, Doran & Co.

Morse, David (1982), *Romanticism,* London: Macmillan.

Nehamas, Alexander (1988), "The School of Eloquence," *Times Literary Supplement,* July, 15–21.

Nelson, Katherine (1977), "Cognitive Development and the Acquisition of Concepts," in R. C. Anderson, R. J. Spiro, and W. E. Montague, (eds.), *Schooling and the Acquisition of Knowledge,* Hillsdale, NJ: Erlbaum.

Nietzsche, Friedrich (1949), *The Use and Abuse of History,* New York: Bobbs-Merrill.

Nolan, Christopher (1987), *Under the Eye of the Clock,* London: Weidenfeld and Nicolson.

Olson, David R. (1977), "From Utterance to Text: The Bias of Language in Speech and Writing," *Harvard Educational Review,* 47, 84–109.

Olson, David R. (1987), "An Introduction to Understanding Literacy," *Interchange,* 18, 1–2.

Olson, David R. (1988), "The Literacy Problem: Myths and Reality," *Globe and Mail,* Toronto, August 15.

Ong, Walter J. (1971), *Rhetoric, Romance, and Technology,* Ithaca, NY: Cornell University Press.

Ong, Walter J. (1977), *Interfaces of the Word,* Ithaca, NY: Cornell University Press.

Ong, Walter (1982), *Orality and Literacy,* London: Methuen.

Paley, Vivian Gussin (1981), *Wally's Stories,* Cambridge, MA: Harvard University Press.

Parry, Milman (1971), The Making of Homeric Verse: The Collected Papers of Milman Parry (Adam Parry ed.), Oxford: Clarendon Press.

Pearson, Lionel (1939), *Early Ionian Historians,* Oxford: Clarendon Press.

Peckham, Morse (1970), *The Triumph of Romanticism,* Columbia: University of South Carolina Press.

Peers, E. Allison (1929), *Ramon Lull,* London: Society for Promoting Christian Knowledge.

Phenix, Philip (1964), *Realms of Meaning,* New York: McGraw Hill.

Piaget, Jean (1951), *Play Dreams and Imitation in Childhood,* New York: Norton.

Piaget, Jean (1952), *The Child's Conception of Number,* London: Humanities Press.

Piaget, Jean (1954), *The Construction of Reality in the Child,* New York: Basic Books.

Piaget, Jean (1964), "Development and Learning," in Richard E. Ripple and Verne N. Rockcastle (eds.), *Piaget Rediscovered,* Ithaca, NY: School of Education, Cornell University.

Plumb, J. H. (1971), *The Death of the Past,* Boston: Houghton Mifflin.

Potter, S. (ed) (1933), *Selected Poetry and Prose of S.T. Coleridge,* London: Nonesuch.

Pound, Ezra (1929), *The Spirit of Romance,* Norfolk, CT: New Directions.

Rahv, Philip (1966), *The Myth and the Powerhouse,* New York: Farrar, Straus & Giroux.

Ravitch, Diane (1987), "Tot Sociology or What Happened to History in the Grade Schools," *American Scholar,* 56, 343–353.

Robinson, Ken (ed.) (1980), *Exploring Theatre and Education*, London: Heinemann.
Romer, John (1988), *Testament*, New York: Henry Holt.
Rorty, Richard (1979), *Philosophy and the Mirror of Nature*, Princeton: Princeton University Press.
Rousseau, Jean-Jacques (1974), *Emile* (Barbara Foxley, trans.), London: Dent. (First published 1762).
Rubin, Louis J. (1985), *Artistry in Teaching*, New York: Random House.
Russell, Bertrand (1926), *On Education*, London: Unwin.
Sagan, Carl (1980), *Cosmos*, New York: Random House.
Sampson, Anthony and Sally (1985), *The Oxford Book of Ages*, Oxford: Oxford University press.
Scribner, S., and Cole, M. (1981), *Psychology of Literacy*, Cambridge, MA: Harvard University Press.
Scriven, Michael (1976), *Reasoning*, New York: McGraw Hill.
Seeley, L. (1906), *Elementary Pedagogics*, New York: Hinds, Noble.
Shaw, Bernard (1988), *Collected Letters*, (Vol. 4), (Dan H. Lawrence, ed.), London: Max Reinhardt.
Shelley, P. B. (1890), *Defense of Poetry*, (Albert S. Cook, ed.) Boston: The Athenaeum Press, Ginn and Company.
Shepard, Roger (1978), "The Mental Image," *American Psychologist*, 33, 123–37.
Shepard, Roger (1988), "The Imagination of the Scientist," in Kieran Egan and Dan Nadaner (eds.), *Imagination and Education*, New York: Teachers College Press; Milton Keynes: Open University Press.
Siebers, Tobin (1984), *The Romantic Fantastic*, Ithaca, NY: Cornell University Press.
Simon, Herbert (1983), *Reason in Human Affairs*, Oxford: Blackwell.
Smith, Frank (1985), "A Metaphor for Literacy: Creating Worlds or Shunting Information," in D. Olson, N. Torrance, and A. Hildyard (eds.), *Literacy, Language, and Learning*, Cambridge, MA: Cambridge University Press.
Snell, Bruno (1960), *The Discovery of the Mind* (T.G. Rosenmeyer, trans.), New York: Harper and Row.
Snow, C. P. (1963), *The Two Cultures: And a Second Look*, New York: The New American Library.
Solmsen, Friedrich (1975), *Intellectual Experiments of the Greek Enlightenment*, Princeton: Princeton University Press.
Spacks, Patricia Meyer (1981), *The Adolescent Idea: Myths of Youth and the Adult Imagination*, New York: Basic Books.
Spencer, Herbert (1861), *Education: Intellectual, Moral and Physical*, London: G. Manwaring.
Sperber, Dan (1986), "The Mind as a Whole," *Times Literary Supplement*, Nov. 21st.
Springhall, John (1986), *Coming of Age: Adolescence in Britain 1860–1960*, Dublin: Gill and Macmillan.
Steiner, George (1988), "Tragic and Counter-tragic," *Times Literary Supplement*, February 12–18.
Stock, Brian (1983), *The Implications of Literacy*, Princeton: Princeton University Press.
Stokes, Michael C. (1967), "Heraclitus of Ephesus," in *The Encyclopaedia of Philosophy* (Vol. 3), New York: Macmillan and The Free Press.
Street, Brian V. (1984), *Literacy in Theory and Practice*, Cambridge: Cambridge University Press.
Sturrock, June (1988), "How the Graminivorous Ruminating Quadruped Jumped over the Moon: A Romantic Approach," in Kieran Egan and Dan Nadaner (eds.), *Imagination and Education*, New York: Teachers College Press.

Temple, Charles, and Gillet, Jean Wallace (1989), *Language Arts* (2nd ed.), Glenview, IL: Scott, Foresman.

Toulmin, Stephen (1972), *Human Understanding*, Princeton: Princeton University Press.

Toulmin, Stephen and Goodfield, June (1965), *The Discovery of Time*, Chicago: University of Chicago Press.

Tyler, Ralph (1949), *Basic Principles of Curriculum and Instruction*, Chicago: University of Chicago Press.

Vernant, Jean-Pierre (1982), *The Origins of Greek Thought*, Ithaca, NY: Cornell University Press.

Vickers, Brian (1988), *In Defense of Rhetoric*, Oxford: Clarendon Press.

Vico, Giambattista (1970), *The New Science* (T. G. Gergin and M. H. Fisch, trans.), Ithaca, NY: Cornell University Press. (First published 1744).

Vygotsky, L. (1966), "Development of the Higher Mental Functions," in *Psychological Research in the USSR* (Vol. 1), Moscow: Progress Publishers.

Vygotsky, L. S. (1978), *Mind in Society: The Development of Higher Psychological Processes* (M. Cole, V. John-Steiner, S. Scribner, and E. Souberman, eds.), Cambridge, MA: Harvard University Press.

Waddell, Helen (1954), *The Wandering Scholars*, Harmondsworth, Middlesex: Penguin. (First published 1927).

Warnock, Mary (1977), *Schools of Thought*, London: Faber and Faber.

Waters, K. H. (1985), *Herodotos the Historian*, Norman, Oklahoma: University of Oklahoma Press.

Wertsch, J. V. (1985), *Vygotsky and the Social Formation of Mind*, Cambridge, MA: Harvard University Press.

Whitehead, A. N. (1967), *The Aims of Education*, New York: Free Press. (London: Macmillan, 1929).

Willinsky, John (1987), "The Paradox of Text," *Interchange*, 18, 147–63.

Wills, C. (1988)," Responses and Allegiances," *Times Literary Supplement*, March 4–10.

Wilson, John (1979), *Fantasy and Common Sense in Education*, Oxford: Martin Robertson.

Wolfe, Tom (1968), *The Pump-House Gang*, New York: Farrar, Strauss & Giroux.

Index